DATE DUE

THE CRISIS OF CONFIDENCE

IDEAS, POWER AND VIOLENCE
IN AMERICA

BY ARTHUR M. SCHLESINGER, JR.

THE CRISIS
OF CONFIDENCE

IDEAS, POWER AND VIOLENCE
IN AMERICA

Arthur M. Schlesinger, Jr.

HOUGHTON MIFFLIN COMPANY BOSTON

1969

Detailed acknowledgments are given on page 303 for earlier published versions of these essays. The author wishes to thank the publishers concerned for permission to use passages from previously copyrighted material: "Intellectuals in American Politics" in *The Great Ideas Today*, *1968* copyright © 1968 by Encyclopaedia Britannica, Inc.; a review article on Noam Chomsky's *American Power and the New Mandarins* © 1969 Postrib Corp.; "Origins of the Cold War" copyright 1967 Council on Foreign Relations, Inc.

First Printing c

Library of Congress Catalog Card Number: 75-79389
Printed in the United States of America

IN MEMORY OF

ROBERT FRANCIS KENNEDY

Before my term is ended, we shall have to test anew whether a nation organized and governed such as ours can endure. The outcome is by no means certain.

JOHN F. KENNEDY, 1961

FOREWORD

As THE SIXTH DECADE of the twentieth century draws to a close, America is undergoing a crisis of self-confidence. For most of our national existence, we have enjoyed a placid faith in our virtue and our invulnerability. There have been dark days, but generally the storms pass quickly and the sun shines again. Except for slavery and the Civil War, ours has been a history without agony. William Dean Howells, after reading *Crime and Punishment*, doubted whether there could be an American Dostoyevsky; anyone striking "a note so profoundly tragic in American fiction would do a false and mistaken thing." Our novelists concern themselves "with the more smiling aspects of life, which are the more American."

That was 1891. Alas, no one would write such a sentence three quarters of a century later. We are a good deal less buoyant today about ourselves and our future. Events seem to have slipped beyond our control; we have lost our immunity to history. Of course, we have had seasons of perplexity in the past. Americans have always (luckily) been addicted to self-criticism; and self-criticism has not seldom been tinged with catastrophic expectation. Yet is one wrong in supposing that pessimism is cutting much closer to the national nerve today than ever before? that it has ceased to be a polemical tactic and is becoming a national reality?

Heaven knows that Americans have faced tough problems in the last forty years — the worst depression in our history, the worst total war in our history, the worst cold war in our history, the most frustrating limited war in our history. Yet, until recently, we have always felt that our leadership and our resources — moral and psychological as well as economic — were equal to any conceivable challenge. Are we so sure of that now? One's impression is that, underneath the continuing babble of self-congratulation, more and more Americans are beginning to wonder whether we will be able to cope in the next years — to cope all at once with the Russians, the Chinese, the French, the Africans, the Latin Americans; with the decaying cities and the blighted countryside; with the jammed freeways and the crowded airways; with the polluted water and the poisoned atmosphere; with the fury of the blacks and the animosity of the low-income whites and the mingled guilt and resentment of the upper-class whites; with the mysterious skepticisms and irascibilities of our own children.

At home we see our cities in travail and revolt; rising mistrust and bitterness on the part of minorities; unraveling ties of social civility; a contagion of violence; a multiplication of fanaticisms on both far right and far left; a spreading impulse, especially among the intellectuals, the young and the blacks, to secede from the established order; and three terrible murders in five years of men who, through their ability to mobilize American idealism, might have held the country together. Abroad we see our nation increasingly disbelieved and disliked, our motives misunderstood and traduced, our labors unavailing. The failure of half a million American soldiers with nearly a million allies, employing the might of modern military technology, to defeat a few thousand guerrillas in black pajamas has shaken our faith in our power, as the destruction we have wrought in the pursuit of what we conceived as noble ends has shaken our faith in our virtue.

A Louis Harris poll in December 1968 reported that Americans doubted by a proportion of 55 to 31 percent there would be a decline in violence in the years ahead and doubted by a proportion of 73 to 16 percent there would be a future without constant tension. We are in a double crisis — the crisis of our internal character as a nation and the crisis of the relationship between America and the world. After so many years of overweening confidence in our ability to fix up all the troubles of mankind, we are now suffering increasing doubt that we can even heal the ills of our own national community. The time has surely come for a reassessment of our institutions and values. The essays which follow are intended as an historian's contribution to this effort.

We must first recognize the mixed nature of our historical inheritance. The "consensus history" of the nineteen-fifties, with its emphasis on the homogeneity of American life and thought, tended to expel the impression of conflict from our American tradition. Nothing is more evident than the relativity of historical judgment; and, as the decade of the fifties projected the blandness of the Eisenhower years onto the screen of the past, so the decade of the sixties, immersed in the savagery of present differences, can no longer repress the theme of discord. We have suddenly been reminded of ambiguous strains in our legacy from history, of national instincts for aggression and destruction which have long warred with a national capacity for civility and idealism. The first chapter in the book attempts to define the problem of violence in American life; the second to suggest the role and responsibility of ideas and intellectuals.

The current phase in our foreign affairs began with the rise of the Cold War, a problem discussed in the third essay. The illusions that have created the crisis of confidence in our external relations came to climax in Vietnam; and the fourth chapter is an inquiry into the lessons we might draw from the Vietnam tragedy. The collapse of our pretensions both at home and abroad has struck our young men and women with devastating impact; the fifth chapter explores the disquietudes among college students. The hope for resolving our problems rests, in large part, with our political leaders, parties and institutions; the final chapter speculates about the prospects for our politics and particularly about the future of the Presidency. Properly the book, having considered the estrangement of the intellectuals and of the young, should also have dealt at length with the issues of national reconciliation presented by the poor, the blacks and the low-income whites. However, I do not have enough fresh ideas or special knowledge in these areas to justify wearying the reader by telling him at length what he may already know. Such reflections as I have on these vital questions appear in the first and last chapters.

This book does not pretend to offer a comprehensive reassessment of our situation. It consists, rather, of some contributions to a reassessment already well under way. This process is taking place in our colleges, our churches, our New Politics, our underground press; one would like to think that it is also taking place in our editorial offices, our boardrooms and our corridors of power. Much of the result is strident, extravagant and delusive. But no one can doubt the reality of the ferment, or the intensity of the frustration lying behind it. Out of this there must come, one hopes, a wider awareness of our limitations and frailties, a deeper comprehension of our predicament and a new determination to fulfill the ideals on which this nation was established.

For the Founding Fathers saw the United States of America not as a finished product but as an experiment. "The preservation of the sacred fire of liberty and the destiny of the republican model of government," as Washington said in his first inaugural address, "are justly considered, perhaps, as *deeply*, as *finally* staked on the experiment intrusted to the hands of the American people." America is still an experiment; it is still intrusted to the hands of the people. Their thoughts, their purposes, their decisions will answer John F. Kennedy's question whether a nation organized and governed such as ours can endure.

ARTHUR M. SCHLESINGER, JR.

New York City
February 4, 1969

CONTENTS

THE CRISIS OF CONFIDENCE

IDEAS, POWER AND VIOLENCE
IN AMERICA

I

VIOLENCE AS AN
AMERICAN WAY OF LIFE

THE CRISIS OF AMERICAN CONFIDENCE begins at home. The murders within five years of John F. Kennedy, Martin Luther King, Jr., and Robert F. Kennedy raise somber questions about the character of contemporary America. One such murder might be explained away as an isolated horror, unrelated to the inner life of our society. But the successive shootings, in a short time, of three men who greatly embodied the idealism of American life suggest not so much a fortuitous set of aberrations as an emerging pattern of response and action — a spreading and ominous belief in the efficacy of violence and the politics of the deed.

Yet, while each of these murders produced a genuine season of national mourning, none has produced a sustained season of national questioning. In every case, remorse has seemed to end not as an incitement to self-examination but as an escape from it. An orgy of sorrow and shame becomes an easy way of purging a bad conscience and returning as quickly as possible to business as usual.

This cannot be enough. How many more such murders will be required before we strive — in a serious and not a ritualistic way — to identify the violent impulses in American society?

For the premonition of violence has become a central fact of American politics. Stewart Alsop wrote of the 1968 presidential campaign, "At every rally, the police were everywhere. There were cops on the rooftops, with rifles — little figures outlined against the sky. There were cops in helicopters, ready to pounce, like a hawk on a rabbit, on some would-be assassin. There were cops in mufti, with slight bulges at their hips or under their arms, who peered, lynx-eyed, at the crowds. Everywhere there were cops, to control the people, to herd them about, to insulate the candidate against them."

Nor is the spread of political assassination the only expression of this alarming national mood. The violent crime rate, according to the Federal Bureau of Investigation, was more than twice as high in 1967 as in 1940. Nothing is more dubious than criminal statistics; yet memory assures us that thirty years ago, with millions of Americans angrily out of work, one could walk equably at night along streets which would be dangerous in the affluent America of today. And, though mass violence has different motives and consequences from individual violence, the growth in one has been matched by a growth in the other. The bitter riots which swept through Washington, Newark, Cleveland, Detroit and Los Angeles in recent years have had their counterparts in more than two hundred other American cities. According to the National Student Association, there were at least 221 major demonstrations in American colleges and universities between January 1 and June 15, 1968; a year later, the campuses were even more embattled. The protest meetings and police bludgeonings during the Democratic convention in Chicago represented an embellishment of the convention process unknown in earlier American history. This spectacle was rendered the more disturbing by the evident incapacity of the presidential candidates of either major party to address themselves to the problem — one screaming against the Supreme Court, the other whimpering, "I don't like to say it but I was targeted by an assassination team." *

Surely we can no longer dodge the fact that violence is becoming a central factor in the American social process — as William Styron recently put it, "that a kind of anarchic murder is in the air; that we're all theoretical victims and we're scared." Our salvation demands an intense national determination to look searchingly at ourselves and our society before the carelessness of hate rushes us on to more destruction and finally tears the nation apart. For the only lasting answer to our contemporary taste for violence is to uncover the roots of hatred and rage and, through self-knowledge, move toward self-control.

* The great Chicago assassination plot evaporated rather quickly. On October 10, 1968, the *Chicago Daily News*, citing federal sources, wrote, "The story of the convention-week assassination plot, already surrounded by clouds of doubt, grew even more hazy recently." Federal officials "know if there was an assassination plot, they should have made arrests. And, so far, they have found nothing on which to base an arrest. . . . A federal grand jury investigation of the plot was quickly terminated, with no indictments." A climate of violence inevitably breeds rumors of violence, but responsible men, including Vice Presidents of the United States, should take care to preserve critical discrimination in potentially explosive situations.

1. A Sick Society?

"It would be . . . self-deceptive," President Johnson said after the shooting of Robert Kennedy, "to conclude from this act that our country is sick, that it has lost its balance, that it has lost its sense of direction, even its common decency. Two hundred million Americans did not strike down Robert Kennedy last night any more than they struck down John F. Kennedy in 1963 or Dr. Martin Luther King in April of this year."

I do not quarrel with these words. Of course two hundred million Americans did not strike down these men. Nor, in my judgment, is this a question of a "sick society" or of "collective guilt." I do not know what such phrases mean, and I am certain that they do not represent useful ways of thinking about our problem. Obviously most Americans are decent and God-fearing people. Obviously most Americans were deeply and honestly appalled by these atrocities. Obviously most Americans rightly resent being told that they were "guilty" of crimes they neither willed nor wished.

Still, it is not enough to dismiss the ideas of a sick society and of collective guilt and suppose that such dismissal closes the question. For the United States has seen a contagion of political murder in the nineteen-sixties unparalleled in its history. After each atrocity, we restore our national complacency with astonishing promptitude. Yet a problem remains which complacency cannot wave away. If we are reluctant to confront this problem ourselves, let us consider for a moment how it looks from two perspectives: how it looks to the rest of the world; and how it looks to the young people of our own country.

No one can doubt that much of the world views contemporary America with misgiving and consternation. After the murder of Robert Kennedy, Lord Harlech, the former British Ambassador to the United States and a strong and tested friend of America, said, "Violence in the United States has become a world scandal." *Le Monde* of Paris asked: "How many men are still to fall before the long and exacting efforts to furnish a sick and extremely tense society with new reasons for a soothing balance are successful?" The *Times of India* said, "The overriding question is whether America will have the moral strength to cure itself of the sickness of which there has been one virulent symptom after another since President Kennedy's assassination." Even such specialists in violence as the Germans and the Russians condescended to us. Thus the *Rheinische Post* of Düsseldorf: "What a country! For more than a century this exclamation reflected the pride the Americans take in their subcontinent. Now it has become an expression of alarm." Thus Yevtushenko, the Soviet poet:

> Who is going to believe hypocritical fairy tales,
> When, behind a facade of noble ideas,
> The price of revolver lubricant rises
> And the price of human life falls? . . .
> The eyes of murderers peer out alike from under
>   hats and caps,
> The steps of murderers are heard at all doorways,
> And a second of the Kennedys falls.

And, incredibly, in a speech published in the United States on the Fourth of July, Leonid Brezhnev, general secretary of the Soviet Communist party, which, except for the Nazis, has been the bloodiest instrument of politics in this century: "A state, which raised violence and terror to a basic principle of policy, is paying for this with the lives of its own political leaders. . . . A social and political system which gives birth to political banditry evokes contempt and aversion throughout the world. A rotting society, a degrading society, a decadent society — this is how the present-day United States is being described even by those who not long ago were praising the American way of life."

The London *Times* summed it up: "The rest of the world will be tempted to turn away from America. . . . Each fresh act of violence spreads fresh doubt about American capacity for leadership" — and again, after the Democratic convention, "In any civilised city successful actions for assault could be brought by the hundreds against the police of Chicago. . . . Yet this violence in Chicago is paralleled by the increasing violence of American life, just as the violence in Czechoslovakia is paralleled by the suppression of intellectual dissent in the Soviet Union. . . . Both these countries should, at the present time, feel a deep shame for the disgraceful impression they have left upon the rest of the world."

We can hardly doubt that in the eyes of much of mankind we have become a frightening people — because in this decade we have permitted murder to become a major technique of domestic politics.

We have become a frightening people — because for three years we have been wrecking a small country on the other side of the world in a war which bears no proportionate relationship to our national security or national interest.

We are frightening — because many around the planet are beginning to wonder about the connection suggested by that devoted student of America, Sir Denis Brogan: "Are we sure it is merely an accident that the most domestically murderous nation in the world was the first — and only — nation to drop the atomic bomb?"

We are above all a frightening people because the atrocities we commit, at home or abroad, seem even now hardly to have touched our official self-righteousness or dented our transcendent conviction of moral infallibility.

America not only strikes much of the world as a frightening society. Worse, it strikes many of our sons and daughters the same way.

The older generation in America worries a good deal about its children. It objects to the drastic judgments the young make on a society which their parents find satisfying and even admirable. It feels that the young, instead of blessing their good fortune in being born in the best and happiest country in the world, are filled with shallow pessimism and deep ingratitude. It finds what they think, say or do irritating and incomprehensible, even threatening. Yet every generation is the prisoner of its own experience. Perhaps the old are at fault for expecting people of twenty to see the world as people of sixty do.

The old lived through turbulent times themselves — times of war, times of depression. Americans often were in trouble; they often disagreed with each other; they often had hard things to say. Yet, in general, they stayed within the fabric of civility. Thirty years ago Franklin Roosevelt was, in some circles, a bitterly hated President. The most shocking remarks were made about him. But no one in the twelve years of his Presidency took a shot at him. (The one attempt to assassinate Roosevelt came a few weeks before his inauguration.) For a good part of the nineteen-thirties America had twelve or fifteen million people out of work through no fault of their own. Many of the unemployed deeply resented the American business community. But they did not go around killing businessmen (though it must be said that businessmen or their hired cops sometimes killed them).

This is the experience that produced the older generation. They had their share of turbulence, but it was turbulence within a society that still respected certain forms of stability. People did not murder leaders with whom they disagreed. Wars had a rational reason and goal. Their children, and grandchildren, have had a different experience. The political memory of a first voter in 1968 goes back to about 1960. These have been the years of the least rational war in our history. And in these years three men have caught the imagination of the young and summoned them to action in service of the highest possibilities in American life. One after another — John F. Kennedy, Martin Luther King, Jr., Robert F. Kennedy — fell before assassins' bullets. Why should not the young begin to despair about such a society? Why should they not make drastic judgments? What has *their* experience of public affairs in America been but a series of ghastly killings at home and a ghastly war abroad?

One can understand why President Johnson, who was born in 1908 and grew up in the years when acrimony did not lead to assassination, should insist that recent deviations from his experience can only be accidents and aberrations, irrelevant to the course of American life. But cannot his generation make some effort to understand why the young must reject statements of national self-exculpation as cruelly sanctimonious after they have seen men in whom they reposed the greatest hope shot down?

Nothing is more dispiriting than this insistence of the old that their own experience is the normal experience. For the young, the normal experience has been the *murder* of leaders who have forcefully asked America to live up to its ideals.

We cannot blame the epidemic of murder at home exclusively on deranged and solitary individuals who are separate from the rest of us. For these individuals are plainly weak and suggestible men, stamped by our society with an instinct for hatred and a compulsion toward violence.

We cannot blame the epidemic of murder abroad exclusively on the perversity of those who will not stop doing things because we think they should stop doing them. For the zeal with which we have pursued an irrational war — a war which makes so little sense in the classical terms of foreign policy — suggests internal impulses of hatred and violence demanding outlet and shaping our foreign policy to their ends.

The terrible things we do to our own people, the terrible things we do to other people — we cannot take the easy course and blame these things on everyone but ourselves. If we continue to say it is all the work of lunatics and foreigners, that nothing is wrong and that our society is beyond criticism, if we cry like Macbeth

> Thou canst not say I did it: never shake
> Thy gory locks at me

then we lose hope of recovering control of the destructive impulse within. Then we will only continue the downward spiral of social decomposition and moral degradation.

2. *Violence as an American Tradition*

Self-knowledge is the indispensable prelude to self-control; and self-knowledge, for a nation as well as for an individual, begins with history. We like to think of ourselves as a peaceful, tolerant, benign people who have always lived under a government of laws and not of men. And, indeed, respect for persons and for law has been one characteristic strain in the American tradition. Most Americans offer this respect most of their lives. Yet this is by no means the only strain in our tradition. For we also have been a violent people. When we refuse to acknowledge the existence of this other strain, we refuse to see our nation as it is.

We must recognize that an impulse to destroy coexists with our impulse to create — that the destructive impulse is in us and that it springs from some dark intolerable tension in our history and our institutions. We began, after all, as a people who killed red men and enslaved black men. No doubt we often did this with a Bible and a prayerbook. But no nation, however righteous its professions, could act as we did without doing something fearful to itself — without burying deep in itself, in its customs, its institutions, its conditioned reflexes and its psyche, a propensity toward violence. However much we pretended that Indians and Negroes were subhuman, we really knew that they were God's children too. It is almost as if this initial experience fixed a primal curse on our nation — a curse which still shadows our life.

It was a curse we have always flinched to acknowledge. In this respect our written history is revealing; for history, after

all, is the record of a nation's consciousness. "To our reproach," Jefferson wrote in 1782, "it must be said that though
for a century and a half we have had under our eyes the races
of black and of red men, they have never yet been viewed
by us as subjects of natural history." This reproach, initially
directed at scientists, applied in the next century and a half
just as much to historians. White historians wrote of Indian
wars, of slavery and so on; but they held racial events at a distance, treated them as isolated phenomena of a remote time
and rarely connected them in any organic way with the development of the American character. They were engaged in
the process Freud called "repression" — "the function of rejecting and keeping something out of consciousness." Repression, Freud added, "is, at bottom, an attempt at flight."

The evidence that such repression took place in the writing
of American history is abundantly provided by American
literature. For, if history is the record of a nation's consciousness, novels, short stories and poems are the mirror of a nation's unconscious. And, where our history has segregated race
from the main course of American development, our literature has involuntarily perceived race as very near the heart
of American life; it has been pervaded, indeed haunted, by
images of racial unrest, aggression and guilt. What white
America declined to confront in its explicit portrayal of the
past, it could not escape in the dreams and fantasies that un-
derlie artistic creation. "The Negro," said Richard Wright,
"is America's metaphor." The colored American has been the
symbol of white America's capacity for sin, the permanent
but forgotten weight on the American conscience.

Our great writers have felt this, even if they did not precisely know what they were feeling. How else to account for
the fact that the relationship between white man and colored

man has been one of the grand themes of American fiction
— a more basic theme, as Leslie Fiedler has insisted, than the
relationship between man and woman? Leatherstocking and
Chingachgook, Ishmael and Queequeg, Huck and Jim —
these have signified the artists' compulsion to come to terms
with the tragedy the historians have suppressed. There has
always been in American literature what Melville called "the
blackness of darkness beyond." But literature could only register this terrible wound; it could not heal it; it left the guilt
hidden and malignant in the national unconscious, finding
outlet in spasms of violence.

Perhaps nothing shaped our national unconscious more
than the institutionalization of violence in the slavery system. "The whole commerce between master and slave,"
wrote Jefferson, "is a perpetual exercise of the most boisterous
passions, the most unremitting despotism on the one part,
and degrading submissions on the other. . . . The parent
storms, the child looks on, catches the lineaments of wrath,
puts on the same airs in the circle of smaller slaves, gives a
loose to the worst of passions, and thus nursed, educated, and
daily exercised in tyranny, cannot but be stamped by it with
odious peculiarities. The man must be a prodigy who can retain his manners and moral undepraved by such circumstances." And Jefferson foresaw that slavery would demand
retribution. "I tremble for my country when I reflect that
God is just; that his justice cannot sleep forever; that con-
sidering numbers, nature and natural means only, a revolution of the wheel of fortune, an exchange of situation is
among possible events. . . . The Almighty has no attribute
which can take side with us in such a contest." Yet Jefferson
himself retained his slaves; and, like him, his countrymen,

denying what they were doing, armed themselves with obliviousness.

Mark Twain's meditation on the French Revolution illuminates with grim exactitude the attitude of white America toward black America, from Nat Turner to the latest ghetto riot:

> There were two "Reigns of Terror" if we would but remember it and consider it; the one wrought murder in hot passion, the other in heartless cold blood; the one lasted mere months, the other had lasted a thousand years; the one inflicted death upon ten thousand persons, the other upon a hundred millions; but our shudders are all for the "horrors" of the minor Terror, the momentary Terror, so to speak; whereas, what is the horror of swift death by the ax compared with lifelong death from hunger, cold, insult, cruelty, and heartbreak? What is swift death by lightning compared with death by slow fire at the stake? A city cemetery could contain the coffins filled by the brief Terror which we have all been so diligently taught to shiver at and mourn over; but all France could hardly contain the coffins filled by the older and real Terror — that unspeakably bitter and awful Terror which none of us has been taught to see in its vastness or pity as it deserves.

Nor did we confine violence to red men and black men. Habits were contagious. The first century after independence were years of indiscriminate violence — wars, slave insurrections, Indian fighting, urban riots, murders, duels, beatings. Members of Congress went armed to the Senate and House. In his first notable speech, in January 1838, before the Young Men's Lyceum of Springfield, Illinois, Abraham Lincoln named internal violence as the supreme threat to American political institutions. He spoke of "the increasing disregard for law which pervades the country; the growing disposition to substitute the wild and furious passions, in lieu of the sober judgment of Courts; and the worse than savage mobs, for the executive ministers of justice." The danger to the American republic, he said, was not from foreign invasion. "At what point then is the approach of danger to be expected? I answer, if it ever reach us, it must spring up amongst us. It cannot come from abroad. If destruction be our lot, we must ourselves be its author and finisher. As a nation of freemen, we must live through all time, or die by suicide."

So the young Lincoln named the American peril — a peril he did not fear to locate within the American breast. Indeed, the sadness of America has been that our worst qualities have so often been the other face of our best. Our commitment to morality and our faith in experiment have been sources of America's greatness. But they have also led Americans into temptation. For our moralists have sometimes condoned murder if the cause was deemed good; so Emerson and Thoreau applauded John Brown of Osawatomie. And our pragmatists have sometimes ignored the means if they approved the result; so Jefferson could write, "To lose our country by a scrupulous adherence to written law, would be to lose the law itself, with life, liberty, property . . . thus absurdly sacrificing the end to the means." Moralism and pragmatism have hardly provided infallible restraints on the destructive instinct.

No one understood the American ambiguity better than Lincoln. No one saw more poignantly the desperate need to control and transcend a national propensity toward violence. This was the preoccupation of his life. "When . . . you have succeeded in dehumanizing the Negro," he said twenty years after his Springfield speech; "when you have put him down to be but as the beasts of the field; when you have extinguished his soul in this world and placed him where the ray of hope is blown out as in the darkness of the damned, are you quite sure that the demon you have roused will not turn and rend you?" It was both ironic and fortunate that a man who so profoundly perceived the curse of violence in American society should have been President during the greatest explosion of internal violence in our history.

Throughout the Civil War Lincoln tried unremittingly to discipline the destructive impulse; this effort produced his most majestic prose. "We are not enemies, but friends," he said of the rebels in his First Inaugural. "Though passion may have strained, it must not break our bonds of affection." And in his Second Inaugural: "With malice toward none; with charity for all; with firmness in the right, as God gives us to see the right, let us strive on to finish the work we are in; to bind up the nation's wounds." In the end our greatest enemy of violence and hate became our greatest victim of violence and hate.

The impulses of violence and civility continued after Lincoln to war within the American breast. The insensate bloodshed of the Civil War exhausted the national capacity for violence and left the nation emotionally and psychologically spent. For half a century America remained substantially at peace (the Spanish-American War lasted only a few weeks). For nearly a century after Appomattox we appeared on the surface the tranquil and friendly people we still like to imagine ourselves to be. The amiability of that society no doubt exerted a restraining influence. There were still crazy individuals, filled with grievance, bitterness and a potential for violence. But most of these people expended their sickness in fantasy; the Guiteaus and the Czolgoszes were the exception. These years of stability, a stability fitfully recaptured after the First World War, created the older generation's image of a "normal" America.

Yet even in the kindly years we did not wholly eradicate the propensity toward violence which history had hidden in the national unconscious. Walt Whitman noted "the battle, advancing, retreating, between democracy's convictions, aspirations, and the people's crudeness, vice, caprices," and William James commented, "Angelic impulses and predatory lusts divide our heart exactly as they divide the hearts of other countries." Mark Twain wrote of "The United States of Lyncherdom" and attributed "To the Person Sitting in Darkness" (i.e., those living in underdeveloped countries) this proposition about the United States: "There must be two Americas: one that sets the captive free, and one that takes a once-captive's new freedom away from him, and picks a quarrel with him with nothing to found it on; then kills him to get his land." Nor was Jack London's *The Iron Heel* a novel about czarist Russia. In certain moods, indeed, we prided ourselves on our violence; we almost considered it evidence of our virility. "Above all," cried Theodore Roosevelt, "let us shrink from no strife, moral or physical, within or without the nation, provided we are certain that the strife is justified." The fatal susceptibility always lurked under the surface, breaking out in Indian wars and vigilantism in the west, in lynchings in the south, in labor riots and race riots and gang wars in the cities.

It is important to distinguish collective from individual violence — the work of mobs from the work of murderers; for the motive and the effect can be very different. There can, of course, be murder by a mob. This was such a national problem at the turn of the century that Theodore Roosevelt,

who as it turned out was not all that gratified by the beauties
of strife, reminded white America in a passionate State of the
Union message

> that every lynching represents by just so much a loosening
> of the bands of civilization; that the spirit of lynching in-
> evitably throws into prominence in the community all the
> foul and evil creatures who dwell therein. No man can take
> part in the torture of a human being without having his own
> moral nature permanently lowered. Every lynching means
> just so much moral deterioration in all the children who have
> any knowledge of it, and therefore just so much additional
> trouble to the next generation of Americans.

But not all mobs aim at murder. Collective violence—rioting against what were considered illegal British taxes in Boston in 1773, or dangerous Papist influence sixty years later,
or inequitable draft laws in New York in 1863, or unfair labor
practices in Chicago in 1937 — is more characteristically directed at property and process than at people. In many cases
(though by no means all), the aim has been to protest rather
than protect the status quo; and the historian is obliged to
concede that collective violence has often forced those in
power to recognize long-denied rights. Extra-legal group action, for better or worse, has been part of the process of
American democracy. Violence, for better or worse, *does*
settle some questions, and for the better. Violence secured
American independence, freed the slaves and stopped Hitler.
But this has ordinarily been the violence of a mass. The
individual who commits violence is less likely to be concerned
with reforming conditions than with punishing persons. On
occasion his purpose is to protect the status quo by destroying men who symbolize or threaten social change (a tactic
which the anarchists employed in reverse). A difference exists

in psychic color and content between spontaneous mass convulsions and the premeditated killing of individuals. The first signifies an unstable society, the second a murderous society. America has exhibited both forms of violence. The second is more ominous. "Of the last seven elected Presidents," Theodore Roosevelt said in 1901 after the assassination of William McKinley, "he is the third who has been murdered, and the bare recital of this fact is sufficient to justify great alarm among all loyal American citizens." Of the ten Presidents who followed McKinley, four at one time or another in their lives were targets of assassination attempts. The United States has compiled a record in this field not often exceeded by those banana republics on whose politics North Americans look with such disdain.

Along with a devotion to law, a covert relish in violence has been an abiding strain in American history. Dr. Karl Menninger's observation about contemporary America applies equally to the American past: "The crime and punishment ritual is part of our lives. . . . We need criminals to identify ourselves with, to envy secretly, and to punish stoutly. They do for us the forbidden, illegal things we *wish* to do and, like scapegoats of old, they bear the burdens of our displaced guilt and punishment." Our popular heroes have been precisely those who joined the themes of violence and law — the quiet, strong, lonely men, from frontier marshals to private eyes, who drew their guns in order to establish order. But can personal violence and public law be truly joined? The effort to do so made America, in the words of Martin Luther King, "a schizophrenic personality, tragically divided against herself."

3. *Happiness Is a Warm Gun*

Now in the third quarter of the twentieth century violence has broken out with new ferocity in our country. What has given our old propensity new life? Why does the fabric of American civility no longer exert restraint? What now incites crazy individuals to act out their murderous dreams? What is it about the climate of this decade that suddenly encourages — that for some evidently legitimatizes — the relish in hate and the resort to violence? According to the Federal Bureau of Investigation, assaults with a gun increased 77 percent in the four years from 1964 through 1967. The FBI also reports a 21 percent increase in crimes of violence for 1968 over 1967, including an increase of 15 percent in murder. In New York City arrests for murder in the first six months of 1968 were 40.2 percent higher than in the same months of 1967, while the number of persons arrested for possession of dangerous weapons more than doubled.

There are many facile explanations for the renewal of violence. Some talk, for example, about the legacy of the frontier. No doubt the frontier has bequeathed us a set of romantic obsessions about six-shooters and gunfighters. But why should this legacy suddenly reassert itself in the nineteen-sixties? Moreover, Canada and Australia were also frontier societies. Canadians and Australians too have robust, brawling traditions; they too like to strike virile poses. Indeed, the Australians exterminated their aborigines more efficiently than we did our Indians. But Canadians and Australians do not feel the need today to prove themselves by killing people.

The homicide rate in Canada and Australia is one quarter that of the United States.

Some talk about the tensions of industrial society. No doubt industrial society generates awful tensions. No doubt the ever-quickening pace of social change depletes and destroys the institutions which make for social stability. No doubt the elimination from daily life of legitimate outlets for the aggressive impulse — hunting, trapping, clearing the wilderness — intensifies the need for forms of illegal expression; as Bruno Bettelheim has written, "The chances of discharging violent tendencies are now so severely curtailed that their regular and safe draining-off is not possible any more." No doubt the sense of helplessness produced by the impotence of the individual before the towering structures of modern life encourages a desperate wish to break out and recapture identity by some violent act.

Yet none of this explains why the United States is more violent than other industrial societies — why Americans shoot and kill so many more Americans than Englishmen kill Englishmen or Japanese kill Japanese. England, Japan and West Germany are, next to the United States, the most heavily industrialized countries in the world. Together they have a population of 214 million people. Among these 214 million, there are 135 gun murders a year. Among the 200 million people of the United States there are 6500 gun murders a year — about *forty-eight times* as many. Philadelphia alone has about the same number of criminal homicides as England, Scotland and Wales combined — as many in a city of two million (and a city of brotherly love, at that) as in a nation of 45 million.

Some talk about the fears and antagonisms generated by racial conflict. Unquestionably this has contributed to the recent increase in violence. The contemporary climate of defiance of the law began to take its shape in the nineteen-fifties when state and local officials in the south urged resistance to the desegregation process and when white terrorists beat and murdered Negroes and civil rights workers. The murders of Dr. King and Senator Kennedy seem directly traceable to ethnic hatreds. Whites and blacks alike are laying in arms, both sides invoking the needs of self-defense. Yet this explanation still does not tell us why in America today we are tending to convert political problems into military problems — problems of adjustment into problems of force.

The right tells us that we are a violent society because of what Mr. Nixon called in his campaign the "fog of permissiveness" in American life — a weakening of the national moral fiber expressed, among other ways, in judicial decisions strengthening the rights of arrested persons. The Supreme Court, Mr. Nixon said, had given the "green light" to "the criminal elements." More third degrees, more wire-tapping, longer jail sentences, a tougher Attorney General, a conservative Supreme Court and presumably the suppression of the child-rearing treatises of Dr. Spock: these would comprise the distinctive elements of the right-wing program for law and order. Yet careful studies by the National Crime Commission fail to bear out the contention that Supreme Court decisions have been a significant factor in the increase in violence; and, while the enlargement and modernization of our police forces (including the payment of better salaries) are an unquestioned necessity, the establishment of a police state would seem another of those cases where the cure would be, in the end, worse than the disease. "We might then have to choose," as Mayor Lindsay has put it, "between the random terror of the criminal and the official terror of the state."

As for the New Left, it tells us that we are a violent society because we are a capitalist society — that capitalism is itself institutionalized violence; and that life under capitalism inevitably deforms relations among men. This view would be more impressive if the greatest violence of man against man in this century had not taken place in noncapitalist societies — in Nazi Germany, in Stalinist Russia, in precapitalist Indonesia. The fact is that every form of society is in some sense based on institutionalized violence or, as Georges Sorel would say, on force.* Man in society always gives up a measure of "liberty" and accepts a measure of authority. Competition for power, moreover, takes place in every community; and it is obviously more healthy to have that competition relatively legitimate, open and routine, as it is in a capitalist democracy, than to deny it all channels and outlets save those of violence.

No, we cannot escape that easily. It is not just that we were a frontier society or have become an industrial society or are a racist or a capitalist society; it is something more specific than that. Nor can we blame the situation on our gun laws, or the lack of them; though here possibly we are getting closer. There is no question, of course, that we need adequate federal gun laws. In 1967, according to the Criminal Division of the Department of Justice, 4,585,000 firearms were sold in the United States for individual use. An estimated 42.5 million Americans — more than a fifth of the population of the country — own firearms; and the estimates of the number of firearms in private hands range from 100 to 200 million. A recent city gun registration ordinance

---

* "The object of force is to impose a certain social order . . . while violence tends to the destruction of that order." *Reflections on Violence* (New York, 1961), Ch. 5.

in Chicago produced 357,598 guns — enough, according to Major General Francis P. Kane, to "equip more than twenty full-strength army divisions with hand weapons." The citizens of Chicago, General Kane said, "probably have more equipment in their hands than the entire active strength of the United States Army."

President Johnson was everlastingly right in calling for an end to what he properly described as "the insane traffic in guns"; and he set forth the essentials of the program in his message to Congress on June 24, 1968:

> A national registration of all firearms, both those already in private hands and those acquired in the future.
> Federal licensing of all possessors of firearms in those states whose laws fail to meet minimum federal standards.

The success of the National Rifle Association in blocking gun controls demanded by the great majority of the American people (by 71 to 23 percent, according to a Harris poll in April 1968) is a national scandal. And the hysteria expressed by some at the thought that guns should be licensed, like automobiles, dogs and marriages, only strengthens the psychiatric suspicion that men doubtful of their own virility cling to the gun (like Clyde in *Bonnie and Clyde*) as a symbolic phallus and unconsciously fear gun control as the equivalent of castration. ("Happiness," the Beatles remind us, "is a warm gun.") There seems wisdom in Attorney General Homer Cummings's remark of thirty years ago: "Show me the man who doesn't want his gun registered, and I will show you a man who shouldn't have a gun."

Statistics make it evident that gun controls have some effect. Sixty percent of all murders in the United States are by firearms; and states with adequate laws — New Jersey, New

York, Massachusetts, Rhode Island — have much lower rates of gun murder than states with no laws or weak ones — Texas, Mississippi, Louisiana, Nevada. The same is true among countries. The American rate of homicide by gunfire is 3.5 murders per 100,000 population. Compare this to countries with strong gun laws: the rate is .04 per 100,000 in Japan, .05 in Britain, .52 in Canada.

The National Rifle Association suggests that, if a person wants to commit a murder and does not have a gun, he will find some other way to do it. This proposition is at best dubious, and it does not apply at all to the murder of political leaders. No one has ever tried to assassinate a President with a bow and arrow. Every assassination and attempted assassination has been by gun; and, if we could reduce that, we would at least gain something. Still, however useful in making it harder for potential murderers to get guns, federal gun legislation deals with the symptoms and not with the causes of our trouble. We must go farther to account for the resurgence in recent years of our historical propensity toward violence.*

* President Johnson inevitably appointed a commission to solve this question. One member was Senator Roman Hruska of Nebraska, the National Rifle Association's chief senatorial spokesman; appointing him to a commission on violence was like sending Typhoid Mary to stop a typhoid epidemic. Another member was Eric Hoffer, who had explained away the murder of Senator Kennedy by saying that it had been done by a foreigner. Had Sirhan Sirhan, who spent half his life in the United States, won the Nobel Prize, Mr. Hoffer would no doubt have claimed him as a model of the American way of life. While the commission included two establishment blacks, an ex-ambassadress and a federal judge, it had no representatives of the alienated groups in American society, no scholars, no scientists, not even a representative of organized labor. When President Johnson made some supplementary appointments, he added not Dr. Kenneth Clark or Cesar Chavez but an aged and conservative ex-senator, a Texas lawyer and a respectable psychiatrist.

4. Televiolence

One reason surely for the enormous tolerance of violence in contemporary America is that our country has now been more or less continuously at war for a generation. The fact that we invented the atomic bomb and have never lost our nuclear superiority has no doubt encouraged us to internationalize our favorite folk myths and to see ourselves as planetary frontier marshals and private eyes now charged with using force to establish order around the globe.

More particularly, the experience of war over a long period devalues human life and habituates people to killing. And the war in which we are now engaged is far more brutalizing than was the Second World War or the Korean War. It is more brutalizing because the destruction we have wrought in Vietnam is so wildly out of proportion to rational considerations of our national security or our national interest. In the other wars we killed for need. In this war we killed beyond need, and, as we do so, we corrupt our national life. When violence is legally sanctioned for a cause in which many see no moral purpose, this is an obvious stimulus to some to use violence for what they may maniacally consider moral purposes of their own.

War is one source of what R. J. Lifton has described as "psychic numbing" — the numbing which leads people to acquiesce in the climate of violence. A second source is surely the zest with which the mass media, and especially television and films, dwell on violence. One must be clear about this. The mass media do not create violence. But they reinforce aggressive and destructive impulses, and they may well teach the morality as well as the methods of violence.

This all cannot be blamed on the electronic media. Comic books have long provided invaluable advance indoctrination. "With rare exceptions," Gershon Legman wrote in 1949, "every child in America who was six years old in 1938 has by now absorbed an absolute minimum of eighteen thousand pictorial beatings, shootings, stranglings, blood-puddles, and torturings-to-death, from comic (ha-ha) books alone, identifying himself — unless he is a complete masochist — with the heroic beater, shooter, strangler, blood-letter, and/or torturer in every case." * We have improved things since 1949. The day after Robert Kennedy's death the comic (ha-ha) strip "Dick Tracy" offered its readers the aphorism: VIOLENCE IS GOLDEN WHEN IT'S USED TO PUT DOWN EVIL. Construed strictly, the proposition may be defensible (like our political Dick Tracy's comparable maxim, "Extremism in the defense of liberty is no vice"). But it depends a good deal on who defines the evil to be put down; one trusts not Dick Tracy or his political equivalents.

The electronic media, however, foster the subculture of violence with far more vividness and in far greater depth than the older typographic forms. Marshall McLuhan has offered the interesting suggestion that the shift from old to new technologies of communication inevitably generates psychic friction. "The TV generation has neither identity nor goals. Its instinct is to plunge into tragic violence as a means of

---

* In that brilliant essay *Love and Death* (New York, 1949), p. 31. This tract, which should be republished, raises a basic question for the theorists of censorship: "We are faced in our culture by the insurmountable schizophrenic contradiction that sex, which is legal in fact, is a crime on paper, while murder — a crime in fact — is, on paper, the best seller of all time. . . . Murder is a crime. Describing murder is not. Sex is not a crime. Describing sex *is*. Why?"

creating a new identity or image." One does not have fully to accept this to recognize that, if people seek identity, or at least historical notoriety, through violence, nothing serves their purpose more effectively than the instantaneous and comprehensive coverage of contemporary television.

In recent years the movies and television have developed a pornography of violence far more demoralizing than the pornography of sex which still monopolizes the attention of the guardians of civic virtue. Popular films of our day like *Rosemary's Baby* and *Bonnie and Clyde* imply a whole culture of human violation, psychological in one case, physical in the other. *Bonnie and Clyde*, indeed, was greatly admired for its blithe acceptance of the world of violence — an acceptance which almost became a celebration. Thus a student in a film course in San Francisco:

> There is a certain spirit that belongs to us. We the American people. It is pragmatic, rebellious, violent, joyous. It can create or kill. Everything about *Bonnie and Clyde* captures this spirit.
>
> John Brown was motivated by this spirit and it has scared the hell out of historians ever since. The Black Panthers have it. Cab drivers, musicians, used-car salesmen and bus drivers understand it, but doctors, dentists and real estate salesmen don't.

Television is the most pervasive influence of all. The children of the electronic age sit hypnotized by the parade of killings, beatings, gunfights, knifings, maimings, brawls which flash incessantly across the tiny screen, and now in "living" color.* In the issue of the *Saturday Review* which came on the newsstands the week before Robert Kennedy was killed,

* Will NBC please sometime explain what in the world "dead" color is?

Richard L. Tobin reported the results of an eight-hour moni-
toring of the three networks and half a dozen local outlets:

> We marked down ninety-three specific incidents involving
> sadistic brutality, murder, cold-blooded killing, sexual cruelty
> and related sadism. . . . We encountered seven different
> kinds of pistols and revolvers, three varieties of rifle, three
> distinct brands of shotgun, half a dozen assorted daggers and
> stilettos, two types of machete, one butcher's cleaver, a
> broadaxe, rapiers galore, a posse of sabers, and electric prod-
> der, and a guillotine. Men (and women and even children)
> were shot by gunpowder, burned at the stake, tortured over
> live coals, trussed and beaten in relays, dropped into molten
> sugar, cut to ribbons (in color), repeatedly kneed in the groin,
> beaten while being held defenseless by other hoodlums, for-
> cibly drowned, whipped with a leather belt. . . . By the end
> of the stint we were quite insensitive, almost immune to the
> shock of seeing a human being in pain.

And, despite the periodic exhortations of the Federal Communications Commission and the periodic pieties of network
magnates, the proportion of time devoted to cruelty has
steadily increased since the beginning of television. A 1954
survey showed that 22.3 percent of the programs between 4
and 10 P.M. featured violence and crime; in 1961 the proportion had increased by more than a third to 34.2 percent. For
"prime time" — 7 to 10 P.M. — the proportion had jumped
even more spectacularly — from 16.6 percent in 1964 to
50.6 percent in 1961. A 1964 survey showed a "perceptible
decline" in the extent to which one network — CBS — went
in for violence; but the other networks took up the slack, and
the aggregate percentages remained about the same.

For a time the television industry comforted itself with the
theory that children listened to children's programs and that,

if by any chance they saw programs for adults, violence would serve as a safety valve, offering a harmless outlet for pent-up aggressions: the more violence on the screen, the less in life. Alas, this turns out not to be necessarily so. As Dr. Wilbur Schramm, director of the Institute of Communication Research at Stanford has reported, children, even in the early elementary school years, view more programs designed for adults than for themselves; "above all, they prefer the more violent type of adult program including the Western, the adventure program, and the crime drama." Experiments show that such programs, far from serving as safety valves for aggression, attract children with high levels of hostility and stimulate them to seek overt means of acting out their aggressions. Evidence suggests that these programs work the same incitement on adults. According to the Senate Subcommittee to Investigate Juvenile Delinquency, "Experiments have shown that normal persons who see a violent film subsequently exhibit nearly twice as much violence as persons who have not seen such a film." *

While the scientific study of these questions is not conclusive, it is surely reasonable to suppose that continuous exposure to the spectacle of violence creates the insensitivity mentioned by Richard L. Tobin; that, in the words of the

---

* An exchange between Congressman Hale Boggs and Dr. Frank Stanton, president of the Columbia Broadcasting System, before the National Commission on the Causes and Prevention of Violence is relevant here:

   Boggs: How much did the sponsors of President Nixon spend at CBS in the last campaign? Would you say it was a substantial sum?
   Stanton: I would.
   Boggs: Why do you think they spent that money?
   Stanton: Because it's an effective medium to reach people.
   Boggs: Well now, why is television effective in reaching people in advertising political campaigns and is not effective when it shows sadism, masochism, murder, mayhem and rape?

Senate Subcommittee, it encourages the "acceptance of excessive violence as the 'normal' way of life." And televiolence does more than condition emotion and behavior. It also may attenuate people's sense of reality. Men murdered on the television screen reappear on another show next week; death is never permanent and is therefore diminished. A child asked a woman in June 1968 where she was headed in her car. "To Washington," she said. "Why?" he asked. "To attend the funeral of Senator Kennedy." The child said, "Oh yeah — they shot him again." And such shooting may well condition the manner in which people approach the perplexities of existence. On television the hero glibly resolves his problems by killing somebody. The *Gunsmoke* ethos, however, is not necessarily the best way to deal with human or social complexity.

The problem of electronic violence raises difficult questions of prescription as well as of analysis. It would be fatal to restrain artistic exploration and portrayal, even of the most extreme and bitter aspects of human experience. No sensible person wants to reestablish a reign of censorship or mobilize new Legions of Decency. Nor is there great gain in making the electronic media scapegoats for propensities which they reflect rather than create — propensities which spring from our history and our hearts.

Yet society retains a certain right of self-defense. Dr. Ralph Garry put the matter succinctly some years ago: "A writer who can resolve a plot only by killing the villain is incompetent; a producer who deliberately employs violence and brutality to attract an audience is unscrupulous; a network which encourages such material, even by default, is irresponsible; and a sponsor which accepts such sadism if it produces sales is unethical." Is it inconceivable that the

television industry might work out forms of self-restraint? *
Beyond this, it should be noted that the networks and the
stations do *not* own the airways; the nation does; and, if the
industry cannot restrain itself, the Communications Act
offers means as yet unused of democratic control.

The standard, it seems to me, must always be the artistic
one. Authentic artistic merit and purpose should never be
censored. But prefabricated trash can properly be subject
to control. Who is to decide which is which? Expert testimony would seem the best answer (and by "expert testimony" one means the testimony of artists and critics, not of
cops and censors; the cultural expert should be a category as
well defined as the ballistics expert). And, whenever possible,
a distinction should be drawn — as Mr. Valenti's Motion
Picture Association has recently done — between adult and
youthful audiences. Walter Lippmann has written: "A continual exposure of a generation to the commercial exploitation
of the enjoyment of violence and cruelty is one way to corrode
the foundations of a civilized society. For my own part, believing as I do in freedom of speech and thought, I see no
objection in principle to censorship of the mass entertain-
ment of the young. Until some more refined way is worked
out of controlling this evil thing, the risks to our liberties are,
I believe, decidedly less than the risks of unmanageable violence."

---

* Apparently it is inconceivable. Six weeks after the murder of Robert Kennedy the *Christian Science Monitor* gave twenty-two staff members the ghastly
assignment of watching 85½ hours of television, including prime evening hours
and Saturday morning cartoons. In seven evenings of viewing the investigators
recorded 81 killings and 210 incidents or threats of violence; an additional 162
incidents were reported on Saturday morning. The most violent evening hours
were between 7:30 and 9:00 — at a time when an estimated 26.7 million
young people between the ages of two and seventeen are watching television.
In these hours violent incidents occurred on an average of once every 16.3
minutes.

Thus war and the mass media have helped give new life to the American propensity to violence. And there is a third reason for the resurgence of the destructive impulse: the rigidity of American customs and institutions. For the sad fact is that certain forms of violence, up to a point, pay off. If individual violence rarely achieves a just end, collective violence may sometimes force a society to do things which it should have done long since but which it has lacked the intelligence, decency or will to do.

So long as black Americans, for example, remained meek, submissive and invisible, white America did exceedingly little to assure them their constitutional rights. It is black self-assertion which has been primarily responsible for our recent, and shamefully belated, progress toward civil equality. Similarly forcible undergraduate protest, for better or worse, has made university administrations at last undertake reforms which should have been carried out years earlier on their merits. It is a gloomy commentary on a society when people are driven to extra-legal actions in order to get those in power to acknowledge and redress justified grievances.

The resort to violence implies the failure of reason. This does not mean that violence is by definition in every circumstance unreasonable; for there are problems which reason cannot solve. Reason cannot always disentangle the log-jam into which history may thrust the structures of society, nor can it pacify a gangster or placate a madman. The resort to violence was necessary to end slavery in America, as it was necessary to save the world from the thousand-year Reich. But violence is justified only when the resources of reason are demonstrably exhausted and when the application of force remains the only way of achieving rational ends.

5. *The Despair of Democracy*

We have a bad inheritance as far as violence is concerned; and in recent years war and the mass media have given new vitality to the darkest strains in our national psyche. How can we master this panic in our souls before it rushes society on toward disintegration? We must begin to realize how fragile the membranes of our civilization are, stretched so thin over a nation so disparate in its composition, so tense in its interior relationships, so cunningly enmeshed in underground fears and antagonisms, so entrapped by history in the ethos of violence.

Today, as our nation grows more centralized and our energy more concentrated, as our inner tensions grow more desperate and our frustrations in our own land and in the world more embittered, we can no longer regard hatred and violence as accidents and aberrations, as nightmares which will pass away when we awake. We must exert every effort to protect and strengthen the membranes of civility against the impulses of destruction. In this effort, I would suggest, a special responsibility rests on our intellectual community. For one can expect primitive emotions on the part of those who detest the life of the mind. But the intellectual community should be the particular custodian of the life of reason. It should be the particular champion of discipline and restraint. It should be the particular enemy of hatred and violence.

Little is more dismaying than the way in which some, a few, in the intellectual community have rejected the process of reason, have succumbed to the national susceptibility for hatred and violence, have, indeed, begun themselves to exalt hatred and violence as if primitivism in emotion constituted a higher morality. One does not suggest that these intellectuals are responsible for the atrocities committed at home and abroad. One does suggest that they have contributed to the atmosphere which has begun to accept and almost to legitimatize hatred and violence. One does suggest that they are reinforcing the assault on civility and hastening the decomposition of the American social process.

What has led to the intellectuals' revolt against reason? It would seem likely that a pervasive incitement has been the war in Vietnam — a war which has tempted our government into its course of appalling and insensate destruction, a war which, through the draft, has demanded that Americans kill and die where they can see no clear connection between personal sacrifice and national interest. But the cause is more than the Vietnam war. For that war has come to prefigure a larger incomprehensibility, a larger absurdity, even a larger wickedness, in our official society. For some it has come to seem the inevitable result of the irremediable corruption of the American system.

I cannot share the belief that there was something foreordained and ineluctable about the war in Vietnam — that the nature of American society would have compelled any set of men in Washington to pursue the same course of folly. This really seems determinist nonsense. One can still understand, though, why the contradictions of our society weigh so heavily on the sensitive — the contradictions between the righteousness of a Secretary of State and the ruthlessness of a B-52; between the notion that violence is fine against simple folk ten thousand miles away and shocking against injustice in our own land; between the equality demanded by our constitutional structure and the equality denied by our social structure.

The very weight of these contradictions has produced a rush of despair about libertarian democracy itself. By libertarian democracy I mean simply the system in which the rule of the majority at any given time rests on the guarantee of the right of minorities to convert themselves into new majorities. Such a system assumes political action to be in its essence a rational process — that is, a deliberate choice of means to achieve desired ends. As a rational process, libertarian democracy requires the widest possible freedom of discussion and debate; and this implies, of course, a considerable indulgence of wrongheadedness and imbecility along the way.

This has been the American theory, as laid down, for example, in the Constitution and the Bill of Rights. And, in the course of our national history, libertarian democracy has led to many useful results. It has also led to many frustrations. It has left problems unsolved, wrongs unredressed, sinners unpunished. It cannot be relied upon to produce rapid and conclusive change. The very insistence on reasonableness and due process has seemed at times a pretext for inaction and therefore a mask for injustice.

This has been particularly the case in recent years. From the moment we started bombing North Vietnam in February 1965, our government appeared rigidly unresponsive to reasoned criticism of its course. The halting pace of the movement toward racial justice further strengthened doubts about the hope of rational reform. Some, persuaded that change was impossible within the constitutional order, started to turn to civil disobedience and emotional agitation, even to violent protest. A sense began to arise that libertarian democracy itself was impotent in the new world of economic, military and intellectual corporatism. One saw a growing conviction that party politics were a façade and fake. One saw a growing cynicism about democratic institutions, a growing defection from the democratic process. In due course, the spreading sense of the impotence of libertarian democracy generated a creed systematically and passionately opposed to libertarian democracy.

6. Existential Politics

This new creed has two parts. The negative part is an attempt to clear away what its theorists regard as the noxious rubbish of the Bill of Rights. The new creed thus perceives the First Amendment as the keystone not of liberty but of a cunning apparatus of tolerance employed by an oppressive social order to thwart basic change. I do not wish to do this new doctrine an injustice, so I will state in the words of its leading advocate — that is, Herbert Marcuse — the belief that it is *necessary* and *right*, as a matter of principle, to howl down views with which one disagrees and to suppress those who utter such views.

Mr. Marcuse begins with the proposition that contemporary society, in his idiom, is defined by "the passing of the historical forces which, at the preceding stage of society, seemed to represent the possibility of new forms of existence." In other words, contemporary society has absorbed and abolished the historic means of social revolution. It has learned the secret of "containing social change — qualitative change which would establish essentially different institutions, a new direction of the productive process, new modes of human existence." It has done this, Mr. Marcuse argues, through an ingenious and despicable combination of welfarism, tolerance and manipulation. Capitalism, in short, subverts potential opponents by offering them a measure of apparent economic security and personal freedom. Mr. Marcuse regards this as a terrible state of affairs. As he sees it, any improvement in the condition of the powerless and the oppressed only plays into the hands of the rulers — and is therefore to be regretted. "The totalitarian tendencies of the one-dimensional society render the traditional ways and means of protest ineffective — perhaps even dangerous because they preserve the illusion of popular sovereignty."

Tolerance is evil because it dissipates the force of protest. It is also evil because it permits the promulgation of evil ideas. Therefore, Mr. Marcuse suggests, the way to revive the dream of social change is to strike at the root of the evil. He is candid about his repudiation of the Bill of Rights.

> The traditional criterion of clear and present danger seems no longer adequate to a stage where the whole society is in the situation of the theater audience when somebody cries: "Fire." . . . The whole post-fascist period is one of clear and present danger. Consequently, true pacification requires the withdrawal of tolerance before the deed, at the stage of communication in word, print, and picture. . . . Certain things cannot be said, certain ideas cannot be expressed, certain policies cannot be proposed, certain behavior cannot be permitted without making tolerance an instrument for the continuation of servitude.

And he is specific about what he would forbid. His program, as he states it, would include the withdrawal of toleration of speech and assembly from groups and movements which promote aggressive policies, armament, chauvinism, discrimination on the grounds of race and religion, or which oppose the extension of public services, medical care, etc. Moreover, the restoration of freedom of thought may necessitate new and rigid restrictions on teachings and practices in the educational institutions.*

Mr. Marcuse's call for the forcible suppression of false ideas is, I have suggested, the first part of the new creed. No one can doubt the relish with which activists have seized the mantle of intellectual respectability thus offered them. So Paul Krassner, editor of a popular underground paper, the *Realist*, in a yippie manifesto: "No more marches. No more speeches. The dialogue is over, baby. Tolerance of rational dissent has become an insidious form of oppression. The goal now is to disrupt an insane society." Of course, this sort of

---

* Mr. Marcuse, enjoying the protection of the Bill of Rights, regards tolerance with contempt and intellectual freedom as a sham and sees American society as far down the road to totalitarianism. How grotesque his arguments must seem to people living in truly totalitarian societies! The Russian physicist Andrei D. Sakharov, writing at great personal risk his underground pamphlet "Thoughts on Progress, Peaceful Coexistence and Intellectual Freedom," is a good deal less disdainful about the disadvantages of liberty. "Intellectual freedom," he says, "is essential to human society — freedom to obtain and distribute information, freedom for open-minded and unfearing debate and freedom from pressure by officialdom and prejudices. . . . The key to a progressive restructuring of the system of government in the interests of mankind lies in an intellectual freedom."

In the summer of 1968, some California reactionaries, perhaps following the Marcuse argument too closely, threatened to murder this champion of intolerance. Subsequently (in the *New York Review of Books*, August 22, 1968) Mr. Marcuse signed a letter about the impending Democratic convention, concluding, "We demand an open Convention," thereby claiming in a somewhat lordly manner for himself what, as a matter of principle, he has argued should be denied to those whose views he dislikes. Ordinarily this would have to be accounted an extraordinary act of impertinence. But perhaps his recent California experience has persuaded my old friend that there may be some point in the Bill of Rights.

assault on the Bill of Rights is not new, even for radicals. The Stalinists of the thirties, for example, had no compunction in arguing in much the same way that civil freedom should be denied those who rejected the Stalinist truth. What particularly distinguishes the New Left of the sixties from previous American radicalisms is the second part of its creed — and here not the summons to revolution, which again is familiar, but the refusal to state revolutionary goals except in the most abstract and empty language. To put it more precisely, what distinguishes the New Left is not only its unwillingness to define what it aims for after the revolution but its belief that such mystification is a virtue.

On its positive side the new creed becomes, so to speak, a kind of existentialism in politics — a rudimentary kind, no doubt, but still rooted in some manner in the existential perception that man dwells in an absurd universe and defines himself through his choices. In extreme cases, this perception may lead to *voyages au bout de la nuit*: as Nietzsche said, "Nihilism represents the ultimate logical conclusion of our great values and ideals — because we must experience nihilism before we can find out what value these 'values' really had." In its serious form, existentialism can lead to an immense and intense sense of individual responsibility as every man realizes that only he can provide his own escape from the enveloping nothingness around him. In its vulgar form, however, with which we are dealing here, existential politics becomes the notion that we must feel and act before we think; it is the illusion that the experience of feeling and action will mysteriously produce the insight and the policy.

Our contemporary existential politics springs much more from Sorel than from Kierkegaard. Sorel drew a distinction between myths, which, he said, were "not descriptions of things, but expressions of a determination to act," and utopias, which were intellectual products, the work of theorists who "seek to establish a model to which they can compare existing society." Sorel regarded utopias — that is, rational programs — as contemptible. The myth must be the basis of action; the myth would produce the revolution, which would thereafter produce its own program; and "the myth," Sorel emphasized, "must be judged as a means of acting on the present; any attempt to discuss how far it can be taken literally as future history is devoid of sense." * So, in the footsteps of Sorel, the New Leftists believe in the omnipotence of the deed and the irrelevance of the goal. The political process is no longer seen as the deliberate choice of means to move toward a desired end. Society is to evolve through the process of struggle itself. Where libertarian democracy ideally demands means consistent with the end, and where the Stalinist Left of the thirties had contended that the end justified the means, the New Left propounds a different doctrine: that the means *create* the end.

Let us not ignore the attractions of the existential approach. After all, there are many absurdities in our world. Our country has never undertaken anything more absurd in its history than the Vietnam war. After all, man does make himself by his decisions. After all, our conventional liberalism is to a discouraging degree a liberalism of promises and excuses. After all, social renewal can only come from personal commitment.

All these things help explain, I think, the appeal of the terrible idealism of the new creed. Yet this creed contains so much in the way of fakery and fallacy — to put it bluntly, it

* *Reflections on Violence*, Introduction, Ch. 4.

is so preposterous and so depraved — that I do not see how it can long be entertained by any serious democrat.

Let us look first at the negative part: the demand for the forcible suppression of false ideas. This immediately raises a self-evident question: How is one to tell which ideas are O.K. and which are to be suppressed? "In the interplay of theory and practice," Mr. Marcuse replies, "true and false solutions become distinguishable. . . . Freedom is liberation, a specific historical process in theory and practice, and as such it has its right and wrong, its truth and falsehood." But who is to make this determination? What agency is the repository of final judgment on truth and falsehood? Here, alas, Mr. Marcuse lets us down, except to introduce hopelessly vague standards, as, for example, that "what is *not* conducive to a free and rational society, what impedes and distorts the possibilities of its creation" should be forbidden. He does not exclude repression: "there is a social and political repression which can foster human progress, which can lead toward a true democracy and a true freedom." In the end, he places his confidence in what he mystically calls "the democratic educational dictatorship of free men."

This is not very satisfactory; so let us pursue the question a step further. I suppose that the new creed does not expect to make such judgments through a man. But, if not through a man, these judgments must be made through a mechanism, which means through men. Such a mechanism would plainly have to have an extraordinary degree of power. What assurance can there ever be that this power would be used disinterestedly — that is, for the good and the true, should there ever be a means of defining the good and the true — rather than in the interests of the men operating the mechanism? What will this mechanism become — what have such mechanisms ever become — but a means to suppress criticism of the manipulators of the mechanism? So the mechanism, in the end, rests on an assumption of human infallibility.

But the assumption of human infallibility has never been justified in the long and varied history of mankind. It implies the rule of those whom Mr. Dooley long ago defined as men who do what they think "th' Lord wud do if He only knew the facts in th' case" — and Mr. Dooley was defining a fanatic. Jefferson in his First Inaugural made a relevant comment: "Sometimes it is said that man cannot be trusted with the government of himself. Can he, then, be trusted with the government of others? Or have we found angels in the form of kings to govern him? Let history answer this question." History has answered the question: man has never found angels in the form of kings, or even of philosopher-kings, to govern him. And, if he should, "the unfortunate thing," Pascal said, "is that he who would act the angel acts the brute."

Not only do men who claim infallibility in politics do far more evil than good, but the systematic suppression of supposedly false ideas would deeply impoverish human knowledge and understanding. "There is no error so crooked," Tupper said, "but it hath in it some lines of truth." Or, as Norman Mailer recently put it, "Sometimes a profound idea is buried in a particularly ugly notion." Human creativity takes a marvelous and sinister diversity of forms. How dare anyone assume the right to deny the unlimited freedom of human expression? "I tolerate with the utmost latitude the right of others to differ from me in opinion without imputing to them criminality," wrote Jefferson. "I know too well the weakness and uncertainty of human reason to wonder at its different result."

The demand for the forcible suppression of "false" ideas would be an enormously effective way of calling a halt to human progress. And the other half of the new creed makes no more sense: that is, the conviction that one should feel and act first and think later, that the struggle generates the program and the means create the end. The kind of action supremely required to strike through the mask of official society, we are told, is violence. Without violence, official society, in its present sophistication, will calmly co-opt and emasculate the opposition. Only violence will force official society to drop the smiling mask of tolerance and reveal its inner viciousness. More than this, violence becomes a means of social and individual redemption. As Frantz Fanon has written, "Violence is a cleaning force. It frees the native from his inferiority complex and from his despair and inaction; it makes him fearless and restores his self-respect. . . . Violence alone, violence committed by the people, violence organized and educated by its leaders, makes it possible for the masses to understand social truths."

This is hardly, of course, a novel doctrine. Others in this century have eloquently propagated the cult of the deed. It was, after all, Mussolini who used to distinguish between "a violence that liberates, and a violence that enslaves . . . a violence that is moral and a violence that is immoral." And it was Hitler who wrote, "The very first essential for success is a perpetually constant and regular employment of violence." It is perfectly obvious why Mussolini and Hitler favored violence: because violence, by abolishing the procedures and civilities of society, opens the way for those who are most adept in the mobilization of force. I do not know about the situation in developing countries; there violence in certain contexts may be an indispensable means of establishing a sense of national identity. But surely little is more pathetic than the view that in American society violence will benefit the left.

A limited amount of collective violence may stimulate the process of democratic change; but, if the left, through the cult of the deed, helps create an atmosphere which destroys the process of democracy itself, the only winners will be those who use violence best, and they will be on the right. "If they want blood to flow from our heads," Tom Hayden cried bravely in Chicago, "the blood will flow from a lot of other heads around this city and around this country. We must take to the streets, for the streets belong to the people. . . . It may well be that the era of organized, peaceful and orderly demonstrations is coming to an end, and that other methods will be needed." If the New Left should finally succeed in making American politics a competition in hysteria and force, does any New Leftist really suppose that Tom Hayden and Eldridge Cleaver will bring more armed men into the streets than George Wallace?

The new creed, with its dismissal of free discussion and its conviction that violence will mystically generate policy and program, represents an assault on rationality in politics — an assault based on the ultimate proposition that rights and wrongs in public affairs are so absolute and so easily ascertainable that opposition can be legitimately forbidden. This assault on the Bill of Rights and on libertarian democracy is in my judgment wrong, because no one is infallible. It is stupid, because the beneficiaries will not be the idealists of the left but the brutalists of the right. It is dangerous because it represents a reversion to and rationalization of the strain of hatred and violence in our own national tradition:

the politics of lynch law against the politics of Lincoln. The New Left, in this respect, casts its vote for the worst against the best in our political ethos.

Above all, the new creed overlooks the fact of human frailty. "Men are not flattered," wrote Lincoln, "by being shown that there has been a difference of purpose between the Almighty and them." Yet men are not gods. That is why absolutism always fails in human society. Democracy requires consent — it insists, that is, that a majority of the electorate eventually be persuaded that one course is preferable to another. If men or mechanisms were infallible, there would be no need for such persuasion. But, because they are not, the discipline of consent is indispensable to civilized society. The discipline of consent means that policies must triumph not through the divine right of kings or of a "democratic educational dictatorship" but through making sense to a majority of the people; and the condition of bringing a majority along is the best guarantee that policies relate, not to private fantasy or personal power, but to the greatest good of the greatest number.

Nietzsche once wrote, "Gaze not too deeply into the abyss, lest the abysss gaze into you." Those who claim to *know* — to be the bearers of absolute truth — are men who have gazed too deeply into the abyss. They have committed what Hawthorne called the Unpardonable Sin — the sin of self-pride, which enslaves people, breeds fanaticism and concludes in madness and catastrophe. It is sad when the derelicts of our society surrender to the Unpardonable Sin; it is contemptible when our intellectuals exemplify it. Worse, these intellectuals who have gazed into the abyss see nothing except the virtue of destruction-for-destruction's-sake; and they then present the absence of intelligible objectives as evidence of the purity of their cause. They should remember Tocqueville: "In a rebellion, as in a novel, the most difficult part to invent is the end."

Let us strike out against the concrete evils of our time. But let us not yield to that awful despair which dissolves all distinctions in thought and action and hurtles us on to the politics of apocalypse. In the long run, any sane society must rest on freedom and reason. If we abandon this, we abandon everything.

7. The Recognition of Responsibility

This discussion of the new creed may seem irrelevant to the pragmatic insurgencies of our society. And, indeed, as long as these insurgencies remain pragmatic — that is, related to specific issues and specific injustices — they represent a desperately needed pressure against the established complacencies of a self-righteous nation. Yet the new creed exists; it has received serious, if not convincing, formulation; it has won support because of the spreading sense in recent years of the impotence of libertarian democracy; and it has created among some of the young a mystical passion for revolutionary upheaval.

I have said that the new creed will only weaken democracy against its enemies. I would say further that it underestimates the power of rational democracy — that is, the power of the people, in one way or another, to modify the system and alter its course. We have had, I noted earlier, a season of despair about our democracy. But those whom despair led on to desperation underestimated the capacity of public opinion eventually to catch on to what is happening, even in fairly controlled and manipulated societies, and to demand a change in things. This has happened even in paternalist states, like France. It has happened even in communist states, like Czechoslovakia. And it has happened in our own country.

Here the democratic process has turned out to be more effective than its critics had supposed. The rebellion against libertarian democracy gathered momentum, we have noted, because of the obstinate determination of our government to pursue a policy of military escalation in Vietnam. Yet in the early months of 1968 the democratic process, working in its own inscrutable way, forced the President to suspend the escalation policy; it forced him to begin preliminary peace talks; it forced him to withdraw from the presidential contest. These were not inconsiderable accomplishments. One cannot contend that the process works swiftly or surely. Yet, with all its tardiness and inconclusiveness, democracy in America continues to show as much vitality and efficacy as the processes of political change in any other land. "The sober, second thought of the people," Martin Van Buren said years ago, "is never wrong, and always efficient." At any rate, it is wiser in the long run than the nonsense of the absolutists.

But the democratic process works only so long as all hands respect the fabric of civility. The preservation of this fabric makes everything else possible. When it is rent, the whole order may begin to unravel, and force will take over — unless the nation rallies to restore the decencies and continuities of society. There is not a problem of collective guilt, but there is a problem of collective responsibility. Certainly two hundred million Americans did not strike down John Kennedy or Martin Luther King or Robert Kennedy. But two hundred million Americans are plainly responsible for the character of a society that works on deranged men and incites them to depraved acts. There were Lee Harvey Oswalds and James Earl Rays and Sirhan Bishara Sirhans in America in the thirties — angry, frustrated, alienated, resentful, marginal men in rootless, unstable cities like Dallas and Memphis and Los Angeles. But our society in the thirties did not stimulate such men to compensate for their own failure by killing leaders the people loved.

Unless, like Lincoln, we acknowledge the existence of the problem, unless we see the destructive impulse as rooted in our history, our society, and ourselves, we will never be able to conquer and transcend the trouble within. Musing by blue Ontario's shore after Lincoln's murder, Walt Whitman wrote of democracy:

(Democracy, the destin'd conquerer, yet treacherous lip-
    smiles everywhere,
And death and infidelity at every step.)

and went on to accept responsibility:

O I see flashing that this America is only you and me,
Its power, weapons, testimony, are you and me,
Its crimes, lies, thefts, defections, are you and me,
Its Congress is you and me, the officers, capitols, armies, ships,
    are you and me . . .

I dare not shirk any part of myself,
Not any part of America good or bad,
Not to build for that which builds for mankind,
Not to balance ranks, complexions, creeds, and the sexes . . .

I will not be outfaced by irrational things,
I will penetrate what it is in them that is sarcastic upon me,
I will make cities and civilizations defer to me,
This is what I have learnt from America — it is the amount,
    and it I teach again. . . .

America isolated yet embodying all, what is it finally except
    myself?
These States, what are they except myself?

The young, I think, understand this. They are tired of alibis
when they see the men they admired most shot down. They
are tired of hearing the older generation say that it was only
some crackpot or foreigner, and that America, this anointed
nation of law and order, had nothing to do with it. They regard such statements as lies, and they can no longer abide the
official hypocrisies. Their sense of our life is the one that
John F. Kennedy expressed in the summer of 1963 when he
concluded an informal talk with representatives of some national organizations by suddenly quoting Blanch of Spain's
speech from *King John:*

> The sun's o'ercast with blood: fair day, adieu!
> Which is the side that I must go withal?
> I am with both: each army hath a hand;
> And in their rage, I having hold of both,
> They whirl asunder and dismember me.

It was this sense of the awful precariousness of existence
which had led President Kennedy to say in his first State of
the Union message: "Before my term is ended, we shall have
to test anew whether a nation organized and governed such
as ours can endure. The outcome is by no means certain."

The outcome is far less certain today. Some of the young
in their despair have come to feel that the answer to reason

is unreason, the answer to violence more violence; but these only hasten the plunge toward the abyss. The more intelligent disagree. They do not want America to beat its breast and go back to the golf course. *They do want America to recognize its responsibility*. They want us to tell it like it is — to confront the darkness in our past and the darkness in our present. They want us to realize that life is not solid and predictable but infinitely chancy, that violence is not the deviation but the ever-present possibility, that we can therefore never rest in the effort to prevent unreason from rendering the skin of civility. They want our leaders to *talk* less about law and order and *do* more about justice. They want to carry forward the fight for decency and rationality in the social and economic arrangements of our society.

If we are to survive as a community, we must acknowledge the destructive impulse. Let us not indulge in utopian fantasies about its abolition: Augustine and Freud unite in testifying to aggression as an organic part of the human disposition. It is safe to predict that there will never be a non-violent human society. But we can resist our inbred instinct for violence instead of capitulating to it or celebrating it. We can resist our inbred instinct for absolutism and finality. As we identify these antihuman impulses, as we strive against them wherever they appear — whether in the gutter press or in the abstractions of intellectuals — we create a chance of defying the winds of unreason. We must, indeed, define ourselves by our choices, but we must do so by making the choices which respect human reason and human dignity, the choices which acknowledge and nourish the human capacity for mutual respect and affection.

When Martin Luther King was murdered, Robert Kennedy

broke the news of his death to a black audience on a street
corner at dusk in Indianapolis. He said:

> In this difficult day, in this difficult time for the United
> States, it is perhaps well to ask what kind of a nation we
> are and what direction we want to move in. For those of
> you who are black . . . you can be filled with bitterness,
> with hatred, and a desire for revenge. We can move in that
> direction as a country, in great polarization — black people
> amongst black, white people amongst white, filled with hatred
> toward one another.
>
> Or we can make an effort, as Martin Luther King did, to
> understand and to comprehend, and to replace that violence,
> that stain of bloodshed that has spread across our land, with
> an effort to understand with compassion and love. . . . I had
> a member of my family killed, but he was killed by a white
> man. But we have to make an effort in the United States, we
> have to make an effort to understand. . . . What we need
> . . . is not division; what we need . . . is not hatred; what
> we need . . . is not violence or lawlessness, but love and wis-
> dom, and compassion toward one another, and a feeling of
> justice towards those who still suffer within our country,
> whether they be white or they be black.

He concluded with a quotation from Aeschylus: "In our
sleep, pain which cannot forget, falls drop by drop upon the
heart until, in our own despair, against our will, comes wisdom through the awful grace of God."

This is the spirit in which Lincoln strove to overcome violence and hate. Perhaps America might now learn from this —
learn that sanctimony is not a persuasive answer to anguish,
and that we can never cure ourselves if we deny the existence
of a disease. If we learn this, if we face up to the schism in our
national tradition, we will have a better chance of subduing

the impulse of destruction and of fulfilling the vision of Lincoln — that noble vision of a serene and just community, united by bonds of affection and mystic chords of memory, dedicated at last to our highest ideals.

II

THE INTELLECTUAL
AND AMERICAN SOCIETY

THE CRISIS OF AMERICAN CONFIDENCE comes in part from a
growing sense of the dissociation between ideas and power.
On the one hand, the spread of violence challenges the old
belief in the efficacy of reason; on the other, the new structures brought into existence by modern industrial society intensify the feelings of individual impotence. The great organizations which tower over us seem to have a life and momentum of their own; they consume human beings and human ideas as they consume steel and electricity. Above all,
the accelerating pace of social and technological change
heightens the impression of a world out of human control.
We all today are constrained to see ourselves as helpless victims of the velocity of history.

The fear that ideas have failed as a means of social control
fills the intellectual community, of course, with particular
anguish. However, the dilemma of the man of ideas in a
world of power is by no means new. Like everything
else, it was pondered by the ancient Greeks, who indicated
well over two thousand years ago the range of ways by
which the mind might relate to the state: the philosopher as
the critic of power (Socrates), the philosopher as tutor of

princes (Aristotle), the philosopher as king (Plato). In the background, moreover, the poets provided a chorus of editorial comment still familiar in its range and inflection: Homer, who converted public men into heroes; Aristophanes, who converted them into fools; Aeschylus, Sophocles and Euripides, the tragic judges. In classical Asian civilizations, men of ideas were often part of the world of power as a natural course. The Brahmans constituted one of the highest castes in India; China recruited its *literati* by competitive examination and commissioned them to run the state as civil servants.

1. *The Rise of the Modern Intellectual*

But in its contemporary form the problem of the relationship between ideas and power emerged in the eighteenth century. For it was in this century that men of ideas and letters — the modern intellectuals — first appeared in the West as a distinct secular group. Several things accounted for the rise of this new vocation. The monopoly of religion over the life of the mind in Christendom had been suffering slow erosion. Now in the eighteenth century its evident breakdown — at least as a system capable of meeting the emerging needs of the national state and the technical economy — set the lay intellectual free. As secularization advanced, the intellectual increasingly usurped the ancient prerogatives of the priest. His philosophy began to displace theology as the means of validating human value and purpose. His science supplemented and then supplanted the Bible as the key to nature and man. His universities succeeded the monasteries as the source of instruction for the present and inspiration for the future. His history assumed the function of confirming social memory and continuity. Even his profane arts took the place of sacred ritual and design in supplying the motive for artistic creation and the substance of aesthetic pleasure.

Other factors contributed to the liberation of the modern intellectual. The diffusion of the scientific world view, the spread of movable type, the increase in literacy, the rise of book publishing and distribution, the modernization of the university — all strengthened the influence of the intellectual; and the steady urbanization of the West concentrated the impact of his ideas. At the same time, the evolving economic arrangements of capitalism challenged the society of prescriptive status and began to establish in its place a new world based on rational calculation, social mobility and the division of labor. "In opulent and commercial societies," wrote Adam Smith, "to think or to reason comes to be, like every other employment, a particular business, which is carried on by a very few people, who furnish the public with all the thought and reason possessed by the vast multitudes that labor."

Above all, perhaps, the modern intellectual was the child of nationalism. The pursuit of nationhood not only excited his enthusiasm but demanded his technical assistance. He invented the national idea, articulated the nationalist ideals, drafted manifestos and constitutions and took an active personal part in establishing the principles and shaping the precedents of the new nation-state. In the Western world two centuries ago, as in the southern hemisphere today, the intellectual thus made himself indispensable to the struggle for national independence and identity. He took advantage of his strategic position to lay down rules that would assure his subsequent freedom of action — rules that appealed at the same time to politicians and entrepreneurs who also needed a regime of liberty, if only to license their own pursuit of power or wealth. The alliance with nationalism, carrying the intellectual from the periphery to the center of authority, clothed him with some sort of legitimacy.

So the intellectuals pushed their way onto the stage of history. Before the end of the eighteenth century, Burke gloomily noted that "a new description of men had grown up . . . I mean the political men of letters." The intellectual stimulated and justified the middle-class assault on the old feudal world of religious and social absolutism. Burke's horror over "this new conquering empire of light and reason" concluded in his famous lament: "The age of chivalry is gone. That of sophisters, economists, and calculators has succeeded; and the glory of Europe is extinguished forever." "There have been three silent revolutions in England," said Coleridge: "— first, when the professions fell off from the church; secondly, when literature fell off from the professions; and, thirdly, when the press fell off from literature." As Tocqueville later observed, "Men of letters, men without wealth, social eminence, responsibilities or official status, became in practice the leading politicians of the age, since despite the fact that others held the reins of government they alone spoke with accents of authority." Writing in 1840 on "The Hero as Man of Letters," Carlyle described the phenomenon and outlined its implications. This Hero, he said, was

altogether a product of these new ages . . . He is new, I say; he has hardly lasted above a century in the world yet.

Never, till about a hundred years ago, was there seen any figure of a Great Soul living apart in that anomalous manner;
endeavouring to speak-forth the inspiration that was in him
by Printed Books, and find place and subsistence by what the
world would please to give him for doing that . . . this same
Man-of-Letters Hero must be regarded as our most important
modern person. He, such as he may be, is the soul of all.
What he teaches, the whole world will do and make. The
world's manner of dealing with him is the most significant
feature of the world's general position.

Secularization, capitalism, typography, nationalism: all
were facets of the process that molded the modern intellectual and discharged him into industrial society. And, as the
widening of industrialism rendered the social order more complex and specialized, the man of ideas acquired technical as
well as philosophical functions. Up to this point I have re-
frained from definition; but the rise of the intellectual technician in the nineteenth century makes it useful to introduce some distinctions.

By an intellectual I mean one whose home is the world of
general ideas. Some people feel instinctively at home in
the world of power: they like to do things, change things, command things, see the concrete effects of their action. Some
people feel instinctively at home in the world of nature: they
can follow trails in the forest, identify bird calls and tell
infallibly which direction is north. Others feel instinctively
at home in the world of images: they can draw pictures, perceive the harmonies of design and respond to color, form and
motion. Still others feel instinctively at home in the world
of machines: they build them, operate them, tinker with them
in their spare time and know which screw to tighten if
something goes wrong. All these groups live, in one
way or another, in a directly apprehended physical world.

The world of the intellectual — the realm of general ideas — is more abstract. Yet the intellectual responds to ideas with the same vivid intensity that the nature lover responds to the burst of color before sunset, or the aesthete to a Goya, or the mechanical-minded man to an electronic computer. He feels happy with ideas, likes to think about them, talk about them, worry them, break them down and build them up, play with them, live by them, die for them. "Nothing affects me," said Hazlitt, "but an abstract idea." He spoke as a true intellectual.

It is important, I think, to distinguish the intellectual from the artist, with whom he is sometimes confused: one is a man of general ideas, the other a man of concrete perceptions. It is equally important to distinguish the man who offers ideas from the man who offers intellectual services — the man who lives for ideas in general, so to speak, from the man who only uses particular ideas for practical purposes — the man for whom ideas are a joy from the man for whom they are only a tool. So in the nineteenth century a new class arose to meet the specialized needs generated by rising living standards and evolving technologies — lawyers, schoolmasters, doctors, engineers, civil servants, journalists, managers, intellectual bureaucrats and technicians of all sorts. Some were true intellectuals in addition, but by no means all. Nor, on the other hand, have all true intellectuals been employed in such quasi-intellectual pursuits. A delight in general ideas may erupt anywhere — even among politicians, bankers, longshoremen and women of leisure. It is the disinterested passion for large ideas, not the professional manipulation of small ideas, which marks the intellectual.

The true intellectual, in short, has served the West from ancient Athens as the carrier of general ideas, and since the eighteenth century he has lived in societies sufficiently sensitive and fluid for ideas to produce astonishing results. Yet the Western intellectual himself has also altered in these last two centuries. The contemporary intellectual, for example, has long since abandoned his alliance with the business classes and, except for the underdeveloped world, has pretty much abandoned his alliance with nationalism. Both shifts are expressions of a deeper change — a change in the attitude of the intellectual power toward itself.

2. *Intellectuals and the American Revolution*

The American experience suggests the character of the change. Here was a new nation established on an idea and by intellectuals; it represented in an exceptional sense the union of mind and state. "When the American Revolution broke," Admiral Morison has reminded us, "it was led by scholars." Scholars wrote the Constitution; indeed, three fifths of the membership of the Constitutional Convention of 1787 — an astonishing proportion at that time — had gone to one of the colonial colleges or to a comparable institution abroad. Franklin was a leading scientist. Hamilton, Madison and Jay expounded the most serious political thought of the times in the *Federalist Papers* without for a moment renouncing party conflict or turning their backs on power. Adams and Jefferson, successive Presidents, conducted in their long correspondence an astute and sustained discussion of the principles of government not likely to be matched, for example, by the Johnson-Nixon letters. The men who organized the struggle for independence and created the new republic were politician-intellectuals, capable at the same time of the most realistic political maneuver and of the most recondite intellectual analysis.

The reasons for this felicitous conjunction of ideas and responsibility have baffled historians ever since. No one can explain the extraordinary *quantity* of genius in the North American colonies in the second half of the eighteenth century. But it is easier to understand why the environment brought potential genius into public affairs. In part, it was because the Western intellectuals of the time, from Turgot, Voltaire and Struensee to Franklin, Adams and Jefferson, assumed collaboration with power as the natural order of things. In part too it was because knowledge itself was not so intricate or esoteric as to discourage men of power from trying to push back the frontiers of intellectual discovery.

The fight for national independence, in addition, not only enlisted the intellectuals of the thirteen colonies in public life but happened to coincide with an odd lull in the cycle of American aspiration. The Revolution was gathering force at just the time when the ministry, the central intellectual vocation of the early colonial days, was losing its authority — and at a time before business or science or education were asserting urgent claims on interest and talent.

In this moment of equipoise, public affairs offered the great outlet for intellectual energy. The mind of young America thus rushed into the vindicaton of the new nation. "I was animated constantly by the belief," wrote the leading physician of the time, Dr. Benjamin Rush, "that I was acting for the benefit of the whole world, and of future ages, by assisting in the formation of new means of political order and general happiness." Politicians invoked ideas without embarrassment, and intellectuals entered politics with no sense that they were doing anything but what was expected of thinkers in their society and their time. The assumption of the age was that intellect and responsibility marched together — that the world of thought naturally and inevitably interpenetrated the world of power.

This, we have seen, was the assumption Americans took from the European Enlightenment. But the specific American version stemmed from the British empirical tradition rather than from continental rationalism. The Americans were, above all, sons of Locke. They believed in natural rights, individual liberty, popular sovereignty and private property. They set it all down in the Declaration of Independence, and their peculiar social circumstances — the absence of a feudal past and thus of a revolutionary present — assured unanimity on the Lockean principles. Though the political arguments were often bitter — as between the agrarian laissez-faire of Jefferson and the industrial mercantilism of Hamilton, or between the particularism of Calhoun and the nationalism of Marshall and Webster — they rarely challenged the Lockean fundamentals. Lacking feudalism, as Louis Hartz has cogently argued, America lacked socialism; lacking a tradition of reaction, it did not need a tradition of revolution. "The great advantage of the Americans," wrote Tocqueville, "is that they have arrived at a state of democracy without having to endure a democratic revolution, and that they are born equal instead of becoming so."

The transatlantic passage, reinforcing the empirical elements in the Lockean tradition, sharpened the contrast with the rationalism of the *philosophes*. It may be useful here to introduce a distinction between *ideas* and *ideologies*. Ideas are particular insights; ideologies are ideas crystallized into universal systems. Ideas are relative, ideologies absolute. In part the difference between the man of ideas and the ideologist is a matter of temperament. Where some men accept the confusions of experience, others require the notion of ultimate rationality in the universe; these yearn for a single, fundamental, all-encompassing, all-explanatory pattern which man can apprehend and which equips him with a body of principles adequate to all the contingencies of politics and life. Tocqueville felt that this "fondness for broad generalizations, cut-and-dried legislative systems and a pedantic symmetry," this "contempt for hard facts," this "desire to reconstruct the entire constitution according to the rules of logic and a preconceived system" were characteristic weaknesses of the political man of letters: "what is a merit in the writer may well be a vice in the statesman and the very qualities which go to make great literature can lead to catastrophic revolutions." Whether Tocqueville was right about all intellectuals, he was certainly right about French intellectuals.

But the difference may in part have sprung too from contrasting social circumstances. Perhaps a stratified society encouraged belief in an ordered universe; while a society in permanent flux might be more ready to rest on contradictions (though this does not altogether account for the case of Britain). At any rate, the American experience was not friendly to systematic and rigid principles. If continental Europe tended toward the politics of ideology, the United States has tended toward the politics of ideas.

The greatest of American philosophers, William James, set forth the American view on this point when he drew his celebrated distinction between the "tender-minded" and the "tough-minded." The mark of the tender-minded man, as James saw it, was his conviction of the essential unity and harmony of things. He was a monist, who believed that the universe could be understood from a single point of view and that there was some ultimate structure which will draw together and reconcile all the conflicting meanings and values of experience. For such people, James wrote, "theory is a passion. . . . The form of inner consistency is pursued far beyond the line at which collateral profits stop. Such men systematize and classify and schematize and make synoptical tables and invent ideal objects for the pure love of unifying." They display "a temper of intellectual absolutism, a demand that the world shall be a solid block, subject to one control."

"The actual universe," James thought, "is a thing wide open, but rationalism makes systems, and systems must be closed." Against the tender-minded assumptions of monism, James urged the tough-minded claims of pluralism. For the pragmatist, "the crudity of experience remains an eternal element thereof. There is no possible point of view from which the world can appear an absolutely single fact." The pragmatist "turns away from abstraction and insufficiency, from verbal solutions, from bad *a priori* reasons, from fixed principles, closed systems, and pretended absolutes and origins. He turns toward concreteness and adequacy, toward facts, toward action, and toward power."

In such passages James clearly defined the characteristic temper of American thought. This is not to suggest that pragmatism itself did not rest, as Hartz has argued, on a "submerged and absolute liberal faith." But a difference remains between a faith which is submerged and one which is formulated and codified in a body of dogma. Nor is it to suggest that Americans have been consistently immune to the ideological temptation. The intellectual origins of the nation were saturated with one of the noblest and most formidable ideological disciplines ever devised, Calvinist theology, and any nation so conditioned was bound to have a certain vulnerability to ideology ever after. Throughout American history men have attempted to endow America with a creed, to translate Americanism into a set of binding propositions and to construe the national tradition in terms of one or another ultimate, ranging from the Natural Law to the Class Struggle.

The tension between ideas and ideology has existed even within the minds of individual American thinkers. Jefferson, for example, was an expounder of both. His ideas — his defense of intellectual liberty, his sense of the relationship between politics and economics, his faith in education, his insights into the meaning of popular government — remain fertile and alive nearly two centuries later. His ideology, however, is today remote and irrelevant. As an ideologist, for example, he believed that agriculture was the only basis of a good society; that the small freehold system was the necessary foundation for freedom; that the virtuous cultivator was the only reliable citizen for democracy; that the great enemies of a free state were urbanization, industry, banking, an industrial working class and a strong national government.

This was Jefferson's ideology, and, had Americans followed it, the United States today would be a feeble and impotent country. By responding to Jefferson's ideas rather than to his ideology, the United States has become a strong modern nation. Happily, Jefferson himself preferred his ideas to his ideology. In case of conflict he chose what concretely helped the nation rather than what conformed to abstract

principle. Indeed, the whole ideological enterprise contradicted Jefferson's temper, which was basically flexible and
experimental. The true Jefferson was not the ideological Jefferson but the Jefferson who said that one generation could
not commit the next to its view of human affairs. Only such
a Jefferson could consummate a Louisiana Purchase.

The difference between the American Revolution, on the
one hand, and the French and Russian Revolutions, on the
other, makes the point — the one a revolution of ideas, the
others revolutions of ideologies. So the revolutionary generation in America — the generation of Jefferson, Hamilton
and Madison — disengaged themselves from the ideological
embrace without, at the same time, rejecting in the slightest
the notion of the intimate connection between the man of
ideas and the world of power.

This was the conception of the intellectual which even
Emerson, the most private of thinkers, celebrated fifty years
after the Constitutional Convention in his Phi Beta Kappa
oration on "The American Scholar." Accepting in effect the
argument of Adam Smith, he said, "In this distribution of
functions the scholar is the delegated intellect. In the
right state he is *Man Thinking*." But Emerson refused to conceive thought as distinct from action or ideas as hostile to
power. "There goes in the world," he continued,

> a notion that the scholar should be a recluse, a valetudinarian,
> — as unfit for any handiwork, or public labor as a penknife
> for an axe. . . . As far as this is true of the studious classes,
> it is not just and wise. Action is with the scholar subordinate,
> but it is essential. Without it he is not yet man. Without it
> thought can never ripen into truth. . . . Inaction is coward
> ice, but there can be no scholar without the heroic mind.
> The preamble of thought, the transition through which it

passes from the unconscious to the conscious, is action. . . .
I do not see how any man can afford, for the sake of his
nerves and his nap, to spare any action in which he can
partake. . . . The true scholar grudges every opportunity
of action past by, as a loss of power.

3. The Nineteenth-Century Withdrawal from Politics

Yet the irony was that, even as Emerson was defining an
activist role for the American intellectual, American intellectuals, encouraged by Emerson himself, were receding from
public action. The last genuine intellectual to serve in the
White House in the nineteenth century — Lincoln had an
intelligence that transcended mere intellectuality — was John
Quincy Adams, whose term expired a decade before Emerson's
Phi Beta Kappa oration.

Conventional history, considerably encouraged by Adams's
grandsons half a century later, has tended to ascribe the divorce of ideas from power and the consequent "degradation
of the democratic dogma" to Adams's defeat in 1828 and the
uncouth upsurge of Jacksonian democracy. The fact, however,
that so many of the primary intellectual figures of the age of
Jackson — Cooper, Bryant, Bancroft, Hawthorne, Irving,
Whitman, Brownson — were ardent Jacksonians suggests that
young Henry and Brooks were making, in the main, a somewhat partisan and familial point. The retreat of the intellectuals had deeper causes. Most basic was the passasge of
the intellectual mind, under the influence of Coleridge

and the German idealists, from the Augustan classicism of the late eighteenth century, cool, rational and objective, to the subjectivism of the early nineteenth century.

What Whitehead has called "the romantic reaction" was now in full tide — the transcendentalist affirmation of intuition and will against the fatalism of science and theology. The object of thought was no longer external: men found the world in their own interior consciousness. Plato replaced Aristotle. Social imagination shifted from the education of statesmen to the design of utopias. Goethe, whom they all read, summed up the implications for public policy: "Let us leave politics to the diplomats and the soldiers." The American intellectual of the middle period was not expelled from public affairs. He withdrew on his own initiative and out of his own preference.

Other conditions reinforced this withdrawal. Public affairs themselves no longer excited the intellectual as they had in the early republic. Then the need for men of ideas had been acute and the opportunity thrilling. "If there is any period one would desire to be born in," said Emerson, "is it not the age of Revolution; when the old and the new stand side by side and admit of being compared; when the energies of all men are searched by fear and by hope?" Fifty years later, the national experiment was well launched; and, as Jackson more or less accurately said, the duties of government were "so plain and simple that men of intelligence may readily qualify themselves for their performance." Political authority, no longer identified with lofty purpose, seemed humdrum and mean. Political issues were few; and, after a time, intellectuals felt there was nothing more of interest to be said about internal improvements, the tariff, the national bank and the public lands. "Of all parties that have existed in the United States," observed Henry Adams, "the famous Whig party was the most feeble in ideas"; and the Democratic party of the day seemed hardly better.

Jeffersonian individualism, moreover, had contained a deep strain of oppposition to power; and this appealed to the romantic individualists of the new generation. As John Taylor of Caroline, the ideologist of Jeffersonianism, put it to James Monroe on the eve of his Presidency, "The moment you are elected, though by my casting vote, carried an hundred miles in a snow storm, my confidence in you would be most confoundedly deminished, and I would instantly join the republican minority." The revolutionary intellectuals had seen themselves as partners in the state; but the romantics, having read Kant rather than Hegel, were beginning to see themselves as the permanent, and not always loyal, opposition.

Even in the absence of the romantic withdrawal, the intellectual community, by its nature, would probably by now have drifted to the opposition. The intellectuals had joined with the commercial classes to overthrow feudalism in Europe and colonialism in the Americas, but in time they began to feel the strains of an awkward association. When their old allies threatened to become their new masters, the intellectuals discovered a new adversary. For, at least outside Germany, the analytical intelligence tended to act against power, and the carrier of ideas was generally in favor of change.

In addition, one cannot ignore a strain of anti-intellectualism always latent in American life, nourished in part by this very association of ideas with change. Indeed, when we speak of ideas, we generally mean *new* ideas; when they have been around long enough, we stop thinking of them as ideas and start regarding them as eternal verities. And obviously new ideas make trouble. "Ideas," wrote Emerson, reporting the orthodox opinion of his day, "are subversive of social order and comfort, and at last make a fool of the possessor." John Dewey later amplified this thought: "Let us admit the case of the conservative. If we once start thinking no one can guarantee what will be the outcome, except that many objects, ends, and institutions will be surely doomed. Every thinker puts some portion of an apparently stable world in peril, and no one can wholly predict what will emerge in its place."

The intellectual's role as the agent of innovation accounts for the peculiar admiration in which he is held in some circles and the peculiar consternation he rouses in others. Not all intellectuals, of course, are innovators. Some are resolute defenders of the status quo. But most American intellectuals have expressed dissatisfaction and argued for change. Those who wish to hold things as they are have no great need for ideas; they can rely on habit and inertia. "The castle, which conservatism is set to defend," wrote Emerson, "is the actual state of things, good and bad." It is the party of reform which must have ideas and people who deal with them. This, of course, helps explain the ill-repute of intellectuals, especially among those who benefit by the existing organization of society.

There are a number of reasons, beyond the inherently subversive character of thought, why the American intellectual has been characteristically inclined toward change. Another perhaps is the social and economic position of intellectuals: as outsiders, with power and status below what they consider their deserts, they tend to succumb to envy and resentment. Another is the impact of external circumstance: observing the fantastic increase in the velocity of history and perceiving before most people the need to adjust old ideas and institutions to a ceaselessly altered environment, they tend to exhort society to get on with it and keep abreast of change.

Such exhortation is no doubt beneficial; for, when society becomes rigid, when it can no longer respond flexibly to the rush of events, when, in short, it runs out of ideas, then it is doomed. But urging people to change their ways may be highly irritating, especially when the intellectual makes as many wrong guesses as anybody else and can be more self-righteous than most. The man of ideas is thus destined to be a man of tension. So Emerson added to his exhortation to the American Scholar a subtle description of what he called "the state of virtual hostility in which [the Scholar] seems to stand to society." The Scholar, Emerson said, "for the pleasure of treading the old road, accepting the fashions, the education, the religion of society . . . takes the cross of making his own, and, of course, the self-accusation, the faint heart, the frequent uncertainty and loss of time, which are the nettles and tangling vines in the way of the self-relying and self-directed." With the startling modernity which so often lurks behind the Emersonian pieties, he put the situation almost in the contemporary idiom: all his statement lacks is the word "alienation."

So, for a variety of reasons, the American intellectual forsook public affairs; the union of ideas and power which had marked the early republic languished; the wall of separation began to arise between mind and state. Slavery and the Civil War for a moment recalled men of ideas to public issues; but most of them by this time — with a few exceptions, like Bancroft — had lost a relationship to government, and their contribution, searching as it was, lay in the field of moral insight rather than policy guidance. The *Federalist Papers* had by now given way to Brook Farm and the cabin at Walden.

After the war, the situation was even more discouraging. The gilded age had no interest at all in general ideas and very little for that matter in public affairs. "The man who commands the attention of his fellows," as the younger Oliver Wendell Holmes said in the eighties, "is the man of wealth. Commerce is the great power. The aspirations of the world are those of commerce." If commercial society before the war had been indifferent to the play of ideas, now it became actively antagonistic, especially when the intellectuals dared challenge the verities, whether the protective tariff or the biblical account of the origin of man. The descendants of John Quincy Adams commenced their brilliant and interminable lamentation over the exclusion of the intellectuals from national responsibility. Politics seemed almost hateful, and the intellectual who paid any attention at all tried to sterilize party conflict through devices ranging through the spectrum from civil service reform to the initiative, referendum and recall.

Yet, if public life did not seem to require intellectuals, it was beginning to require ideas. Industrialization and urbanization were confronting American society with new and unprecedented problems — problems for which the conventional wisdom of the post-Civil War years was hardly adequate. The prevailing faith in a sound currency, a high tariff and a negative state had arisen as a series of practical responses to specific situations. But in the years after the war the influence of Herbert Spencer and Social Darwinism transmuted these positions from ideas into absolutes. The Supreme Court, led by Stephen J. Field, now read the dogmatic and comprehensive ideology of laissez-faire into the Constitution. The result was to deny government the power to act — at the very time when the movement toward economic concentration, the persisting agricultural deflation, the long and grinding depressions of the seventies and nineties, the mounting tension between labor and management, the increase in immigration and the spreading squalor of city slums were all placing the system under acute strain. The questions raised by these new social developments could only be answered by new social conceptions.

4. The Return of the Intellectuals

Intellectuals quickly responded to the need. But they did so at first — like Henry George in *Progress and Poverty* (1879), Edward Bellamy in *Looking Backward* (1888), Henry Demarest Lloyd in *Wealth Against Commonwealth* (1894) — from points well outside the world of power. Nonetheless, ideas were beginning to make their way back into political life. When the Populist party held its first national convention in 1892, its platform flung down a challenge to ideology: "We believe that the power of government — in other words, of the people — should be expanded . . . as rapidly and as far as the good sense of an intelligent people and the teachings of experience shall justify, to the end that oppression, injustice, and poverty shall eventually cease in the land." With the Populists and their revival of the Hamiltonian conception of affirmative government came a new burst of social and administrative invention in politics. Populist proposals on income taxation, railroad regulation, currency and credit expansion, farm income support, postal savings banks, direct election of senators and so on affected the course of legislation for years to come. Then in the first decade of the twentieth century, the Progressive movement, operating from an urban rather than from a rural base, carried forward the movement toward social control of private enterprise.

The basic purpose of Progressivism was to humanize the new industrial society. All Progressives rejected the ideology of laissez-faire; but the movement was divided within itself on the question of the strategy of dealing with economic concentration. One wing, whose political leader was Theodore Roosevelt and whose intellectual spokesman was Herbert Croly (*The Promise of American Life*, 1909), regarded economic concentration as irreversible and proposed to offset the bigness of business by enlarging the authority of the national government. "Every man holds his property," as Roosevelt put it in 1910, "subject to the general right of the community to regulate its use to whatever degree the public welfare may require it." The other wing had Woodrow Wilson as its political leader and Louis D. Brandeis (*Other People's Money*, 1914) as its intellectual spokesman; it was concerned with "the curse of bigness" and hoped, by breaking up large units, to restore a competitive economy. The debate between these two views brought ideas back into the heart of the political process. At the same time, Progressive leaders on the local level — notably Robert M. La Follette in Wisconsin — made a systematic effort to recruit academic experts for public service.

While industrial growth was thus creating a new role for ideas and intellectuals in domestic affairs, it was also transforming the United States into a world power and thereby creating a similar demand for new conceptions in foreign affairs. The naval intellectual Alfred Thayer Mahan began to work out the strategic implications of America's new international position in *The Influence of Sea Power upon History, 1660–1783* (1890) and other works; and Brooks Adams explored the economic implications in such books as *America's Economic Supremacy* (1900) and *The New Empire* (1902). The idea of isolationism — the opposition to what Jefferson called "entangling alliances" — had prevailed since the early republic. Mahan and Adams now formulated the first stage of the critique of isolationism. Their ideas influenced Theodore Roosevelt and the young Franklin D. Roosevelt and helped shape the terms of America's participation in international power politics.

The reunion between ideas and power was on its way. The turn of the century marked the accession to the White House of the first President since the younger Adams to feel at home in the world of general ideas. In another decade a professional political scientist who had served most of his life as a college professor and president was elected President of the nation. But the reentry of the intellectuals was pretty much confined to lawyers, economists and strategists. Indeed, politicians and even the electorate perceived that intellectuals had enlarging roles and constituencies long before this became fully evident to the intellectuals themselves. For most intellectuals power had too long bred resentment and timidity, and, with the *fin-de-siècle* imperialism of the Spanish-American War, it began to breed guilt. The state of "virtual hostility" noted by Emerson now seemed irrevocable. The intellectual class was coming to appear impotent and even ridiculous — "an indistinct herd of intellectual eunuchs," as H. L. Mencken put it in 1919, "chiefly professors . . . feeble and vacillating . . . unorganized and without authority. . . . It lacks experience of the world, assurance, the consciousness of class solidarity and security. Of no definite position in our national life, exposed alike to the clamors of the mob and the discipline of the plutocracy, it gets no public respect and is deficient in self-respect." In the next decade, intellectuals even began to flee the country, deciding that things were better ordered in France.

Yet at this very time the changes in the environment that had recalled intellectuals to politics at the turn of the century were gathering momentum. The First World War brought scholars into active, if sometimes dubious, government service. The twenties were a season of business supremacy and therefore of official anti-intellectualism; but after 1929 the depression exposed the bankruptcy of the laissez-faire state, and in 1933 Franklin Roosevelt began the systematic mobilization of social intelligence in his brain trust.

The warfare of ideas in the nineteen-thirties was perhaps the last battle between ideology and pragmatism in the conduct of American domestic affairs. A quarter of the labor force was unemployed; the national income fell to below $40 billion; and a sense of paralysis and despair was settling over American life. Winston Churchill said in 1930: "This problem of unemployment is the most torturing that can be presented to civilized society," and America faced the question what could be done to end this torture. The critical issue soon became the question of how far the national government could intervene in the economy — in other words, whether it was possible to work out a mixed and regulated economic system that would give the state enough power to assure economic and social security but still not so much as to destroy liberty.

To this question, ideology — whether of laissez-faire on the right or socialism on the left — had in the early thirties a clear and emphatic answer. Dogma revealed that there was no possible middle road between capitalism and socialism, no alternative between laissez-faire and dictatorship. Ogden Mills, who served as Secretary of the Treasury in Herbert Hoover's administration, put it this way: "We can have a free country or a socialistic one. We cannot have both. Our economic system cannot be half free and half socialistic. . . . There is no middle ground between governing and being governed, between absolute sovereignty and liberty, between tyranny and freedom."

Hoover himself was equally categorical. "Even partial regimentation cannot be made to work," he wrote, "and still maintain live democratic institutions." And in such sentiments Hoover and Mills commanded the enthusiastic assent of communists and fascists alike. Harold Laski and Norman Thomas vied in attacking the notion of deficit-spending and an unbalanced budget. They all — the prophets of laissez-faire and the prophets of collectivism — agreed on this if nothing else: no system of modified capitalism was possible, no mixed economy, no middle way.

Confronting the certitudes of ideology, Roosevelt spoke for the possibilities of ideas. He scorned the bleak doctrine of either-or in the confidence that democracy offered room for a much larger measure of experiment than the dogmatisms of right or left would concede. Instead of sacrificing human beings to abstractions, the New Deal tried in one manner or another to *do* things. Its whole point lay in its indifference to ideology, its belief in ideas, its faith in experiment, its conviction that a managed and modified capitalist order achieved by piecemeal reform could combine personal freedom and economic growth. And it gained its support from the instinctive rebellion of practical and energetic people against a set of dogmatic absolutes which told them that, because of some abstract doctrine, they could not do what was necessary to save their society and themselves.

For a time, the fight between ideology and pragmatism divided the intellectuals. Some for a moment rejected the confused and groping experimentalism of the New Deal in favor of the drastic, if delusive, clarity of dogma. But in due course this passed. By the end of the thirties, tough-mindedness triumphed over tender-mindedness, ideas over ideology, pragmatism over dogmatism, and America moved beyond the abstract models of laissez-faire and socialism to build precisely the sort of mixed economic order which the ideologists on both sides had pronounced impossible. Then the onset of the Second World War confirmed the reunion between mind and state, enlisting intellectuals to clarify the aims and purposes of the war and, later, to justify American objectives in the subsequent Cold War.

The New Deal thus broke the grip of laissez-faire ideology on domestic policy — a development confirmed by the failure of Senator Barry Goldwater to revive the absolutist approach as Republican presidential candidate in 1964. But the ideological impulse, repressed at home, found a new outlet in foreign affairs. This had begun in a mild way with Wilsonian doctrines of collective security and national self-determination. Then the reaction in the twenties against Wilsonianism hardened isolationism into an ideology. The rising menace of Germany and Japan in the late thirties produced from 1939 to 1941 a vigorous debate between isolationism and internationalism — a debate abruptly terminated by the Japanese attack on Pearl Harbor. During the war, American internationalism tended to take a "universalist" form; that is, it sought not just to assure American interests in its zone of primary security (which would have implied an acquiescence in corresponding policies by the other leading powers) but to establish general principles of international decency and human right through the United Nations. Some, more euphoric, spoke, like Henry R. Luce, of "the American Century." The Cold War distorted part of this internationalism into the notion of a crusade against communism. By the nineteen-fifties the ideology of anticommunism, as expounded by John Foster Dulles, James Burnham, Senator Joseph McCarthy and others, became almost as rigid and misleading, if not so cruel, as the ideology of communism itself. By the nineteen-sixties the euphoria of internationalism and the messianic anticommunist thesis had embroiled the United States deeply in a hopeless war on the mainland of Asia, and this in turn produced a reaction in favor of a more sober sense of national priorities and of the limits of American power.

The brief administration of John F. Kennedy represented a resurgence of ideas as against ideology both in foreign and domestic policy. In 1958 Kennedy had called on Americans to repudiate the proposition that "we should enter every military conflict as a moral crusade requiring the unconditional surrender of the enemy." As President, he urged the nation to understand the limits of American power. Against the idea of the American century he contended for "the world of diversity." "No one who examines the modern world," he said, "can doubt that the great currents of history are carrying the world away from the monolithic toward the pluralist idea."

He was equally opposed to the tyranny of cant and stereotype — of ideology — in domestic affairs. "The great enemy of the truth," he wrote, "is very often not the lie — deliberate, contrived and dishonest — but the myth, persistent, persuasive and unrealistic. Too often we hold fast to the clichés of our forebears. We subject all facts to a prefabricated set of interpretations." His effort was to identify the distinctive problems of his own time and to apply pragmatic remedies.

To fulfill this objective, Kennedy hoped to achieve a reunion of intellect and power in the style of the early republic. His purpose was wholly explicit. "Our nation's first great politicians," he had written in the nineteen-fifties, " — those who presided at its birth in 1776 and at its christening in 1787 — included among their ranks most of the nation's first great writers and scholars." But "the gap between the intellectual and the politician seems to be growing. . . . Today this link is all but gone. Where are the scholar-statesmen?" His New Frontier was a culmination of the tendency that had begun with the Progressive movement sixty years before: the application of trained intelligence to the affairs of state.

Kennedy's summons to the scholar-statesmen expressed a growing reality in the political community: almost a seventh of the members of the United States Senate in the mid-sixties were former college professors. It also responded to the changes in the environment which were offering the American intellectual new functions, new constituencies and a new access into the mainstream of national life. In the longest perspective, this was a consequence of the nation's movement into a new stage of economic development. Intellectuals, we have seen, play a vital role in the formative years of nationhood. In the next stage — the stage of entry into self-sustaining economic growth — national energies tend to flow into technological innovation, organization of production and markets and the other tasks required for the maximization of output. But a developed nation achieves a new plateau, where rudimentary economic needs are largely met, emphasis shifts from production to consumption and public policy must consider not only output but allocation, not only wealth but welfare. Increasing involvement in world affairs further increased the need of the state for intellectuals. The Second World War in particular almost made government service a routine part of an academic or literary career; and the Cold War drew heavily on the intellectual community for assistance on everything from economic development and scientific research to diplomatic and intelligence activity.

The advanced society of the United States thus began to face both a growing complexity of technical structure and a widening range of economic and moral choice at home and abroad, all demanding new ideas and new levels of knowledge and understanding in public administration and political leadership. The duties of government were no longer so plain and simple that men of intelligence could readily qualify themselves for their performance; goodness of heart, despite the celebrated aphorism of William Jennings Bryan, was not enough to enable a man to write a currency law. The state could simply not run effectively without ideas and the intellectual.

At the same time that public affairs were creating a new need for the intellectual, other developments were giving him a new constituency. For the high-technology society required an educated citizenry — a requirement which, as

America moves into the electronic age, will become all the
more urgent. No doubt our schools have for this reason over-
concentrated on technical and vocational instruction as well
as on vapid courses designed to hold the interest of unwilling
students. But, no matter how much emphasis an educational system places on adjustment to the environment, it
cannot totally avoid the incitement of ideas. Moreover, in
recent years we not only have increased the national investment in education and research but have to some degree revised the curriculum to give more scope and status to the
training of the mind. The result of this new concern with
general ideas may not always please the conservative critics
of progressive education. For the reform of the curriculum,
on top of the vast postwar increase in the size and weight of
the academic community, is already bringing into existence
a new and active force for national discontent.

There are today twice as many students enrolled in institutions of higher education in this country as there were a
short decade ago. By the early seventies there will be almost three quarters of a million teachers in our colleges and
universities and seven million students. The educational interest will constitute by 1970 a body about twice as large as
the farmers of the nation. Moreover, the processes of selec-
tion will assure for it many of the brightest, most ambitious,
most articulate and most irascible people in the country.
Despite the diversity of view and value that education brings
— despite, too, the fact that many college students and even
more college graduates will have their primary allegiances elsewhere — this group will have to a degree a common morale
and certain common purposes.

If it will not have the immediate influence on public policy that the much smaller agricultural interest will retain,

in part because the agricultural interest is geographically more concentrated, the educational interest will nonetheless begin to formulate its demands and fight for them. If thwarted, this new constituency, no longer feeble and vacillating, now enjoying a definite position in our national life, will begin to strike back — whether using reason to operate on public opinion or demonstrations to ventilate resentment and outrage. If all this should appear unseemly in a quarter presumably devoted to austere standards of rationality and judgment — and no doubt it is — one can only say that the educational interest would be doing no more than to act as selfishly as the business interest, the labor interest and the agricultural interest have acted under duress throughout American history.

Some of the demands set forth by the new interest will be claims on the educational community itself — essentially for a more humane and rational organization of American education. Others will be claims on external society — not only more money for schools and research but more freedom for intellectual inquiry and more recognition and representation for intellectuals in the agencies of national power. In any case, the universities will become a growing source of political ferment. It is already notable that politicians with an intelligent understanding of the dynamics of American society spend time on college campuses out of all proportion to the number of eligible voters they find there. Social change, by rendering ideas and experts indispensable to the workings of the high-technology, high-consumption society, has thus given intellectuals a new power to influence public policy.

5. *The New Hostility to Politics*

Yet, despite the conditions now favoring the influence of the intellectual, the summons to scholar-statesmen has encountered a surprising resistance in the intellectual community itself. This has arisen in part from a certain — and understandable — skepticism on the part of intellectuals about the uses to which power seeks to put intellect. Most of the time power wants the intellectual not at all as an intellectual — that is, as a man with a critical and speculative interest in general ideas — but rather as a technician, as a man who can perform specified intellectual services. This is displayed in the notion, for example, that scientists should go about their work of inventing new and more dreadful nuclear weapons but should have no opinion as to the place of these weapons in the larger scheme of things.

This situation has led some contemporary intellectuals to regard power with automatic and inflexible mistrust and to suppose that the intellectual who accepts political responsibility has lost his purity and forfeited his franchise. The estrangement between mind and state hardened into dogma. This was true in Europe as well as in America. Julien Benda's book of 1927, *Le Trahison des Clercs*, gave this dogma its phrase, if not its philosophy.

Actually *Le Trahison* is a muddled and superficial work, committed to the medieval ideal of intellectuals united in adherence to an abstract and comprehensive body of received truth. In his devotion to the realm of universals, Benda denounced pluralism, pragmatism, radical empiricism and those thinkers, like James and Bergson, who preferred existence to essence. But Benda's phrase captivated many who would have rejected his philosophy if they had known what it was. So some intellectuals today contend that, despite Emerson, the American Scholar should be something of a recluse and a valetudinarian, on principle and in all circumstances opposed to power. The model, if it cannot be Plato, must be Socrates; never Aristotle.

This position has its obvious attractions. Greed for power is one of the most squalid of human impulses, as pleasure in power is one of the most comic. Moreover, power is always tainted and often wicked; association with it generally compels compromise and often leads to corruption; and the prudent course is to stay one's distance and keep one's hands clean. Even the fact that he is now valued creates problems for the intellectual. If the old days of poverty menaced the scholar's security, the new age of plenty menaces his freedom. Now he constantly faces the question whether he should do what he wants to do — or what his foundation or the government want him to do. For most intellectuals and artists, in consequence, the farther from authority the better; and if their study or their sensibility freely brings them to criticize authority, all society, whether it realizes it or not, stands to benefit. Wise political leaders understand this in general, even if they do not always appreciate the consequences in particular. Where Frost hailed the onset of the "next Augustan age . . . A golden age of poetry and power," Kennedy saw the relation between poetry and power less as a coalition than a dialogue:

> When power leads man toward arrogance, poetry reminds him of his limitations. When power narrows the area of man's concern, poetry reminds him of the richness and di-

versity of existence. When power corrupts, poetry cleanses.
. . . The men who create power make an indispensable
contribution to the nation's greatness, but the men who
question power make a contribution just as indispensable
. . . for they determine whether we use power or power
uses us.

The question is not whether *all* intellectuals should plunge
into public affairs: no one asserts so ludicrous a proposition.
The question is whether *any* intellectual can take part in
public affairs without betraying his vocation. But, on examination, even this question becomes more apparent than real.
Most of the intellectual protest against political involvement
is a protest less against the involvement than against the
politics. This was even true of Julien Benda, who fully approved of intellectuals in politics if they were on the right
side. The real question is this: If intellectuals do take part
in public affairs, are they to be permitted by their fellows any
role save that of intransigent opposition? If they accept political responsibility, must they be chastised by intellectual
excommunication?

Two theories about the proper role of the intellectual have
made an impression on the contemporary left. One is the
view espoused by Herbert Marcuse that there are right ideas
and wrong ideas; that these two classes of ideas are readily
distinguishable; and that it is the duty of the intellectual to
impose the good and suppress the bad. This view, with its
candid rejection of intellectual freedom, belongs in a discussion of violence rather than a discussion of the intellectual
community.* Another influential view, espoused by Noam
Chomsky, excludes violence and presumably supports the
Bill of Rights. The Chomsky approach has, however, de-

* See earlier, "Violence as an American Way of Life," parts 5–6.

fects of its own, and the Chomsky phenomenon may be worth examination.

Half a century ago Mencken described the eruption of Thorstein Veblen on the American intellectual scene: "Of a sudden, Siss! Boom! Ah! Then, overnight, the upspringing of the intellectual soviets, the headlong assault upon all the old axioms of pedagogical speculation, the nihilistic dethronement of Prof. Dewey — and rah, rah, rah for Prof. Dr. Veblen! . . . In a few months — almost it seemed a few days — he was all over the *Nation,* the *Dial,* the *New Republic* and the rest of them, and his books and pamphlets began to pour from the presses, and newspapers reported his every wink and whisper, and everybody who was anybody began gabbling about him."

One is tempted to write in the same way about the emergence of Noam Chomsky. A distinguished student of linguistics, he quietly pursued arcane studies in a highly specialized field. Then, of a sudden, he burst forth as an all-purpose expert on history, strategy, foreign policy, social psychology, political science, political ethics, ethical politics. He settled every issue with ecclesiastical certitude. His sermons covered interminable pages in the *New York Review of Books.* He was cited with reverence by the young. It was rah, rah, rah for Prof. Dr. Chomsky.

American Power and the New Mandarins, a collection of his essays, offered a chance to see what the shouting is all about. The Vietnam war drove Dr. Chomsky into the public arena; it has obviously been the formative experience in his political thought, and it provides the perspective through which he sees both the American past and the American future. He views this war not as the result of miscalculation or stupidity but as the expression of profound aggressive drives rooted in the American commercial and industrial system. Looking back at earlier history in the light of Vietnam, he finds the quest for world domination a major and abiding American impulse.

Thus, in one long digression, he wonders whether American policy did not, after all, force Japan into the attack on Pearl Harbor. "It is an open question whether a more conciliatory American diplomacy that took into account some of the real problems faced by Japan might have helped. . . . It is hardly astonishing, then, that in 1937 Japan began to expand at the expense of China." Dr. Chomsky surmises that when Roosevelt rejected a policy of appeasement and made an issue of Japan's alliance with Germany the underlying motive was to justify the forthcoming American involvement in the European war. In any event, American terms, by November 1941, would have made Japan a "mere 'subcontractor' in the emerging American world system." Confronted by such pressure from American imperialism, what else could Japan do but act in self-defense? There is an agreeable symmetry after all these years in watching the New Left join hands with the Old Right.

American imperialism has reached, Dr. Chomsky thinks, its culmination in Vietnam. "By any objective standard," he writes, "the United States has become the most aggressive power in the world, the greatest threat to peace, to national self-determination, and to international cooperation" — a proposition that might conceivably be read with skepticism in Prague. "If one wishes to pursue the Munich analogy," Dr. Chomsky adds, "there is only one plausible contender for the role of Hitler," and he does not mean Brezhnev. The challenge that the existence of this Nazi-like America offers to the American intellectual community gives Dr. Chomsky's book its unifying theme.

He sees American intellectuals as divided into two main groups: the Mandarins (bad) and the Resistance (good). The Mandarins are those who use the knowledge and technique demanded by industrial society to achieve personal power in collaboration with the state. They are elitist, reformist, pragmatic, managerial, manipulative, technocratic, counterrevolutionary, opposed to popular movements and mass participation in decision making, addicted to the behavioral sciences, contemptuous of principles, moral issues and human rights. Their allegiance is not to truth and justice, but to power and the effective use of power.

There are Mandarins in all advanced societies, including the Soviet Union, but the worst ones are in America. These believe "that the United States has the right to extend its power and control without limit, insofar as is feasible," and the Vietnam war testifies to the concept of humanity and civilization they are likely to bring to the exercise of power. The Resistance, on the other hand, is spontaneous, democratic, humane, principled, anti-organization, pro-community, a "moral elite" dedicated to truth, justice and the creative search for alternatives. Dr. Chomsky opposes the cries of the hard New Left for revolution; but even his soft New Left seems to believe that the Mandarins deserve punishment, and he himself proposes what he obscurely calls "a kind of denazification."

All this purports to be political analysis. But Dr. Chomsky, it soon becomes evident, does not understand the rudiments of political analysis. Indeed, despite occasional pretenses of reasoned discussion, he is not much interested in the analytical process:

> By entering into the arena of argument and counterargument, of technical feasibility and tactics, of footnotes and citations, by accepting the presumption of legitimacy of debate on certain issues, one has already lost one's humanity. . . . [Anyone] going through the motions of building a case against the American war in Vietnam . . . degrades himself, and insults beyond measure the victims of our violence and our moral blindness. . . .

Dr. Chomsky in short, is not a political analyst at all. Like John Foster Dulles and Dean Rusk, he believes in reducing political questions to rather confident and facile moral judgments. Now the historian's rule here must be *de minimis*. A few questions, like slavery or nazism, do qualify for unequivocal moral judgments; but, as one supposed Reinhold Niebuhr had demonstrated long since, most secular questions intermingle good and evil in problematic proportions and are more usefully handled in other than moralistic categories. Moreover, those who rush around ladling out moral judgments quickly arrogate to themselves an alarming and repellent sense of their own moral infallibility. Dr. Chomsky should remember his Chekhov: "You will not become a saint through other people's sins."

Political analysis requires a belief in the application of reason to *all* questions. Dr. Chomsky rejects this belief. It also requires a capacity to make distinctions. This too Dr. Chomsky lacks. Take the first sentence of his book: "Three years have passed since American intervention in a civil war in Vietnam was converted into a colonial war of the classic type." One may say many things about the Vietnam war;

but one thing it is not is "a colonial war of the classic type" — i.e., a war in which a developed nation aims at the territorial annexation of an underdeveloped land. Indeed, Dr. Chomsky himself never claims that the United States wants to make Vietnam an American colony in the classic sense; it is just that he scorns precision in the use of language. Or, to consider another example, Dr. Chomsky calls Senator Mike Mansfield "the kind of man who is the terror of our age." If one uses language of this sort about Senator Mansfield, what words does one have left for Hitler or Stalin? Or, a more personal example, Dr. Chomsky, writing about Vietnam, talks about a "Rusk-Schlesinger concept" — a notion which the former Secretary of State and I would find equally distasteful.

Political analysis requires in addition a reasonable sense of logic. Thus, in making his case against the Vietnam war, Dr. Chomsky mentions a newspaper photograph showing Vietnamese children in the Mekong Delta wounded by fire from American helicopters. "How many hundreds of such pictures must we see," he writes, "before we begin to care and to act?" The incident could hardly have been more horrifying; but it simply does not by itself justify political conclusions. Would the photograph of German children in Dresden or Hamburg wounded by bombs from Allied planes have led Dr. Chomsky to argue that we should stop the war against Hitler? In short, logic prescribes that the case against the Vietnam war must be established — as it easily can be — on other grounds than the tragic fact of the killing or maiming of innocent bystanders. But Dr. Chomsky has no particular regard for logic.

Political analysis requires, above all, some respect for facts. This, despite a showy apparatus of footnotes and citations,

Dr. Chomsky also lacks. Consider, for example, the way he deals with a President of the United States. Thus he writes: "These words recall the characteristically direct formulations of Harry Truman, who proclaimed in 1947 that 'all freedom is dependent on freedom of enterprise. . . . The whole world should adopt the American system. . . . The American system can survive in America only if it becomes a world system.'" In case anyone does not get the point, Dr. Chomsky, who is rarely content with saying anything once, writes some pages later: ". . . the principles that were crudely outlined by President Truman almost twenty years ago when he observed in a famous and important speech that 'all freedom is dependent on freedom of enterprise,' that 'the whole world should adopt the American system,' that 'the American system can survive in America only if it becomes a world system.'" On the first occasion, Dr. Chomsky cites as his source for this "famous and important speech" a book by D. F. Fleming called *The Cold War and Its Origins*. The Fleming book refers to a speech given by Truman at Baylor University on March 6, 1947. This speech is readily available in Truman's *Public Papers*. An examination of the speech shows that Truman said none of the things which Dr. Chomsky says he said. And, while D. F. Fleming is hardly celebrated for the rigor of his scholarship, even he does not claim that Truman said them. The last two quotations, as the Fleming text makes clear, were not from Truman at all but from a book by J. P. Warburg in which Warburg was giving his own theory as to what was in Truman's mind. The first quotation does not appear on the page cited in Fleming and may well have been invented by Dr. Chomsky. (This quotation alone bears a distant resemblance to actual words of the Baylor speech, though what Truman said was essentially different:

"Freedom of worship — freedom of speech — freedom of enterprise. It must be true that the first two of these freedoms are related to the third.") In a field of linguistics, Dr. Chomsky would, I am sure, be merciless on a scholar who misquoted, misattributed and made up language in order to strengthen an argument. But his contempt for political writing is evidently such that he has no hesitation in doing exactly this himself in the field of public affairs.

Somewhere in the book Dr. Chomsky writes with his usual sententiousness, "It is the responsibility of intellectuals to speak the truth and to expose lies." Chomsky must be putting us on. His argument contradicts the first half of this responsibility and his practice the second. Judging by *American Power and the New Mandarins*, one can only conclude that Dr. Chomsky's idea of the responsibility of intellectuals is to forswear reasoned analysis, indulge in moralistic declamation, fabricate evidence when necessary and shout always at the top of one's voice.

It may well be that doctrines of Herbert Marcuse and Noam Chomsky represent an even greater example of the treason of the intellectuals than, say, the actions of those who have committed the occasional sin of association with power. The Marcuse vision sees the intellectual as the ultimate wielder of power, the Chomsky vision as the permanent opponent of power; but both, in different ways, reveal an obsession with power, a mixture of fascination and fear. Yet intellectuals surely should not thus be rattled by the fact of power. Power is here to stay. It is neutral. It can be used for good purposes as well as bad. If not used for good, it will almost certainly be used for bad. Those for whom power breeds alarm and guilt have no business in the realm of public affairs.

Nor is power the only thing in politics that corrupts. "The integrity of a writer," Auden has said, "is more threatened by appeals to his social conscience, his political or religious convictions, than by appeals to his cupidity." No cause is perfect enough to justify the total dedication of man; and commitment to an ideology of intransigent opposition may well invite a captivity more destructive than commitment to power. Ideology, after all, embraces the individual far more comprehensively than democracy does. Its discipline is more stringent, its penetration deeper into mind and soul. Democratic politics, as George Orwell has observed, permits the participant "to keep part of yourself inviolate." But the ideological despotisms, in the phrase of Camus, "no longer admit of silence or neutrality." In retrospect, would anyone argue that the intellectuals of the thirties who joined the New Deal were less pure, or less intellectual, than those who joined the Communist party? Yet this was the view of some intellectuals at the time, and its equivalent is the view of some intellectuals today.

6. *Intellectuals and Power in a Democracy*

What should the relationship be between intellectuals and power in a democratic society? The answer surely is that there is no single answer. The strength of the intellectual community lies, among other things, in its diversity. According to temperament or preoccupation, some intellectuals will participate in the world of power, some will criticize, some will denounce, some will cultivate their own gardens, some will, at one time or another, do all these things. A spectrum of opinion and action among intellectuals is indispensable if reason is to civilize power.

The notion that the duty of the intellectual is unrelenting hostility to his society is as wrong as the opposite notion that the duty of the intellectual is unqualified support. Both positions are wrong because their insistence on a single role for the intellectual binds the free mind and contracts the whole premise of intellectual life — the belief in the diversity and spontaneity of ideas. They are wrong, moreover, because the role appointed either denies the intellectual's essential responsibility, which is the search for knowledge and understanding, or else forecloses that search by assuming its conclusion in advance. More than that, the radical version is stupidly self-defeating because those who acquiesce in the idea, more characteristically propagated by anti-intellectuals, that intelligence has no role in public affairs, voluntarily resign power to Goethe's diplomats and soldiers — as if the ordinary course of things had not given diplomats and soldiers power enough already.

The New Left theory is that, in any conjunction between mind and state, the state will always win. Doubtless this happens often in practice; even perhaps most of the time. But there is no ontological necessity about it. Obviously the exercise of power, above all in a democracy, requires compromise; and the New Left assumption is that compromise means corruption. But somewhere this syllogism has gone off the track. For it is entirely possible to deal with practical realities without yielding inner convictions; it is entirely possible to compromise in program and action without compromis-

ing in ideas and values. Indeed, conscientious politicians —
and there are more than most intellectuals think — must
make precisely the same judgment as intellectuals in politics
about the point where compromise becomes betrayal. The
recognition of political realities does not inexorably mean the
relinquishment of political principles. Whether or not power
corrupts is a matter of the strength or weakness of the individual mind and conscience. Moreover, the intellectual in
government is never alone. He is there in part because he
serves as a broker between the political community and the
intellectual community; and he knows he can count on the
legion of incorruptibles left behind to act with relish as his
conscience and his critics. This pressure of the intellectual
community has some effect in helping the intellectual in government to keep straight.

The assumption that power will inexorably subvert intelligence exhibits a fatal lack of confidence in the force of facts,
ideas and reason. Over the longer run, it may become evident that intelligence may begin to subvert power. Though
the state does its best to employ the intellectual as a technician and keep him in the back room, it cannot forever escape
him as a carrier of general ideas. The habit of thought is in-
fectious; and, as it begins to infiltrate government, it may affect government as much as government affects it. No doubt
some intellectuals, anxious to blend with their new environment, prove themselves more cautious than the diplomats
and more belligerent than the soldiers. Yet in time one will,
I believe, start to discern certain consequences of raising the
educational level of government — an acceptance, for example, of the role of debate, a new susceptibility to reading,
even of books, a heightened interest in ideas, a growing commitment to analysis and thinking ahead, a sense perhaps even

of intellectual honesty in acknowledging the differences between profession and performance.

There is no need to issue a blanket defense of intellectuals. Like everyone else, they are vulnerable, vain and corruptible. But ideas are another matter. "The ideas of economic and political philosophers, both when they are right and when they are wrong," Keynes wrote thirty years ago, "are more powerful than is commonly understood. Indeed, the world is ruled by little else." John Kenneth Galbraith has added in our own day, "The intellectual community, far from being powerless in these matters, is almost the only source of power."

Ideas are the means by which a rational society comes to terms with a changing environment. The turbulent and unpredictable world in which we live makes good ideas — ideas which comprehend the present and anticipate the future — more indispensable than ever. But ideas to exert power must bear some relation to actuality. Intellectuals too often rush into public affairs armed only with emotion and ignorance. If they really wish to shape events, they must join the expertise of the intellectual technician with the passion and creativity of the man of general ideas. They will influence government most effectively not by learning the art of public relations, not by transforming themselves into publicists or hucksters, not by organizing pressure groups and marches on Washington but by thinking hard about basic problems and coming up with basic answers. Thinkers are most powerful when they think.

Marx and Keynes, for example, changed the world because they had large conceptions, worked hard, mastered their subject and knew what they were talking about. Marcuse and Chomsky are unlikely to affect things very much because, when they get to the field of public policy, they don't know what they are talking about. In the end, the influence of intellectuals will depend more on the merits of their ideas than on the passion with which they speak on subjects they have not mastered. As Hannah Arendt has reminded us, "Truth, though powerless and always defeated in a head-on clash with the powers that be, possesses a strength of its own: whatever those in power may contrive, they are unable to discover or invent a viable substitute for it. Persuasion and violence can destroy truth, but they cannot replace it."

Public affairs will never involve more than a small minority of intellectuals, and rightly so, for the vitality of intellectual life depends on the endless diversity of intellectual roles and interests. Since most governments will pursue more or less hopeless policies, most intellectuals will continue to criticize them. Emerson's state of "virtual hostility" will not come to an end, and the word "alienation" will not disappear from fashionable vocabularies. Yet the breach is closing between mind and state, and this will not necessarily mean the capitulation of intelligence to power. It may well mean rather a resumption in contemporary terms of the partnership between ideas and responsibility that gave the early republic its luster — and not simply a bilateral arrangement between scholars and statesmen, which tends to be a matter of mutual exploitation and has no great consequence, but something far more fundamental: a union of thought and action within political leaders themselves. Ideas will permeate public policy once again; and the intellectual community, at last liberating itself from the cult of impotence, may finally fulfill the prophecy of Emerson.

However, in a true partnership of ideas and responsibility the intellectual must remember that his abiding obligation is neither to power nor to ideology but to the integrity of reason. He must, as Emerson said, be free and brave and defer never to the popular cry. He must stand by "his belief that a popgun is a popgun, though the ancient and honorable of the earth affirm it to be the crack of doom." He "must take up into himself all the ability of the time, all the contributions of the past, all the hopes of the future." Recalling that mighty phrase of Yeats, he must hold "reality and justice in a single thought." He must reject the attempt to divorce passion from reason and exalt commitment-for-commitment's-sake. Reason without passion is sterile; passion without reason is hysterical; and the two must be united in effective public action.

If the man of ideas remains faithful to his vocation — which is neither automatic obeisance nor automatic hostility to power but the disciplined and, if need be, passionate use of reason in pursuit of understanding — he need not fear his capacity to live and move in the world of power. But if intellectuals themselves conspire to destroy the discipline of reason, if they help turn our politics into a competition in unreason and fanaticism, we reduce the chance of solving any of our problems and abandon our society to those most skilled and ruthless in the use of force.

III

THE ORIGINS
OF THE COLD WAR

THE CONTEMPORARY CRISIS OF CONFIDENCE has become acute because of growing national bafflement before the dilemmas of American society. But it is also acute because of an equal bafflement over America's role in the world. That role, so apparently clear and splendid in the years between Pearl Harbor and Korea, has latterly become clouded in doubt and, in Vietnam, touched with shame. The Vietnam adventure, undertaken, it was supposed, for high motives, has ended in squalor; and this has encouraged a reexamination of the American foreign policy of the last generation, and especially of the Cold War, of which the Vietnam commitment was so melancholy an expression.

The Cold War in its original form was a presumably mortal antagonism, arising in the wake of the Second World War, between two rigidly hostile blocs, one led by the Soviet Union, the other by the United States. For nearly two somber and dangerous decades this antagonism dominated the fears of mankind; it may even, on occasion, have come close to blowing up the planet. In recent years, however, the once implacable struggle has lost its familiar clarity of outline. With the passing of old issues and the emergence of new conflicts and contestants, there is a natural tendency, especially on the part of the generation that grew up during the Cold War, to take a fresh look at the causes of the great contention between Russia and America.

Some exercises in reappraisal have merely elaborated the orthodoxies promulgated in Washington or Moscow during the boom years of the Cold War. But others, especially in the United States (there are no signs, alas, of this in the Soviet Union), represent what American historians call "revisionism" — that is, a readiness to challenge official explanations. No one should be surprised by this phenomenon. Every war in American history has been followed in due course by skeptical reassessments of supposedly sacred assumptions. So the War of 1812, fought at the time for the freedom of the seas, was in later years ascribed to the expansionist ambitions of congressional war hawks; so the Mexican War became a slaveholders' conspiracy. So the Civil War has been pronounced a "needless war," and Lincoln has even been accused of provoking the rebel attack on Fort Sumter. So too the Spanish-American War and the First and Second World Wars have, each in its turn, undergone revisionist critiques. It is not to be supposed that the Cold War would remain exempt.

1. *The Rise of Revisionism*

In the case of the Cold War, special factors reinforce the predictable historiographical rhythm. The outburst of polycentrism in the communist empire has made people wonder whether communism was ever so monolithic as official theories of the Cold War supposed. A generation with no vivid memories of Stalinism may see the Russia of the forties in the image of the seedy and mediocre Russia of the sixties. And for this same generation the American course of widening the war in Vietnam — which even nonrevisionists can easily regard as folly — has unquestionably stirred doubts about the wisdom of American foreign policy in the sixties which younger historians may have begun to read back into the forties.

It is useful to remember that, on the whole, past exercises in revisionism have failed to stick. Few historians today believe that the war hawks caused the War of 1812 or the slaveholders the Mexican War, or that the Civil War was needless, or that the House of Morgan brought America into the First World War or that Franklin Roosevelt schemed to produce the attack on Pearl Harbor. But this does not mean that one should deplore the rise of Cold War revisionism.* For revisionism is an essential part of the process by which history, through the posing of new problems and the investigation of new possibilities, enlarges its perspectives and enriches its insights.

* As this writer somewhat intemperately did in a letter to the *New York Review of Books,* October 20, 1966.

More than this, in the present context, revisionism expresses a deep, legitimate and tragic apprehension. As the Cold War has begun to lose its purity of definition, as the moral absolutes of the fifties become the moralistic clichés of the sixties, some have begun to ask whether the appalling risks that humanity ran during the Cold War were, after all, necessary and inevitable; whether more restrained and rational policies might not have guided the energies of man from the perils of conflict into the potentialities of collaboration. The fact that such questions are in their nature unanswerable does not mean that it is not right and useful to raise them. Nor does it mean that our sons and daughters are not entitled to an accounting from the generation of Russians and Americans who produced the Cold War.

The orthodox American view, as originally set forth by the American government and as reaffirmed until recently by most American scholars, has been that the Cold War was the brave and essential response of free men to communist aggression. Some have gone back well before the Second World War to lay open the sources of Russian expansionism. Geopoliticians traced the Cold War to imperial Russian strategic ambitions which in the nineteenth century led to the Crimean War, to Russian penetration of the Balkans and the Middle East and to Russian pressure on Britain's "lifeline" to India. Ideologists traced it to the Communist Manifesto of 1848 ("the violent overthrow of the bourgeoisie lays the foundation for the sway of the proletariat"). Thoughtful observers (a phrase meant to exclude those who speak in Dullese about the unlimited evil of godless, atheistic, militant communism) concluded that classical Russian imperialism and pan-slavism, compounded after 1917 by Leninist messianism, confronted the West at the end of the Second World War with an inexorable drive for domination.*

The revisionist thesis is very different.† In its extreme

---

* Every student of the Cold War must acknowledge his debt to William H. McNeill's remarkable account, *America, Britain and Russia: Their Co-operation and Conflict, 1941–1946* (New York, 1953) and to the brilliant and indispensable series by Herbert Feis: *Churchill, Roosevelt, Stalin: The War They Waged and the Peace They Sought* (Princeton, 1957); *Between War and Peace: The Potsdam Conference* (Princeton, 1960); and *The Atomic Bomb and the End of World War II* (Princeton, 1966). Useful recent analyses include: André Fontaine, *Histoire de la Guerre Froide* (2 vols., Paris, 1965, 1967); Norman A. Graebner, *Cold War Diplomacy, 1945–1960* (Princeton, 1962); Louis J. Halle, *The Cold War as History* (New York, 1967); Martin F. Herz, *Beginnings of the Cold War* (Bloomington, Ind., 1966) and William L. Neumann, *After Victory: Churchill, Roosevelt, Stalin and the Making of the Peace* (New York, 1967).

† The fullest statement of this case is to be found in Denna F. Fleming's voluminous *The Cold War and Its Origins* (New York, 1961). For a shorter version of this argument, see David Horowitz, *The Free World Colossus* (New York, 1965); the most subtle and ingenious statements come in William A. Williams' *The Tragedy of American Diplomacy* (rev. ed., New York, 1962) and in Gar Alperovitz's *Atomic Diplomacy: Hiroshima and Potsdam* (New York, 1965) and in subsequent articles and reviews by Mr. Alperovitz in the *New York Review of Books*. The fact that in some aspects the revisionist thesis parallels the official Soviet argument must not, of course, prevent consideration of the case on its merits, nor raise questions about the motives of the writers, all of whom, so far as I know, are independent-minded scholars.

I might further add that all these books, in spite of their ostentatious display of scholarly apparatus, must be used with caution. Professor Fleming, for example, relies heavily on newspaper articles and even columnists. While Mr. Alperovitz bases his case on official documents or authoritative reminiscences, he sometimes twists his material in a most unscholarly way. For example, on p. 27 Mr. Alperovitz writes that Under Secretary of State Joseph C. Grew "was *already* convinced that 'a future war with Soviet Russia is as certain as anything in this world can be certain.' " Obviously this seems an alarming expression of the inner state of mind of American policy-makers. But what Mr. Alperovitz did was to omit the proviso with which Grew specifically qualified this remark (*Turbulent Era* [Boston, 1952], II, 1447): "*unless we recognize the danger and take steps to meet it in time*" (Grew's italics). This is a rather different thought. Or, again, in describing Ambassador Harriman's talk with President Truman on April 20, 1945, Mr. Alperovitz writes, "He argued that a reconsideration of Roosevelt's policy was necessary" (p. 22, repeated on p. 24). The citation is to pp. 70–72 in President Truman's *Year of Decisions* (Garden City, N.Y., 1955). What President Truman reported Harriman as saying was the exact opposite: "Before leaving, Harriman took me aside and said, 'Frankly, one of the reasons that made me rush back to Wash-

form, it is that, after the death of Franklin Roosevelt and the end of the Second World War, the United States deliberately abandoned the wartime policy of collaboration and, exhilarated by the possession of the atomic bomb, undertook a course of aggression of its own designed to expel all Russian influence from Eastern Europe and to establish democratic-capitalist states on the very border of the Soviet Union. As the revisionists see it, this radically new American policy — or rather this resumption by Truman of the pre-Roosevelt policy of insensate anticommunism — left Moscow no alternative but to take measures in defense of its own borders. The result was the Cold War.

These two views, of course, could not be more starkly contrasting. It is therefore not unreasonable to look again at the half-dozen critical years between June 22, 1941, when Hitler attacked Russia, and July 2, 1947, when the Russians walked out of the Marshall Plan meeting in Paris. Several things should be borne in mind as this reexamination is made. For one thing, we have thought a great deal more in recent years, in part because of writers like Roberta Wohlstetter and T. C. Schelling, about the problems of communication in diplo-

---

ington was the fear that you did not understand, as I had seen Roosevelt understand, that Stalin is breaking his agreements.' " Similarly, in an appendix (p. 271) Mr. Alperovitz writes that the Hopkins and Davies missions of May 1945 "were opposed by the 'firm' advisers." Actually the Hopkins mission was proposed by Harriman and Charles E. Bohlen, who Mr. Alperovitz elsewhere suggests were the firmest of the firm — and was proposed by them precisely to impress on Stalin the continuity of American policy from Roosevelt to Truman. While the idea that Truman reversed Roosevelt's policy is tempting dramatically, it is a myth. See, for example, the testimony of Anna Rosenberg Hoffman, who lunched with Roosevelt on March 24, 1945, the last day he spent in Washington. After luncheon, Roosevelt was handed a cable. "He read it and became quite angry. He banged his fists on the arms of his wheelchair and said, 'Averell is right; we can't do business with Stalin. He has broken every one of the promises he made at Yalta.' He was very upset and continued in the same vein on the subject."

macy — the signals that one nation, by word or by deed, gives, inadvertently or intentionally, to another. Any honest reappraisal of the origins of the Cold War requires the imaginative leap — which should in any case be as instinctive for the historian as it is prudent for the statesman — into the adversary's viewpoint. We must strive to see how, given Soviet perspectives, the Russians might conceivably have misread our signals, as we must reconsider how intelligently we read theirs.

For another, the historian must not overindulge the man of power in the illusion cherished by those in office that high position carries with it the easy ability to shape history. Violating the statesman's creed, Lincoln once blurted out the truth in his letter of 1864 to A. G. Hodges: "I claim not to have controlled events, but confess plainly that events have controlled me." He was not asserting Tolstoyan fatalism but rather suggesting how greatly events limit the capacity of the statesman to bend history to his will. The physical course of the Second World War — the military operations undertaken, the position of the respective armies at the war's end, the momentum generated by victory and the vacuums created by defeat — all these determined the future as much as the character of individual leaders and the substance of national ideology and purpose.

Nor can the historian forget the conditions under which decisions are made, especially in a time like the Second World War. These were tired, overworked, aging men: in 1945, Churchill was 71 years old, Stalin had governed his country for 17 exacting years, Roosevelt his for 12 years nearly as exacting. During the war, moreover, the importunities of military operations had shoved postwar questions to the margins of their minds. All — even Stalin, behind his screen of ideology — had become addicts of improvisation, relying on authority and virtuosity to conceal the fact that they were constantly surprised by developments. Like Eliza, they leaped from one cake of ice to the next in the effort to reach the other side of the river. None showed great tactical consistency, or cared much about it; all employed a certain ambiguity to preserve their power to decide big issues; and it is hard to know how to interpret anything any one of them said on any specific occasion. This was partly because, like all princes, they designed their expressions to have particular effects on particular audiences; partly because the entirely genuine intellectual difficulty of the questions they faced made a degree of vacillation and mind-changing eminently reasonable. If historians cannot solve these problems in retrospect, who are they to blame Roosevelt, Stalin and Churchill for not having solved them at the time?

2. *Universalism*

Peacemaking after the Second World War was not so much a tapestry as it was a hopelessly raveled and knotted mess of yarn. Yet, for purposes of clarity, it is essential to follow certain threads. One theme indispensable to an understanding of the Cold War is the contrast between two clashing views of world order: the "universalist" view, by which all nations shared a common interest in all the affairs of the world, and the "sphere-of-influence" view, by which each great power would be assured by the other great powers of an acknowledged predominance in its own area of special interest. The universalist view assumed that national security would be guaranteed by an international organization. The sphere-of-influence view assumed that national security would be guaranteed by the balance of power. While in practice these views have by no means been incompatible (indeed, our shaky peace has been based on a combination of the two), in the abstract they involved sharp contradictions.

The tradition of American thought in these matters was universalist — i.e., Wilsonian. Roosevelt had been a member of Wilson's subcabinet; in 1920, as candidate for Vice President, he had campaigned for the League of Nations. It is true that, within Roosevelt's infinitely complex mind, Wilsonianism warred with the perception of vital strategic interests he had imbibed from Mahan. Moreover, his temperamental inclination to settle things with fellow princes around the conference table led him to regard the Big Three — or Four — as trustees for the rest of the world. On occasion, as this narrative will show, he was beguiled into flirtation with the sphere-of-influence heresy. But in principle he believed in joint action and remained a Wilsonian. His hope for Yalta, as he told the Congress on his return, was that it would "spell the end of the system of unilateral action, the exclusive alliances, the spheres of influence, the balances of power, and all the other expedients that have been tried for centuries — and have always failed."

Whenever Roosevelt backslid, he had at his side that Wilsonian fundamentalist, Secretary of State Cordell Hull, to recall him to the pure faith. After his visit to Moscow in

1943, Hull characteristically said that, with the Declaration of Four Nations on General Security (in which America, Russia, Britain and China pledged "united action . . . for the organization and maintenance of peace and security"), "there will no longer be need for spheres of influence, for alliances, for balance of power, or any other of the special arrangements through which, in the unhappy past, the nations strove to safeguard their security or to promote their interests."

Remembering the corruption of the Wilsonian vision by the secret treaties of the First World War, Hull was determined to prevent any sphere-of-influence nonsense after the Second World War. He therefore fought all proposals to settle border questions while the war was still on and, excluded as he largely was from wartime diplomacy, poured his not inconsiderable moral energy and frustration into the promulgation of virtuous and spacious general principles.

In adopting the universalist view, Roosevelt and Hull were not indulging personal hobbies. Sumner Welles, Adolf Berle, Averell Harriman, Charles Bohlen — all, if with a variety of nuances, opposed the sphere-of-influence approach. And here the State Department was expressing what seems clearly to have been the predominant mood of the American people, so long mistrustful of European power politics. The Republicans shared the true faith. John Foster Dulles argued that the great threat to peace after the war would lie in the revival of sphere-of-influence thinking. The United States, he said, must not permit Britain and Russia to revert to these bad old ways; it must therefore insist on American participation in all policy decisions for all territories in the world. Dulles wrote pessimistically in January 1945, "The three great powers which at Moscow agreed upon the 'closest cooperation' about European questions have shifted to a practice of separate, regional responsibility."

It is true that critics, and even friends, of the United States sometimes noted a discrepancy between the American passion for universalism when it applied to territory far from American shores and the preeminence the United States accorded its own interests nearer home. Churchill, seeking Washington's blessing for a sphere-of-influence initiative in Eastern Europe, could not forbear reminding the Americans, "We follow the lead of the United States in South America"; nor did any universalist of record propose the abolition of the Monroe Doctrine. But a convenient myopia prevented such inconsistencies from qualifying the ardency of the universalist faith.

There seem only to have been three officials in the United States Government who dissented. One was the Secretary of War, Henry L. Stimson, a classical balance-of-power man, who in 1944 opposed the creation of a vacuum in Central Europe by the pastoralization of Germany and in 1945 urged "the settlement of all territorial acquisitions in the shape of defense posts which each of these four powers may deem to be necessary for their own safety" in advance of any effort to establish a peacetime United Nations. Stimson considered the claim of Russia to a preferred position in Eastern Europe as not unreasonable: as he told President Truman, he "thought the Russians perhaps were being more realistic than we were in regard to their own security." Such a position for Russia seemed to him comparable to the preferred American position in Latin America; he even spoke of "our respective orbits." Stimson was therefore skeptical of what he regarded as the prevailing tendency "to hang on to exaggerated views of the Monroe Doctrine and at the same time butt into every question that comes up in Central Europe." Acceptance of spheres of influence seemed to him the way to avoid "a head-on collision."

A second official opponent of universalism was George Kennan, an eloquent advocate from the American embassy in Moscow of "a prompt and clear recognition of the division of Europe into spheres of influence and of a policy based on the fact of such division." Kennan argued that nothing we could do would possibly alter the course of events in Eastern Europe; that we were deceiving ourselves by supposing that these countries had any future but Russian domination; that we should therefore relinquish Eastern Europe to the Soviet Union and avoid anything which would make things easier for the Russians by giving them economic assistance or by sharing moral responsibility for their actions.

A third voice within the government against universalism was (at least after the war) Henry A. Wallace. As Secretary of Commerce, he stated the sphere-of-influence case with trenchancy in the famous Madison Square Garden speech of September 1946 which led to his dismissal by President Truman:

> On our part, we should recognize that we have no more business in the *political* affairs of Eastern Europe than Russia has in the *political* affairs of Latin America, Western Europe, and the United States. . . . Whether we like it or not, the Russians will try to socialize their sphere of influence just as we try to democratize our sphere of influence. . . . The Russians have no more business stirring up native Communists to political activity in Western Europe, Latin America, and the United States than we have in interfering with the politics of Eastern Europe and Russia.

Stimson, Kennan and Wallace seem to have been alone in the government, however, in taking these views. They were very much minority voices. Meanwhile universalism, rooted in the American legal and moral tradition, overwhelmingly backed by public opinion, received successive enshrinements in the Atlantic Charter of 1941, in the Declaration of the United Nations in 1942 and in the Moscow Declaration of 1943.

3. *Spheres of Influence*

The Kremlin, on the other hand, thought *only* of spheres of interest; above all, the Russians were determined to protect their frontiers, and especially their border to the west, crossed so often and so bloodily in the dark course of their history. These western frontiers lacked natural means of defense — no great oceans, rugged mountains, steaming swamps or impenetrable jungles. The history of Russia had been the history of invasion, the last of which was by now horribly killing up to twenty millions of its people. The protection of Russia therefore meant the enlargement of the area of Russian influence. Kennan himself wrote (in May 1944), "Behind Russia's stubborn expansion lies only the age-old sense of insecurity of a sedentary people reared on an exposed plain in the neighborhood of fierce nomadic peoples," and he called this "urge" a "permanent feature of Russian psychology."

In earlier times the "urge" had produced the czarist search for buffer states and maritime outlets. In 1939 the Soviet-Nazi pact and its secret protocol had enabled Russia to begin to satisfy in the Baltic states, Karelian Finland and Poland, part of what it conceived as its security requirements in Eastern Europe. But the "urge" persisted, causing the friction between Russia and Germany in 1940 as each jostled for position in the area which separated them. Later it led to Molotov's new demands on Hitler in November 1940 — a free hand in Finland, Soviet predominance in Rumania and Bulgaria, bases in the Dardanelles — the demands which convinced Hitler that he had no choice but to attack Russia. Now Stalin hoped to gain from the West what Hitler, a closer neighbor, had not dared yield him.

It is true that, so long as Russian survival appeared to require a second front to relieve the Nazi pressure, Moscow's demand for Eastern Europe was a little muffled. Thus the Soviet government adhered to the Atlantic Charter (though with a significant if obscure reservation about adapting its principles to "the circumstances, needs, and historic peculiarities of particular countries"). Thus it also adhered to the Moscow Declaration of 1943, and Molotov then, with his easy mendacity, even denied that Russia had any desire to divide Europe into spheres of influence. But this was guff that the Russians were perfectly willing to ladle out if it would keep the Americans, and especially Secretary Hull (who made a strong personal impression at the Moscow conference), happy. "A declaration," as Stalin once observed to Eden, "I regard as algebra, but an agreement as practical arithmetic. I do not wish to decry algebra, but I prefer practical arithmetic."

The more consistent Russian purpose was revealed when

Stalin offered the British a straight sphere-of-influence deal at the end of 1941. Britain, he suggested, should recognize the Russian absorption of the Baltic states, part of Finland, eastern Poland and Bessarabia; in return, Russia would support any special British need for bases or security arrangements in Western Europe. There was nothing specifically communist about these ambitions. If Stalin achieved them, he would be fulfilling an age-old dream of the czars. The British reaction was mixed. "Soviet policy is amoral," as Anthony Eden noted at the time; "United States policy is exaggeratedly moral, at least where non-American interests are concerned." If Roosevelt was a universalist with occasional leanings toward spheres of influence and Stalin was a sphere-of-influence man with occasional gestures toward universalism, Churchill seemed evenly poised between the familiar realism of the balance of power, which he had so long recorded as an historian and manipulated as a statesman, and the hope that there must be some better way of doing things. His 1943 proposal of a world organization divided into regional councils represented an effort to blend universalist and sphere-of-interest conceptions. His initial rejection of Stalin's proposal in December 1941 as "directly contrary to the first, second and third articles of the Atlantic Charter" thus did not spring entirely from a desire to propitiate the United States. On the other hand, he had himself already reinterpreted the Atlantic Charter as applying only to Europe (and thus not to the British Empire), and he was, above all, an empiricist who never believed in sacrificing reality on the altar of doctrine.

So in April 1942 he wrote Roosevelt that "the increasing gravity of the war" had led him to feel that the Charter "ought not to be construed so as to deny Russia the frontiers she occupied when Germany attacked her." Hull, however, remained fiercely hostile to the inclusion of territorial provisions in the Anglo-Russian treaty; the American position, Eden noted, "chilled me with Wilsonian memories." Though Stalin complained that it looked "as if the Atlantic Charter was directed against the U.S.S.R.," it was the Russian season of military adversity in the spring of 1942, and he dropped his demands.

He did not, however, change his intentions. A year later Ambassador Standley could cable Washington from Moscow: "In 1918 Western Europe attempted to set up a *cordon sanitaire* to protect it from the influence of bolshevism. Might not now the Kremlin envisage the formation of a belt of pro-Soviet states to protect it from the influences of the West?" It well might; and that purpose became increasingly clear as the war approached its end. Indeed, it derived sustenance from Western policy in the first area of liberation.

The unconditional surrender of Italy in July 1943 created the first major test of the Western devotion to universalism. America and Britain, having won the Italian war, handled the capitulation, keeping Moscow informed at a distance. Stalin complained:

> The United States and Great Britain made agreements but the Soviet Union received information about the results . . . just as a passive third observer. I have to tell you that it is impossible to tolerate the situation any longer. I propose that the [tripartite military-political commission] be established and that Sicily be assigned . . . as its place of residence.

Roosevelt, who had no intention of sharing the control of Italy with the Russians, suavely replied with the suggestion that Stalin send an officer "to General Eisenhower's headquarters in connection with the commission." Unimpressed, Stalin continued to press for a tripartite body; but his Western allies were adamant in keeping the Soviet Union off the Control Commission for Italy, and the Russians in the end had to be satisfied with a seat, along with minor Allied states, on a meaningless Inter-Allied Advisory Council. Their acquiescence in this was doubtless not unconnected with a desire to establish precedents for Eastern Europe.

Teheran in December 1943 marked the high point of three-power collaboration. Still, when Churchill asked about Russian territorial interests, Stalin replied a little ominously, "There is no need to speak at the present time about any Soviet desires, but when the time comes we will speak." In the next weeks, there were increasing indications of a Soviet determination to deal unilaterally with Eastern Europe — so much so that in early February 1944 Hull cabled Harriman in Moscow:

> Matters are rapidly approaching the point where the Soviet Government will have to choose between the development and extension of the foundation of international cooperation as the guiding principle of the postwar world as against the continuance of a unilateral and arbitrary method of dealing with its special problems even though these problems are admittedly of more direct interest to the Soviet Union than to other great powers.

As against this approach, however, Churchill, more tolerant of sphere-of-influence deviations, soon proposed that, with the impending liberation of the Balkans, Russia should run things in Rumania and Britain in Greece. Hull strongly opposed this suggestion but made the mistake of leaving Washington for a few days; and Roosevelt, momentarily free from his Wilsonian conscience, yielded to Churchill's plea for a three-month trial. Hull resumed the fight on his return, and Churchill postponed the matter.

The Red Army continued its advance into Eastern Europe. In August the Polish Home Army, urged on by Polish-language broadcasts from Moscow, rose up against the Nazis in Warsaw. For sixty-three terrible days, the Poles fought valiantly on, while the Red Army halted on the banks of the Vistula a few miles away, and in Moscow Stalin for more than half this time declined to cooperate with the Western effort to drop supplies to the Warsaw Resistance. It appeared a calculated Soviet decision to let the Nazis slaughter the anti-Soviet Polish underground; and, indeed, the result was to destroy any substantial alternative to a Soviet solution in Poland. The agony of Warsaw caused the most deep and genuine moral shock in Britain and America and provoked dark forebodings about Soviet postwar purposes.

Again history enjoins the imaginative leap in order to see things for a moment from Moscow's viewpoint. The Polish question, Churchill would say at Yalta, was for Britain a question of honor. "It is not only a question of honor for Russia," Stalin replied, "but one of life and death. . . . Throughout history Poland had been the corridor for attack on Russia." A top postwar priority for any Russian regime must be to close that corridor. The Home Army was led by anticommunists. It clearly hoped by its action to forestall the Soviet occupation of Warsaw and, in Russian eyes, to prepare the way for an anti-Russian Poland. In addition, the uprising from a strictly operational viewpoint was premature. The Russians, it is evident in retrospect, had real military problems at the Vistula. The Soviet attempt in September to send Polish units from the Red Army across the river to join forces with the Home Army was a disaster. Heavy German shelling thereafter prevented the ferrying of tanks necessary for an assault on the German position. The Red Army itself did not take Warsaw for another three months. Nonetheless, Stalin's indifference to the human tragedy, his effort to blackmail the London Poles during the ordeal, his sanctimonious opposition during five precious weeks to aerial resupply, the invariable coldness of his explanations ("the Soviet command has come to the conclusion that it must dissociate itself from the Warsaw adventure") and the obvious political benefit to the Soviet Union from the destruction of the Home Army — all these had the effect of suddenly dropping the mask of wartime comradeship and displaying to the West the hard face of Soviet policy. In now pursuing what he grimly regarded as the minimal requirements for the postwar security of his country, Stalin was inadvertently showing the irreconcilability of both his means and his ends with the Anglo-American conception of the peace.

Meanwhile Eastern Europe presented the Alliance with still another crisis that same September. Bulgaria, which was not at war with Russia, decided to surrender to the Western allies while it still could; and the English and Americans at Cairo began to discuss armistice terms with Bulgarian envoys. Moscow, challenged by what it plainly saw as a Western intrusion into its own zone of vital interest, promptly declared war on Bulgaria, took over the surrender negotiations and, invoking the Italian precedent, denied its Western allies any role in the Bulgarian Control Commission. In a long and thoughtful cable, Ambassador Harriman meditated on the problems of communication with the Soviet Union.

"Words," he reflected, "have a different connotation to the Soviets than they have to us. When they speak of insisting on 'friendly governments' in their neighboring countries, they have in mind something quite different from what we would mean." The Russians, he surmised, really believed that Washington accepted "their position that although they would keep us informed they had the right to settle their problems with their western neighbors unilaterally." But the Soviet position was still in flux: "the Soviet Government is not one mind." The problem, as Harriman had earlier told Harry Hopkins, was "to strengthen the hands of those around Stalin who want to play the game along our lines." The way to do this, he now told Hull, was to

> be understanding of their sensitivity, meet them much more than half way, encourage them and support them wherever we can, and yet oppose them promptly with greatest of firmness where we see them going wrong. . . . The only way we can eventually come to an understanding with the Soviet Union on the question of non-interference in the internal affairs of other countries is for us to take a definite interest in the solution of the problems of each individual country as they arise.

As against Harriman's sophisticated universalist strategy, however, Churchill, increasingly fearful of the consequences of unrestrained competition in Eastern Europe, decided in early October to carry his sphere-of-influence proposal directly to Moscow. Roosevelt was at first content to have Churchill speak for him too and even prepared a cable to that effect. But Hopkins, a more rigorous universalist, took it upon himself to stop the cable and warn Roosevelt of its possible implications. Eventually Roosevelt sent a message to

Harriman in Moscow emphasizing that he expected to "retain complete freedom of action after this conference is over." It was now that Churchill quickly proposed — and Stalin as quickly accepted — the celebrated division of southeastern Europe: ending (after further haggling between Eden and Molotov) with 90 percent Soviet predominance in Rumania, 80 percent in Bulgaria and Hungary, fifty-fifty in Yugoslavia, 90 percent British predominance in Greece.

Churchill in discussing this with Harriman used the phrase "spheres of influence." But he insisted that these were only "immediate wartime arrangements" and received a highly general blessing from Roosevelt. Yet, whatever Churchill intended, there is reason to believe that Stalin construed the percentages as an agreement, not a declaration; as practical arithmetic, not algebra. For Stalin, it should be understood, the sphere-of-influence idea did not mean that he would abandon all efforts to spread communism in some other nation's sphere; it did mean that, if he tried this and the other side cracked down, he could not feel he had serious cause for complaint. As Kennan wrote to Harriman at the end of 1944:

> As far as border states are concerned the Soviet government has never ceased to think in terms of spheres of interest. They expect us to support them in whatever action they wish to take in those regions, regardless of whether that action seems to us or to the rest of the world to be right or wrong. . . . I have no doubt that this position is honestly maintained on their part, and that they would be equally prepared to reserve moral judgment on any actions which we might wish to carry out, i.e., in the Caribbean area.

In any case, the matter was already under test a good deal closer to Moscow than the Caribbean. The communist-dominated resistance movement in Greece was in open revolt against the effort of the Papandreou government to disarm and disband the guerrillas. Churchill now called in British Army units to crush the insurrection. This action produced a storm of criticism in his own country and in the United States; the American government even publicly disassociated itself from the intervention, thereby emphasizing its detachment from the sphere-of-influence deal. But Stalin, Churchill later claimed, "adhered strictly and faithfully to our agreement of October, and during all the long weeks of fighting the Communists in the streets of Athens not one word of reproach came from *Pravda* or *Izvestia*," though there is no evidence that he tried to call off the Greek communists. Still, when the communist rebellion later broke out again in Greece, Stalin told Kardelj and Djilas of Yugoslavia in 1948, "The uprising in Greece must be stopped, and as quickly as possible."

No one, of course, can know what really was in the minds of the Russian leaders. The Kremlin archives are locked; of the primary actors, only Molotov survives, and he has not yet indicated any desire to collaborate with the Columbia Oral History Project. We do know that Stalin did not wholly surrender to sentimental illusion about his new friends. In June 1944, on the night before the landings in Normandy, he told Djilas that the English "find nothing sweeter than to trick their allies. . . . And Churchill? Churchill is the kind who, if you don't watch him, will slip a kopeck out of your pocket. Yes, a kopeck out of your pocket! . . . Roosevelt is not like that. He dips in his hand only for bigger coins." But, whatever his views of his colleagues, it is not unreasonable to suppose that Stalin would have been satisfied at the end of the war to secure what Kennan has called "a protective glacis along Russia's western border," and that, in exchange for a free hand in Eastern Europe, he was prepared to give the British and Americans equally free hands in their zones of vital interest, including in nations as close to Russia as Greece (for the British) and, very probably — or at least so the Yugoslavs believe — China (for the United States). In other words, his initial objectives were very probably not world conquest but Russian security.

4. The American Analysis

It is now pertinent to inquire why the United States rejected the idea of stabilizing the world by division into spheres of influence and insisted on an East European strategy. One should warn against rushing to the conclusion that it was all a row between hard-nosed, balance-of-power realists and starry-eyed Wilsonians. Roosevelt, Hopkins, Welles, Harriman, Bohlen, Berle, Dulles and other universalists were tough and serious men. Why then did they rebuff the sphere-of-influence solution?

The first reason is that they regarded this solution as containing within itself the seeds of a third world war. The balance-of-power idea seemed inherently unstable. It had always broken down in the past. It held out to each power the permanent temptation to try to alter the balance in its own favor, and it built this temptation into the international order. It would turn the great powers of 1945 away from the objective of concerting common policies toward competition for postwar advantage. As Hopkins told Molotov at Teheran, "The President feels it essential to world peace that Russia, Great Britain and the United States work out this control question in a manner which will not start each of the three powers arming against the others." "The greatest likelihood of eventual conflict," said the Joint Chiefs of Staff in 1944 (the only conflict which the JCS, in its wisdom, could then glimpse "in the foreseeable future" was between Britain and Russia), ". . . would seem to grow out of either nation initiating attempts to build up its strength, by seeking to attach to herself parts of Europe to the disadvantage and possible danger of her potential adversary." The Americans were perfectly ready to acknowledge that Russia was entitled to convincing assurance of her national security — but not this way. "I could not sympathize fully with Stalin's desire to protect his western borders from future attack," as Hull put it. "But I felt that this security could best be obtained through a strong postwar peace organization."

Hull's remark suggests the second objection: that the sphere-of-influence approach would, in the words of the State Department in 1945, "militate against the establishment and effective functioning of a broader system of general security in which all countries will have their part." The United Nations, in short, was seen as the alternative to the balance of power. Nor did the universalists see any necessary incompatibility between the Russian desire for "friendly governments" on its frontier and the American desire for self-determination in Eastern Europe. Before Yalta the State Department judged the general mood of Europe as "to the left and strongly in favor of far-reaching economic and social reforms, but not, however, in favor of a left-wing totalitarian regime to achieve these reforms." Governments in Eastern Europe could be sufficiently to the left "to allay Soviet suspicions" but sufficiently representative "of the center and *petit bourgeois* elements" not to seem a prelude to communist dictatorship. The American criteria were therefore that the government "should be dedicated to the preservation of civil liberties" and "should favor social and economic reforms." A string of New Deal states — of Finlands and Czechoslovakias — seemed a reasonable compromise solution.

Third, the universalists feared that the sphere-of-interest approach would be what Hull termed "a haven for the isolationists," who would advocate America's participation in western hemisphere affairs on condition that it did not participate in European or Asian affairs. Hull also feared that spheres of interest would lead to "closed trade areas or discriminatory systems" and thus defeat his cherished dream of a low-tariff, freely trading world.

Fourth, the sphere-of-interest solution meant the betrayal of the principles for which the Second World War was being fought — the Atlantic Charter, the Four Freedoms, the Declaration of the United Nations. Poland summed up the problem. Britain, having gone to war to defend the independence of Poland from the Germans, could not easily conclude the war by surrendering the independence of Poland to the Russians. Thus, as Hopkins told Stalin after Roosevelt's death in 1945, Poland had "become the symbol of our ability to work out problems with the Soviet Union." Nor could American liberals in general watch with equanimity while the police state spread into countries which, if they had mostly not been real democracies, had mostly not been tyrannies either. The execution in 1943 of Ehrlich and Alter, the Polish socialist trade union leaders, excited deep concern. "I have particularly in mind," Harriman cabled in 1944, "objection to the institution of secret police who may become involved in the persecution of persons of truly democratic convictions who may not be willing to conform to Soviet methods."

Fifth, the sphere-of-influence solution would create difficult domestic problems in American politics. Roosevelt was aware of the six million or more Polish votes in the 1944 election; even more acutely, he was aware of the broader and deeper attack which would follow if, after going to war to stop the Nazi conquest of Europe, he permitted the war to end with the communist conquest of Eastern Europe. As Archibald MacLeish, then Assistant Secretary of State for Public Affairs, warned in January 1945, "The wave of disillusionment which has distressed us in the last several weeks will be increased if the impression is permitted to get abroad that potentially totalitarian provisional governments are to be set up without adequate safeguards as to the holding of free elections and the realization of the principles of the Atlantic Charter." Roosevelt believed that no administration could survive which did not try everything short of war to save Eastern Europe, and he was the supreme American politician of the century.

Sixth, if the Russians were allowed to overrun Eastern Europe without argument, would that satisfy them? Even Kennan, in a dispatch of May 1944, admitted that the "urge" had dreadful potentialities: "If initially successful, will it know where to stop? Will it not be inexorably carried forward, by its very nature, in a struggle to reach the whole — to attain complete mastery of the shores of the Atlantic and the Pacific?" His own answer was that there were inherent limits to the Russian capacity to expand — "that Russia will not have an easy time in maintaining the power which it has seized over other people in Eastern and Central Europe unless it receives both moral and material assistance from the West." Subsequent developments have vindicated Kennan's argument. By the late forties, Yugoslavia and Albania, the two East European states farthest from the Soviet Union and the two in which communism was imposed from within rather than from without, had declared their independence of Moscow. But, given Russia's success in maintaining centralized control over the international communist movement for a quarter of a century, who in 1944 could have had much confidence in the idea of communist revolts against Moscow?

Most of those involved therefore rejected Kennan's answer and stayed with his question. If the West turned its back on Eastern Europe, the higher probability, in their view, was that the Russians would use their security zone, not just for defensive purposes, but as a springboard from which to mount an attack on Western Europe, now shattered by war, a vacuum of power awaiting its master. "If the policy is accepted that the Soviet Union has a right to penetrate her immediate neighbors for security," Harriman said in 1944, "penetration of the next immediate neighbors becomes at a certain time equally logical." If a row with Russia were inevitable, every consideration of prudence dictated that it should take place in Eastern rather than Western Europe.

Thus idealism and realism joined in opposition to the sphere-of-influence solution. The consequence was a determination to assert an American interest in the postwar destiny of all nations, including those of Eastern Europe. In the message which Roosevelt and Hopkins drafted after Hopkins had stopped Roosevelt's initial cable authorizing Churchill to speak for the United States at the Moscow meeting of October 1944, Roosevelt now said, "There is in this global war literally no question, either military or political, in which the United States is not interested." After Roosevelt's death Hopkins repeated the point to Stalin: "The cardinal basis of President Roosevelt's policy which the American people had fully supported had been the concept that the interests of the U.S. were worldwide and not confined to North and South America and the Pacific Ocean."

5. Confusions at the Summit

For better or worse, this was the American position. It is now necessary to attempt the imaginative leap and consider the impact of this position on the leaders of the Soviet Union who, also for better or for worse, had reached the bitter conclusion that the survival of their country depended on their unchallenged control of the corridors through which enemies had so often invaded their homeland. They could claim to have been keeping their own side of the sphere-of-influence bargain. Of course, they were working to capture the resistance movements of Western Europe; indeed, with the appointment of Oumansky as Ambassador to Mexico they were even beginning to enlarge underground operations in the western hemisphere. But, from their viewpoint, if the West permitted this, the more fools they; and, if the West stopped it, it was within their right to do so. In overt political matters the Russians were scrupulously playing the game. They had watched in silence while the British shot down communists in Greece. In Yugoslavia Stalin was urging Tito (as Djilas later revealed) to keep King Peter. They had not only acknowledged Western preeminence in Italy but had recognized the Badoglio regime; the Italian communists had even voted (against the Socialists and the Liberals) for the renewal of the Lateran Pacts.

They would not regard anticommunist action in a Western zone as a *casus belli*; and they expected reciprocal license to assert their own authority in the East. But the principle of self-determination was carrying the United States into a deeper entanglement in Eastern Europe than the Soviet Union claimed as a right (whatever it was doing underground) in the affairs of Italy, Greece or China. When the Russians now exercised in Eastern Europe the same brutal control they were prepared to have Washington exercise in the American sphere of influence, the American protests, given the paranoia produced alike by Russian history and Leninist ideology, no doubt seemed not only an act of hypocrisy but a threat to security. To the Russians, a stroll into the neighborhood easily became a plot to burn down the house: when, for example, damaged American planes made emergency landings in Poland and Hungary, Moscow took this as attempts to organize the local resistance. It is not unusual to suspect one's adversary of doing what one is already doing oneself. At the same time, the cruelty with which the Russians executed their idea of spheres of influence — in a sense, perhaps, an unwitting cruelty, since Stalin treated the East Europeans no worse than he had treated the Russians in the thirties — discouraged the West from accepting the equation (for example, Italy = Rumania) which seemed so self-evident to the Kremlin.

So Moscow very probably, and not unnaturally, perceived the emphasis on self-determination as a systematic and deliberate pressure on Russia's western frontiers. Moreover, the restoration of capitalism to countries freed at frightful cost by the Red Army no doubt struck the Russians as the betrayal of the principles for which *they* were fighting. "That they, the victors," Isaac Deutscher has suggested, "should now preserve an order from which they had experienced nothing but hostility, and could expect nothing but hostility . . . would have been the most miserable anti-climax to their great 'war of liberation.'" By 1944 Poland was the critical issue; Harriman later said that "under instructions from President Roosevelt, I talked about Poland with Stalin more frequently than any other subject." While the West saw the point of Stalin's demand for a "friendly government" in Warsaw, the American insistence on the sovereign virtues of free elections (ironically in the spirit of the 1917 Bolshevik decree of peace, which affirmed "the right" of a nation "to decide the forms of its state existence by a free vote, taken after the complete evacuation of the incorporating or, generally, of the stronger nation") created an insoluble problem in those countries, like Poland (and Rumania) where free elections would almost certainly produce anti-Soviet governments.

The Russians thus may well have estimated the Western pressures as calculated to encourage their enemies in Eastern Europe and to defeat their own minimum objective of a protective glacis. Everything still hung, however, on the course of military operations. The wartime collaboration had been created by one thing, and one thing alone: the threat of Nazi victory. So long as this threat was real, so was the collaboration. In late December 1944, Rundstedt launched his counteroffensive in the Ardennes. A few weeks later, when Roosevelt, Churchill and Stalin gathered in the Crimea, it was in the shadow of this last considerable explosion of German power. The meeting at Yalta was still dominated by the mood of war.

Yalta remains something of an historical perplexity — less, from the perspective of 1967, because of a mythical American deference to the sphere-of-influence thesis than because of the documentable Russian deference to the universalist thesis. Why should Stalin in 1945 have accepted the Declaration on Liberated Europe and an agreement on Poland pledging that "the three governments will jointly" act to assure "free elections of governments responsive to the will of the people"? There are several probable answers: that the war was not over and the Russians still wanted the Americans to intensify their military effort in the West; that one clause in the Declaration premised action on "the opinion of the three governments" and thus implied a Soviet veto, though the Polish agreement was more definite; most of all that the universalist algebra of the Declaration was plainly in Stalin's mind to be construed in terms of the practical arithmetic of his sphere-of-influence agreement with Churchill the previous October. Stalin's assurance to Churchill at Yalta that a proposed Russian amendment to the Declaration would not apply to Greece makes it clear that Roosevelt's pieties did not, in Stalin's mind, nullify Churchill's percentages. He could well have been strengthened in this supposition by the fact that *after* Yalta, Churchill himself repeatedly reasserted the terms of the October agreement as if he regarded it, despite Yalta, as controlling.

Harriman still had the feeling before Yalta that the Kremlin had "two approaches to their postwar policies" and that

Stalin himself was "of two minds." One approach emphasized the internal reconstruction and development of Russia; the other its external expansion. But in the meantime the fact which dominated all political decisions — that is, the war against Germany — was moving into its final phase. In the weeks after Yalta, the military situation changed with great rapidity. As the Nazi threat declined, so too did the need for cooperation. The Soviet Union, feeling itself menaced by the American idea of self-determination and the borderlands diplomacy to which it was leading, skeptical whether the United Nations would protect its frontiers as reliably as its own domination in Eastern Europe, began to fulfill its security requirements unilaterally.

In March Stalin expressed his evaluation of the United Nations by rejecting Roosevelt's plea that Molotov come to the San Francisco conference, if only for the opening sessions. In the next weeks the Russians emphatically and crudely worked their will in Eastern Europe, above all in the test country of Poland. They were ignoring the Declaration on Liberated Europe, ignoring the Atlantic Charter, self-determination, human freedom and everything else the Americans considered essential for a stable peace. "We must clearly recognize," Harriman wired Washington a few days before Roosevelt's death, "that the Soviet program is the establishment of totalitarianism, ending personal liberty and democracy as we know and respect it."

At the same time, the Russians also began to mobilize communist resources in the United States itself to block American universalism. In April 1945 Jacques Duclos, who had been the Comintern official responsible for the Western communist parties, launched in *Cahiers du Communisme* an uncompromising attack on the policy of the American Communist party. Duclos sharply condemned the revisionism of Earl Browder, the American communist leader, as "expressed in the concept of a long-term class peace in the United States, of the possibility of the suppression of the class struggle in the postwar period and of establishment of harmony between labor and capital." Browder was specifically rebuked for favoring the "self-determination" of Europe "west of the Soviet Union" on a bourgeois-democratic basis. The excommunication of Browderism was plainly the Politburo's considered reaction to the impending defeat of Germany; it was a signal to the communist parties of the West that they should recover their identity; it was Moscow's alert to communists everywhere that they should prepare for new policies in the postwar world.

The Duclos piece obviously could not have been planned and written much later than the Yalta conference — that is, well before a number of events which revisionists now cite in order to demonstrate American responsibility for the Cold War: before Allen Dulles, for example, began to negotiate the surrender of the German armies in Italy (the episode which provoked Stalin to charge Roosevelt with seeking a separate peace and provoked Roosevelt to denounce the "vile misrepresentations" of Stalin's informants); well before Roosevelt died; many months before the testing of the atomic bomb; even more months before Truman ordered that the bomb be dropped on Japan. William Z. Foster, who soon replaced Browder as the leader of the American Communist party and embodied the new Moscow line, later boasted of having said in January 1944, "A post-war Roosevelt administration would continue to be, as it is now, an imperialist government." With ancient suspicions revived by the American insistence on universalism, this was no doubt the conclusion which the Russians were reaching at the same time. The Soviet canonization of Roosevelt (like their present-day canonization of Kennedy) took place after the American President's death.

The atmosphere of mutual suspicion was beginning to rise. In January 1945 Molotov formally proposed that the United States grant Russia a $6 billion credit for postwar reconstruction. With characteristic tact he explained that he was doing this as a favor to save America from a postwar depression. The proposal seems to have been diffidently made and diffidently received. Roosevelt requested that the matter "not be pressed further" on the American side until he had a chance to talk with Stalin; but the Russians did not follow it up either at Yalta in February (save for a single glancing reference) or during the Stalin-Hopkins talks in May or at Potsdam. Finally the proposal was renewed in the very different political atmosphere of August. This time Washington inexplicably mislaid the request during the transfer of the records of the Foreign Economic Administration to the State Department. It did not turn up again until March 1946. Of course this was impossible for the Russians to believe; it is hard enough even for those acquainted with the capacity of the American government for incompetence to believe; and it only strengthened Soviet suspicions of American purposes.

The American credit was one conceivable form of Western contribution to Russian reconstruction. Another was Lend-Lease, and the possibility of reconstruction aid under the Lend-Lease protocol had already been discussed in 1944. But in May 1945 Russia, like Britain, suffered from Truman's abrupt termination of Lend-Lease shipments — "unfortunate and even brutal," Stalin told Hopkins, adding that, if it was "designed as pressure on the Russians in order to soften them up, then it was a fundamental mistake." A third form was German reparations. Here Stalin in demanding $10 billion in reparations for the Soviet Union made his strongest fight at Yalta. Roosevelt, while agreeing essentially with Churchill's opposition, tried to postpone the matter by accepting the Soviet figure as a "basis for discussion" — a formula that led to future misunderstanding. In short, the Russian hope for major Western assistance in postwar reconstruction foundered on three events the Kremlin could well have interpreted respectively as deliberate sabotage (the loan request), blackmail (Lend-Lease cancellation) and pro-Germanism (reparations).

Actually the American attempt to settle the fourth Lend-Lease protocol was generous and the Russians for their own reasons declined to come to an agreement. It is not clear, though, that satisfying Moscow on any of these financial scores would have made much essential difference. It might have persuaded some doves in the Kremlin that the United States Government was genuinely friendly; it might have persuaded some hawks that the American anxiety for Soviet friendship was such that Moscow could do as it wished without inviting challenge from the United States. It would, in short, merely have reinforced both sides of the Kremlin debate; it would hardly have reversed deeper tendencies toward the deterioration of political relationships. Economic deals were surely subordinate to the quality of mutual political confidence; and here, in the months after Yalta, the decay was steady.

The Cold War had now begun. It was the product not of a decision but of a dilemma. Each side felt compelled to adopt policies that the other could not but regard as a threat to the principles of the peace. Each then felt compelled to undertake defensive measures. Thus the Russians saw no choice but to consolidate their security in Eastern Europe. The Americans, regarding Eastern Europe as the first step toward Western Europe, responded by asserting their interest in the zone the Russians deemed vital to their security. The Russians concluded that the West was resuming its old course of capitalist encirclement; that it was purposefully laying the foundation for anti-Soviet regimes in the area defined by the blood of centuries as crucial to Russian survival. Each side believed with passion that future international stability depended on the success of its own conception of world order. Each side, in pursuing its own clearly indicated and deeply cherished principles, was only confirming the fear of the other that it was bent on aggression.

Very soon the process began to acquire a cumulative momentum. The impending collapse of Germany thus provoked new troubles: the Russians, for example, sincerely feared that the West was planning a separate surrender of the German armies in Italy in a way which would release troops for Hitler's eastern front, as they subsequently feared that the Nazis might succeed in surrendering Berlin to the West. This was the context in which the atomic bomb now appeared. Though the revisionist argument that Truman dropped the bomb less to defeat Japan than to intimidate Russia is not convincing, this thought unquestionably appealed to some in Washington as at least an advantageous side-effect of Hiroshima.

So the machinery of suspicion and countersuspicion, action and counteraction, was set in motion. But, given relations among traditional national states, there was still no reason, even with all the postwar jostling, why this should not have remained a manageable situation. What made it unmanageable, what caused the rapid escalation of the Cold War and in another two years completed the division of Europe, was a set of considerations this account has thus far excluded.

6. The Asymmetry of Totalitarianism

Up to this point, the discussion has considered the schism within the wartime coalition as if it were entirely the result of disagreements among national states. Assuming this framework, there was unquestionably a failure of communication between America and Russia, a misperception of signals and, as time went on, a mounting tendency to ascribe ominous motives to the other side. It seems hard, for example, to deny that American postwar policy created genuine difficulties for the Russians and even assumed a threatening aspect for them. All this the revisionists have rightly and usefully emphasized.

But the great omission of the revisionists — and also the fundamental explanation of the speed with which the Cold War escalated — lies precisely in the fact that the Soviet Union was *not* a traditional national state.* This is where the

* This is the classical revisionist fallacy — the assumption of the rationality, or at least of the traditionalism, of states where ideology and social organization have created a different range of motives. So the Second World War revisionists omit the totalitarian dynamism of nazism and the fanaticism of Hitler, as the Civil War revisionists omit the fact that the slavery system was producing a doctrinaire closed society in the American South. For a consideration of some of these issues, see "The Causes of the Civil War: A Note on Historical Sentimentalism" in my *The Politics of Hope* (Boston, 1963).

"mirror image," invoked by some psychologists, falls down. For the Soviet Union was a phenomenon very different from America or Britain: it was a totalitarian state, endowed with an all-explanatory, all-consuming ideology, committed to the infallibility of government and party, still in a somewhat messianic mood, equating dissent with treason, and ruled by a dictator who, for all his quite extraordinary abilities, had his paranoid moments.

Marxism-Leninism gave the Russian leaders a view of the world according to which all societies were inexorably destined to proceed along appointed roads by appointed stages until they achieved the classless nirvana. Moreover, given the resistance of the capitalists to this development, the existence of any noncommunist state was *by definition* a threat to the Soviet Union. "As long as capitalism and socialism exist," Lenin wrote, "we cannot live in peace: in the end, one or the other will triumph — a funeral dirge will be sung either over the Soviet Republic or over world capitalism."

Stalin and his associates, whatever Roosevelt or Truman did or failed to do, were bound to regard the United States as the enemy, not because of this deed or that, but because of the primordial fact that America was the leading capitalist power and thus, by Leninist syllogism, unappeasably hostile, driven by the logic of its system to oppose, encircle and destroy Soviet Russia. Nothing the United States could have done in 1944–1945 would have abolished this mistrust, required and sanctified as it was by Marxist gospel — nothing short of the conversion of the United States into a Stalinist despotism; and even this would not have sufficed, as the experience of Yugoslavia and China soon showed, unless it were accompanied by total subservience to Moscow. So long as the United States remained a capitalist democracy, no American policy, given Moscow's theology, could hope to win basic Soviet confidence, and every American action was poisoned from the source. So long as the Soviet Union remained a messianic state, ideology compelled a steady expansion of communist power.

It is easy, of course, to exaggerate the capacity of ideology to control events. The tension of acting according to revolutionary abstractions is too much for most nations to sustain over a long period: that is why Mao Tse-tung launched his Cultural Revolution, hoping thereby to create a permanent revolutionary mood and save Chinese communism from the degeneration which, in his view, had overtaken Russian communism. Still, as any revolution grows older, normal human and social motives will increasingly reassert themselves. In due course, we can be sure, Leninism will be about as effective in governing the daily lives of Russians as Christianity is in governing the daily lives of Americans. Like the Ten Commandments and the Sermon on the Mount, the Leninist verities will increasingly become platitudes for ritual observance, not guides to secular decision. There can be no worse fallacy (even if respectable people practiced it diligently for a season in the United States) than that of drawing from a nation's ideology permanent conclusions about its behavior.

A temporary recession of ideology was already taking place during the Second World War when Stalin, to rally his people against the invader, had to replace the appeal of Marxism by that of nationalism. ("We are under no illusions that they are fighting for us," Stalin once said to Harriman. "They are fighting for Mother Russia.") But this was still taking place within the strictest limitations. The Soviet Union remained as much a police state as ever; the regime was as infallible as ever; foreigners and their ideas were as suspect as ever. "Never, except possibly during my later experience as ambassador in Moscow," Kennan has written, "did the insistence of the Soviet authorities on isolation of the diplomatic corps weigh more heavily on me . . . than in these first weeks following my return to Russia in the final months of the war. . . . [We were] treated as though we were the bearers of some species of the plague" — which, of course, from the Soviet viewpoint, they were: the plague of skepticism.

Paradoxically, of the forces capable of bringing about a modification of ideology, the most practical and effective was the Soviet dictatorship itself. If Stalin was an ideologist, he was also a pragmatist. If he saw everything through the lenses of Marxism-Leninism, he also, as the infallible expositor of the faith, could reinterpret Marxism-Leninism to justify anything he wanted to do at any given moment. No doubt Roosevelt's ignorance of Marxism-Leninism was inexcusable and led to grievous miscalculations. But Roosevelt's efforts to work on and through Stalin were not so hopelessly naïve as it used to be fashionable to think. With the extraordinary instinct of a great political leader, Roosevelt intuitively understood that Stalin was the *only* lever available to the West against the Leninist ideology and the Soviet system. "What helps a lot," he told the White House physician, "is that Stalin is the only man I have to convince. Joe doesn't worry about a congress or a Parliament. He's the whole world." If Stalin could be reached, then alone was there a chance of getting the Russians to act contrary to the prescriptions of their faith. The best evidence is that Roosevelt retained a certain capacity to influence Stalin to the end; the nominal Soviet acquiescence in American universalism as late as Yalta was perhaps an indication of that. It is in this way that the death of Roosevelt was crucial — not in the vulgar sense that his policy was then reversed by his successor, which did not happen, but in the sense that no other American could hope to have the restraining impact on Stalin that Roosevelt might for a while have had.

Stalin alone could have made any difference. Yet Stalin, in spite of the impression of sobriety and realism he made on Westerners who saw him during the Second World War, was plainly a man of deep and morbid obsessions and compulsions. When he was still young, Lenin had criticized his rude and arbitrary ways. A reasonably authoritative observer (N. S. Khrushchev) later commented, "These negative characteristics of his developed steadily and during the last years acquired an absolutely insufferable character." His paranoia, probably set off by the suicide of his wife in 1932, led to the terrible purges of the mid-thirties and the wanton murder of thousands of his Bolshevik comrades. "Everywhere and in everything," Khrushchev says of this period, "he saw 'enemies,' 'double-dealers' and 'spies.' " The crisis of war evidently steadied him in some way, though Khrushchev speaks of his "nervousness and hysteria . . . even after the war began." The madness, so rigidly controlled for a time, burst out with new and shocking intensity in the postwar years. "After the war," Khrushchev testifies,

> the situation became even more complicated. Stalin became even more capricious, irritable and brutal; in particular, his suspicion grew. His persecution mania reached unbelievable dimensions. . . . He decided everything, without any consideration for anyone or anything.
>
> Stalin's wilfulness showed itself . . . also in the international relations of the Soviet Union. . . . He had completely lost a sense of reality; he demonstrated his suspicion

and haughtiness not only in relation to individuals in the USSR, but in relation to whole parties and nations.

A revisionist fallacy has been to treat Stalin as just another Realpolitik statesman, as Second World War revisionists see Hitler as just another Stresemann or Bismarck. But the record makes it clear that in the end nothing could satisfy Stalin's paranoia. His own associates failed. Why does anyone suppose that any conceivable American policy would have succeeded?

An analysis of the origins of the Cold War which leaves out these factors — the intransigence of Leninist ideology, the sinister dynamics of a totalitarian society and the madness of Stalin — is obviously incomplete. It was these factors which made it hard for the West to accept the thesis that Russia was moved only by a desire to protect its security and would be satisfied by the control of Eastern Europe; it was these factors which charged the debate between universalism and spheres of influence with apocalyptic potentiality.

Leninism and totalitarianism created a structure of thought and behavior that made postwar collaboration between Russia and America — in any normal sense of civilized intercourse between national states — inherently impossible. The Soviet dictatorship of 1945 simply could not have survived such a collaboration. Indeed, nearly a quarter century later, the Soviet regime, though it has meanwhile moved a good distance, could still hardly survive it without risking the release inside Russia of energies profoundly opposed to communist despotism. As for Stalin, he may have represented the only force in 1945 capable of overcoming Stalinism, but the very traits which enabled him to win absolute power expressed terrifying instabilities of mind and temperament and hardly offered a solid foundation for a peaceful world.

7. Confrontation

The difference between America and Russia in 1945 was that some Americans fundamentally believed in the possibility, over the long run, of a modus vivendi with Russia; while no Russians, so far as one can tell, believed in more than a short-run modus vivendi with the United States.

Harriman and Kennan, this narrative has made clear, took the lead in warning Washington about the difficulties of short-run dealings with the Soviet Union. But both argued that, if the United States developed a rational policy and stuck to it, there would be, after long and rough passages, the prospect of eventual clearing. "I am, as you know," Harriman cabled Washington in early April, "a most earnest advocate of the closest possible understanding with the Soviet Union so that what I am saying relates only to how best to attain such understanding." Kennan has similarly made it clear that the function of his containment policy was "to tide us over a difficult time and bring us to the point where we could discuss effectively with the Russians the dangers and drawbacks this status quo involved, and to arrange with them for its peaceful replacement by a better and sounder one." The subsequent careers of both men attest to the honesty of these statements.

There is no corresponding evidence on the Russian side that anyone seriously sought a modus vivendi in these terms. Stalin's choice was whether his long-term ideological and national interests would be better served by a short-run truce with the West or by an immediate resumption of pressure.

In October 1945 Stalin indicated to Harriman at Sochi that he planned to adopt the second course — that the Soviet Union was going isolationist. No doubt the succession of problems with the United States contributed to this decision, but the basic causes most probably lay elsewhere: in the developing situations in Eastern Europe, in Western Europe and in the United States.

In Eastern Europe, Stalin was still for a moment experimenting with techniques of control. But he must by now have begun to conclude that he had underestimated the hostility of the people to Russian dominion. The Hungarian elections in November would finally convince him that the Yalta formula was a road to anti-Soviet governments. At the same time, he was feeling more strongly than ever a sense of his opportunities in Western Europe. The other half of the continent lay unexpectedly before him, politically demoralized, economically prostrate, militarily defenseless. The hunting would be better and safer than he had anticipated. As for the United States, the alacrity of postwar demobilization must have recalled Roosevelt's offhand remark at Yalta that "two years would be the limit" for keeping American troops in Europe. And, despite Dr. Eugene Varga's doubts about the imminence of American economic breakdown, Marxist theology assured Stalin that the United States was heading into a bitter postwar depression and would be consumed with its own problems. If the condition of Eastern Europe made unilateral action seem essential in the interests of Russian security, the condition of Western Europe and the United States offered new temptations for communist expansion. The Cold War was now in full swing.

It still had its year of modulations and accommodations. Secretary Byrnes conducted his long and fruitless campaign to persuade the Russians that America only sought governments in Eastern Europe "both friendly to the Soviet Union and representative of all the democratic elements of the country." Finally he traded Russian dominance in Eastern Europe for American dominance in Japan. Crises were surmounted in Trieste and Iran. Secretary Marshall evidently did not give up hope of a modus vivendi until the Moscow conference of foreign secretaries of March 1947. Even then, the Soviet Union was invited to participate in the Marshall Plan.

The point of no return came on July 2, 1947, when Molotov, after bringing eighty-nine technical specialists with him to Paris and evincing initial interest in the project for European reconstruction, received the hot flash from the Kremlin, denounced the whole idea and walked out of the conference. For the next fifteen years the Cold War raged unabated, passing out of historical ambiguity into the realm of good versus evil and breeding on both sides simplifications, stereotypes and self-serving absolutes, often couched in interchangeable phrases. Under the pressure even America, for a deplorable decade, forsook its pragmatic and pluralist traditions, posed as God's appointed messenger to ignorant and sinful man and followed the Soviet example in looking to a world remade in its own image.

In retrospect, if it is impossible to see the Cold War as a case of American aggression and Russian response, it is also hard to see it as a pure case of Russian aggression and American response. "In what is truly tragic," wrote Hegel, "there must be valid moral powers on both the sides which come into collision. . . . Both suffer loss and yet both are mutually justified." In this sense, the Cold War had its tragic elements. The question remains whether it was an instance of Greek tragedy — as Auden has called it, "the tragedy of necessity," where the feeling aroused in the spectator is "What a pity it had to be this way" — or of Christian tragedy, "the tragedy of possibility," where the feeling aroused is "What a pity it was this way when it might have been otherwise."

Once something has happened, the historian is tempted to assume that it had to happen; but this may often be a highly unphilosophical assumption. The Cold War could have been avoided only if the Soviet Union had not been possessed by convictions both of the infallibility of the communist word and of the inevitability of a communist world. These convictions transformed an impasse between national states into a religious war, a tragedy of possibility into one of necessity. One might wish that America had preserved the poise and proportion of the first years of the Cold War and had not in time succumbed to its own forms of self-righteousness. But the most rational of American policies could hardly have averted the Cold War. Only today, if Russia begins to recede from its messianic mission and to accept, in practice if not yet in principle, the permanence of the world of diversity, only now can the hope flicker that this long, dreary, costly contest may at last be taking on forms less dramatic, less obsessive and less dangerous to the future of mankind.

IV

VIETNAM: LESSONS OF
THE TRAGEDY

THE CONTEMPORARY CRISIS of American confidence comes in
great part from a growing sense of our inability to manage
violence. The rise of violence at home has done more than
anything else to create doubt about the internal prospects of
American life; while, ironically, it has been the failure of violence to achieve our aims in Vietnam that has created equal
doubt about the prospects of our foreign policy.

When President Johnson spoke to the nation about Vietnam on March 31, 1968, he did more than suspend military
escalation, intensify the search for negotiation and remove
himself from the impending presidential contest. Though he
did not of course put it this way, he announced the collapse
of a policy and even perhaps the end of an era. His speech implied a rejection, or at least a drastic modification, of the
premises that have governed American foreign policy since the
end of the Second World War.

The folly of Vietnam, if properly understood, can perhaps
save us from more folly in the years to come; and it would be
useful now to make explicit what President Johnson inadvertently implied. The March 31 speech suggested in particular a retreat from the universalism that has been so sig-

nificant a strain in American foreign policy for half a century. By "universalism" I mean the belief that the United States has an active and vital interest in the destiny of every nation on the planet. To understand how we wandered into this conception, we must understand that the roots of American universalism reach deep into our national past. For the universalism that led us into Vietnam represented the extension — in the end, I think, the illegitimate extension — of two entirely honorable assumptions of American foreign policy over the last half century: the assumption that the United States has an obligation to create and defend a global structure of order; and the assumption that the United States has a democratizing mission to the world.

Before the Second World War these propositions remained largely hortatory. But the war itself and the geopolitical chaos in its wake gave American universalism a new sense of responsibility and of opportunity. We have seen how the clash between the American commitment to universalism and the Soviet faith in spheres-of-influence led to the Cold War. Universalism thereby gained new fervor from the conviction that, in pursuing a universal mission, we were confronting a universal enemy — communism. And, as universalism expanded American operations around the world, it brought into existence a power group new to American peacetime society — a military class with a vested interest in the institutionalization and indefinite enlargement of interventionist policies.

American universalism has by no means been an unequivocal disaster. It has produced acts of national generosity unparalleled in the history of man. Without it the quantity of human woe on our planet would be infinitely greater. But, as it led to policies of indiscriminate physical intervention, it displayed large and increasing limitations. In recent years, the balance between benefit and damage has shifted — a process which reached tragic culmination in Vietnam. In the succeeding sections, I will attempt to show why the Vietnam involvement proceeded with such apparent logic from the American past and why decent men should therefore have defended that involvement with such invincible self-righteousness.

1. *The Legacy of Collective Security*

Historic experience from a very early time committed North Americans, in spite of an abhorrence, partly real, partly professed, for "power politics," to an interest in the maintenance of a balance of power in Europe. As early as the seventeenth century, the prospect of the monopolization of the continent by any single aggressive state appeared a source of danger. The nation that conquered Europe, it seemed, would inevitably move across the seas; and every European war with major naval operations in the North Atlantic therefore ended by involving North America, first the English colonies and then the American republic, from the Wars of the Spanish and Austrian Succession and the Seven Years' War through the Napoleonic Wars to the First and Second World Wars. As Jefferson put it, the United States could not afford to "see the whole force of Europe wielded by a single hand." The same concern to maintain the European balance of power lay behind the Cold War. Thus for nearly three centuries American self-interest produced American opposition to any power which threatened to dominate and organize Europe — first France, then Germany, then Russia — and therefore recurrent American involvement in restoring a European balance of power.

Though the notion of equipoise in relations among states had a long history, the balance-of-power system in its classical sense prevailed in Europe only from the sixteenth century. It was a rather complex system, requiring specific preconditions for success; and, when the First World War shook the system to its foundations, Western leaders moved to give the crumbling equilibrium both a new framework and new means of action through the League of Nations. Wilson thought the League would abolish the idea of the balance of power. But Clemenceau was nearer right in seeing the League as a new and, hopefully, more civilized setting for power politics. The international community, in this view, had to have the capacity to support idealism by force.

If the belief in an American obligation to help build a global structure of order began with Wilson, the added belief in a consequent American obligation to defend that structure by force at every significant point received its first powerful advocacy from Henry L. Stimson as Secretary of State during the Manchurian crisis of 1931. Stimson's view was that great-power aggression anywhere, if unchecked and unpunished, threatened peace everywhere. This view — "collective security," as it was known in the thirties — represented a wise and courageous effort to prevent the outbreak of new world wars.

Franklin Roosevelt shared this view, and in 1940 he made Stimson his Secretary of War. Stimson, a man of lofty character and great moral force, left the imprint of his convictions on several generations of able public servants. One can trace his influence in a personal sense on the evolution of American policy in Vietnam. Stimson's closest associate during the Second World War was General George C. Marshall; and after the war Marshall became both the patron and the idol of Dean Rusk. One of Stimson's Assistant Secretaries in the State Department was Harvey Bundy, whose brilliant sons played so vital a role in deepening the American involvement in Vietnam.

The essence of the collective-security position remains correct. This essence is the perception that clearcut acts of aggression by major powers constitute threats to world peace, are intolerable and require the restoration of an equilibrium of power through counteraction by the international community. Thus Stimson was plainly right about Manchuria, Roosevelt about Germany and Japan, Truman about Greece and Korea (for the North Korean invasion of South Korea took place at a time when communism was still a relatively unified world movement and when the extension of communism therefore meant the automatic extension of the national power of Soviet Russia).

But the followers of Stimson soon plunged beyond this essence. The inflation of Stimsonianism took place primarily at the hands of John Foster Dulles, who had a complacent conviction of American moral infallibility — all other nations acted according to selfish motives; America was pure — and a rigid belief that the secret of world order lay in the expansion of American military commitments through a network of security treaties. In carrying through his transformation of the collective security policy, Dulles went beyond Stimson in several fundamental respects.

First, our government began to apply the collective-security doctrine not just to cases demonstrably involving major powers but also to cases where major power involvement was tenuous or speculative or, if genuine, ineffectual and very likely doomed to failure.

Second, our government began to apply the collective-security doctrine not just to cases where there was a balance of power to be restored but also to cases where no balance of power had existed and the prospect for its establishment was remote. For the classical equilibrium, we have noted, assumed specific preconditions. Above all, there had to be a rational state system; there had to be units of power to be balanced and criteria of power to be accepted and employed. Southeast Asia had no rational state system, nor any traditional understanding of a power equilibrium. It simply did not fulfill the conditions for a balance-of-power policy. The goal of the restoration of the balance of power could be realistically pursued by the United States in Europe. It could be realistically pursued in the Pacific. Conceivably, it could have been realistically pursued, as Stimson had believed, between Japan and China. It could not be realistically pursued in Southeast Asia. The scales that aim to equilibrate power cannot be set in quicksand.

Third, our government began to apply the collective-security doctrine not just to cases of clearcut aggression but also to cases of internal upheaval. I do not pretend that, in an age when revolution has so often been encouraged or even organized from outside, the distinction between the two is always easy to draw. But our government in recent times — in Vietnam, in the Dominican Republic — has made no serious effort to weigh one possibility against the other. Instead, as in Vietnam, we construed almost from the start as external aggression what began and ran a good deal of its course as internal rebellion.

Fourth, our government began to apply the collective-security doctrine not in genuine and equal consultation with our allies but as their self-appointed trustee and leader. In this way, the collective-security doctrine began to narrow into a doctrine of unilateral American intervention.

The Stimson doctrine held that *clearcut* acts of aggression by *major* powers require *collective* intervention to *restore* the balance of power. The result of the Dulles amendments was in effect to create a new doctrine that almost any form of foreign trouble, whether caused by large or small powers, whether or not the elements of a balance-of-power system exist, whether the trouble is external or internal in origin, requires intervention, if necessary by America alone.

What tempted us thus to change a limited into an unlimited policy? One reason is that our rhetoric tends to carry us to extremes. Rhetoric has always been the pitfall of democratic leaders. Tocqueville, in his note on "Why American Writers and Orators Often Use an Inflated Style," remarked that the ideas of a citizen in a democracy

> are all either extremely minute and clear or extremely general and vague: what lies between is void. When he has been drawn out of his own sphere, therefore, he always expects that some amazing object will be offered to his attention; and it is on these terms alone that he consents to tear himself for an instant from the petty, complicated cares that form the charm and excitement of his life. . . . They perpetually inflate their imaginations, and, expanding them beyond all bounds, they not infrequently abandon the great in order to reach the gigantic. By these means they hope to attract the observation of the multitude.

How precisely Tocqueville forecast the American style in foreign policy! Thus Truman took an entirely sensible action in helping Greece and Turkey in 1947, but he felt compelled to justify this action not in local but in universalist terms. "I believe," he said, "that it must be the policy of the United States to support free peoples who are resisting attempted subjugation by armed minorities or outside pressure." What began as a specific act ended as a universal maxim. Dulles, an incorrigible moralizer, could not take a concrete step without proclaiming it as an eternal principle.

The generalizing compulsions in our political rhetoric were reinforced by an uncritical addiction to historical analogy. The men who Americanized the war in Vietnam in 1965 mostly crystallized their ideas of foreign policy from 1938 to 1948 — in the decade between Munich and the Berlin blockade. The memory of these harsh and vivid years possessed their minds, and they tended to see every act of insurrection or aggression in terms of the appeasement syndrome. "The peace and security of Asia and the Pacific and, indeed, of the entire world are indivisible," we resolved at the Manila conference of October 1966. ". . . Successful aggression anywhere endangers the peace." Soon our leaders incredibly talked as if the threat to American security presented by the Viet Cong and Ho Chi Minh was comparable to the threat presented by Hitler in the thirties and by Stalin in the forties. President Johnson, three weeks before his recantation of March 31, rambled on like this in Beaumont, Texas:

> In 1940, with most of Europe in flames, four Democratic senators . . . said that President Roosevelt could negotiate a just peace — that is, with Hitler — if he would only make an effort. Sounds kind of familiar doesn't it? . . . We are not going to be Quislings and we are not going to be appeasers, and we are not going to cut and run. . . . We do believe that if Hitler starts marching across the face of

Europe that [sic] we ought not wait until the last minute
to let him know that might doesn't make right.

When skeptics began to wonder whether Ho Chi Minh and
his ragged bands could really be equated with Hitler, the
Administration responded by inflating the threat: the Viet
Cong and Ho Minh became the spearhead first of the presumably unified force of "Asian Communism" ("It is not
very attractive to think of the world cut in two by Asian
Communism" — Secretary Rusk, October 1967) and then,
to make it all the more terrifying, of a premeditated Chinese
system of aggression. "The threat to world peace," said Vice
President Humphrey in October 15, 1967, "is militant, aggressive Asian communism, with its headquarters in Peking,
China. . . . The aggression of North Vietnam is but the
most current and immediate action of militant Asian communism."

So in the postwar years the idea of collective security grew
beyond all rational bounds and turned into a sanction for
indiscriminate unilateral intervention.

2. *The Legacy of Liberal Evangelism*

The idea of collective security, we have noted, began with
Wilson. A great and creative President, he also started another idea that ended up, after due transformation, in Vietnam. Or, rather, he took an old American preoccupation and

gave it new significance. This was the idea of America's re-
generative mission to suffering mankind.

This was not in its essence a new idea. The men who
founded the American republic believed they were under-
taking an experiment that in time would revolutionize the
world. But they insisted that this would come about *by example*, not by Americans moving into other countries and
setting things straight. John Quincy Adams well stated the
original creed:

> Wherever the standard of freedom and independence has
> been or shall be unfurled, there will be America's heart, her
> benedictions, and her prayers. But she goes not abroad in
> search of monsters to destroy. She is the well-wisher to the
> freedom and independence of all. She is the champion and
> vindicator only of her own. She will recommend the general
> cause by the countenance of her voice, and by the benignant
> sympathy of her example. She well knows that by once
> enlisting under other banners than her own, were they even
> the banners of foreign independence, she would involve her-
> self beyond the power of extrication, in all the wars of in-
> terest and intrigue, of individual avarice, envy and ambition,
> which assume the colors and usurp the standards of freedom.
> The fundamental maxims of her policy would insensibly
> change from liberty to force. . . . She might become the
> dictatress of the world. She would no longer be the ruler
> of her own spirit.

As American power grew, however, so also grew the American conviction that we must discharge our mission not only
by the example we set in our own national life but by the
direct tutelage — the "leadership" — we can bring to other
nations. This began with tentative imperial experiments at
the turn of the century. Wilson carried the process a step

further when he said, "The world must be made safe for democracy." Franklin Roosevelt went still further. The world of the Four Freedoms, he said, "is no vision of a distant millennium. It is a definite basis for a kind of world attainable in our own time and generation." Others went beyond Roosevelt in suggesting a primary American responsibility for the creation of this new world. Henry R. Luce talked of "the American Century." Henry A. Wallace preferred to speak of "the century of the common man," but added, "Perhaps it will be America's opportunity to suggest the freedoms and duties by which the common man must live."

The intellectual genealogy of liberal evangelism, like that of collective security, can be traced to Vietnam in personal terms: from Wilson through Franklin Roosevelt, his Assistant Secretary of the Navy, to such fervent and energetic young New Dealers of the late thirties and early forties as Lyndon B. Johnson and Hubert Humphrey. It is a small step from Henry Wallace remarking to Mme. Litvinov, "The object of this war is to make sure that everybody in the world has the privilege of drinking a quart of milk a day" to President Johnson talking about TVA's on the Mekong and comparing Marshal Ky to Rexford G. Tugwell.

The point emerges with particular poignancy in an interview with Vice President Humphrey in the spring of 1966.* Mr. Humphrey has since repented these views, but his remarks during the euphoria of the Vietnam intervention illuminate some of the motives behind the Americanization of the war. Speaking shortly after the Honolulu conference between President Johnson and Marshal Ky, he said that the Honolulu Declaration "has as much significance for the fu-

---

* CBS News Special Report, April 19, 1966.

ture of Asia as the Atlantic Charter had for the future of Europe."

Mr. Agronsky: This was the articulation of a Johnson doctrine for Asia?

Vice President Humphrey: Yes, I think it was. . . . What was said in this declaration was a pledge to ourselves and to posterity to defeat aggression, to defeat social misery, to build viable, free political institutions and to achieve peace. Now, those are broad terms, but these are great commitments. . . . I think there is a tremendous new opening here for realizing the dream of the Great Society in the great area of Asia, not just here at home. . . .

We are going to be in Asia for a long, long time. . . . We can't be a great power like America with a half world or, as I have said so many times, a world power with a half world involvement. . . . This will be the test of our leadership capability. We have great military men in our nation. We have powerful weapons. I think we can be very proud of their achievements and their competence. The question is do we have the same statesmanship quality to help build nations. . . . I have said to many of my good liberal friends in government — I said, "Look, we ought to be excited about this challenge, because here is where we can put to work some of our ideas of how a — nation building, of new concepts of education, development of local government, the improvement of the health standards of people, and really the achievement and the fulfillment of social justice."

This is the authentic language of American social reform. Nothing has exalted America more than this sense of world mission — this decent and admirable feeling of responsibility for the welfare of others. Yet little is more dangerous than a sense of world mission pushed too far or perceived too absolutely. The delusion of "nation-building" appealed to

Americans as social reformers, social workers and social engineers; but in the end can anyone build a nation but the people of the nation themselves? Do we know enough to build other people's nations for them? Do we know enough to build our own? World-helping can easily turn into world-saving; mission into messianism. At the very least, the sense of mission since the Second World War has tempted Americans into what I have elsewhere called "sentimental imperialism" — the belief that we know better than other people do what is good for them. At its worst, it has tempted us into becoming not just the world's social reformer but the world's judge, jury and executioner — the role so horribly enacted in Vietnam.

In this process the limited policy of helping others to help themselves grew into the unlimited policy of imposing our own preferences on others; so that, if the Vietnamese would not do out of respect for our superior wisdom what we thought was good for them, we were determined to make them do it out of respect for our superior strength. The Army major standing in the rubble of Ben Tre summed up the ultimate logic of American messianism: "It became necessary to destroy the town to save it."

Like Stimsonianism, liberal evangelism underwent inflation; and again universalism perverted a rational idea into irrationality.

3. The Legacy of Geopolitics

To understand why the ideas of collective security and of liberal evangelism — ideas entirely sound and necessary in themselves — expanded beyond reason in the years after the Second World War, one must move from questions of ideology to questions of power.

The First World War had begun the erosion of the classical European structure of power; the Second World War completed the devastation of the old structure at the same time that it redefined the issues of international relations on a world scale. The defeat of the Axis states meant the elimination, for a while in any case, of Germany, Italy and Japan from the global power equation. It meant, for a while, the exhaustion and demoralization of Europe, victors as well as vanquished. It meant the disintegration of the European colonial empires; it meant, in particular, the unraveling of the British Empire, which so long, for better or for worse, had provided a network of stability through what we have come to call the Third World. And, as the colonial empires fell to pieces, it meant the release of confused and chaotic energies in those parts of the world no longer willing to continue under white domination.

It meant, in short, the emergence of great vacuums of power — in Europe, in Asia, in Africa. And, at the same time, the war left only two nations with the capacity to fill those vacuums of power. Only two nations — America and Russia — survived the war with strong and active military force; one with the world's monopoly of atomic weapons, the other with the world's largest ground army. Each of these nations had grown accustomed during the war to the habit of global assessment and global action. Each came out of the war with marked political and ideological self-confidence. Each was more or less in command of its own armed camp, and each in time formalized this command by setting up systems of alliance. The philosophical disagreement between a capitalist democracy and a communist dictatorship gave edge to the structural conflict; but, even without the philosophical disagreement, the existence of the vacuums of power would no doubt have sucked dynamic states into competition and collision.

A century earlier Tocqueville had made a famous prophecy. He had seen two great nations in the world, starting from different points but tending toward the same end. Both, he said, had grown up unnoticed, while the attention of mankind was directed elsewhere; but, while other nations seemed to have reached their natural limits, these two were still in the act of growth. The Anglo-American, Tocqueville wrote,

> relies upon personal interest to accomplish his ends and gives free scope to the unguided strength and common sense of the people; the Russian centers all the authority of society in a single arm. The principal instrument of the former is freedom; of the latter, servitude. Their starting-point is different and their courses are not the same; yet each of them seems marked out by the will of Heaven to sway the destinies of half the globe.

In 1945 Tocqueville's vision seemed at last on the brink of fulfillment. America and Russia now appeared as the first truly global powers in the history of man, exerting their influence everywhere around the planet, encountering no serious opposition anywhere, except from each other. For a decade — roughly from the end of the Second World War to the end of the war in Korea — these two nations bestrode the narrow world; their writs seemed to run without limits. This was the Age of the Superpowers. And this era generated distinctive habits of mind and action in both Washington and Moscow. Above all, it instilled the feeling that their appointments as Superpowers were permanent and irrevocable, and that each could expect indefinitely to shape destinies wherever they wished. These habits soon became enshrined in national doctrine and embodied in national institutions.

In Russia Superpowership was the logical expression of an absolutist ideology which had already conferred on communism the blessing of historical inevitability. In America Superpowership, lacking a prepared ideological foundation, took the ideas of collective security, liberal evangelism and anticommunism and tried to give them absolute form. In these years illusions of American omnipotence and American omniscience began to arise and prevail — the illusions that we as a nation were all-powerful and all-wise and endowed with the responsibility and the right of "world leadership."

4. The Legacy of Conservative Absolutism

Manes, the Persian philosopher, taught long ago that good and evil were independent and co-eternal realities locked in mortal combat. Both Superpowers tended to take a Manichean view of world affairs in the forties and fifties. In Russia anticapitalism had always been a central and implacable doctrine. In America anticommunism became a doctrine not nearly so central or so implacable but still sufficiently intrusive to distort judgment and to mislead decision.

This is not to imply that anticommunism *per se* is a bad thing. Indeed, I would regard anticommunism as a moral necessity for any believer in democracy. After the last thirty years of world history, one hardly need insist that liberalism and communism have very little in common, either as to the means or the ends of government, either as to principle or practice. But it is essential to distinguish between *rational* and *obsessive* anticommunism: between anticommunism as an element in a larger position, an element addressed to specific situations and graduated in mode and substance according to the character of the threat; and anticommunism as a total position, addressed to some great, all-pervading evil and requiring the subordination of every other consideration and value.

Liberal anticommunism in America consisted in the main of entirely sensible and practical objections to Stalinism, its cruel internal tyranny, its hectoring and aggressive foreign policy and its conspiratorial penetration of the American liberal community, the American labor movement and the American government. Conservative anticommunism, on the other hand, tended to be obsessive and absolute. It inculcated the Manichean view that communism was a changeless, unalterable, monolithic doctrine of total discipline and total evil. This led to the conclusion, for example, that every person involved in whatever way with the communist movement must be an active and (unless he proved his rejection by naming all his associates) a permanent agent of the communist conspiracy. It led to the conclusion that every Communist party or communist state by definition must forever be an obedient instrument of Soviet Russia. It led Dean Rusk as Assistant Secretary of State for Far Eastern Affairs in 1951 to call the communist regime in Peking "a colonial Russian government — a Slavic Manchukuo on a larger scale. It is not the government of China. It does not pass the first test. It is not Chinese." (The spectacular failure of this prophecy did not, alas, prevent Mr. Rusk as Secretary of State from offering new and equally confident forecasts about Chinese behavior.) It led to the delusion that guerrilla wars could not just be, as some might think, local insurrections in which local leadership exploited local grievances but must rather represent "wars of national liberation" organized by Moscow or Peking to "test the will" of the United States. (The absolutists were not very clear toward the end about the location of central communist headquarters. As late as May 1965, the number-three man in the State Department was babbling on about "instruments of Sino-Soviet power" and "orders from the Sino-Soviet military bloc"; even Mr. Rusk, an intelligent man, could remain on occasion resolutely oblivious to communist fragmentation, thus speaking in 1966 about "the Communists," their "larger design" and "their world revolution.") The will-testing doctrine proved a convenient way to transform every dreary local squabble into a great global contest between America and communism.

One major reason our leaders gave us for sending half a million American troops to Vietnam was to stop Moscow or Peking from instigating other guerrilla wars elsewhere. The Vietnam war, according to President Johnson, "is meant to be the opening salvo in a series of bombardments or, as they are called in Peking, 'wars of liberation.'" If this technique worked one week in Vietnam, the Administration assured us, it would be tried next week in Uganda and Peru. But, if it were defeated in Vietnam, the communists would know that we would not let it succeed elsewhere. "What happens in South Vietnam," said President Johnson, "will determine — yes, it will determine — whether ambitious and aggressive nations can use guerrilla warfare to conquer their weaker neighbors."

Next to the Secretary of State's claim that the SEATO treaty *required* American military intervention in Vietnam, the above nonsense was perhaps the most intellectually ludicrous argument invoked in support of the Vietnam tragedy. More than any other form of warfare, guerrilla warfare is dependent on conditions and opportunities within the countries themselves. Defeating communist guerrillas in Greece, the Philippines, Malaya and Venezuela did not prevent guerrilla warfare in Vietnam, nor would the defeat of the Viet Cong have prevented the outbreak of insurrection in Uganda or Peru. Whether there are "wars of national liberation" in Uganda and Peru will depend not on what happens in Vietnam but on what happens in Uganda and Peru.

By defining the Vietnam war as a test case of "wars of national liberation" and then making such a botch of it, our leaders only encouraged what they thought they were combatting. As the RAND Corporation recently concluded, "Our belief that we could cope with what Khrushchev called 'wars of national liberation' by providing expert advice and economic and military assistance proved to be wrong in this instance; and three years of major combat involvement have failed to yield the military and political results intended." Even had we achieved the desired results in Vietnam, there is no reason to suppose that our action would "determine" the future of guerrilla warfare everywhere. As even Richard M. Nixon in his superhawk phase conceded in 1967, "One of the legacies of Vietnam almost certainly will be a deep reluctance on the part of the United States to become involved once again on a similar basis. . . . If another friendly country should be faced with an externally supported Communist insurrection — whether in Asia or in Africa or even Latin America — there is serious question whether the American public or the American Congress would now support a unilateral American intervention, even at the request of the host government."

Under obscure masochistic compulsions, some liberals today like to blame the Vietnam mess on rational anticommunism and even have taken to calling it "the liberals' war." American liberalism, as we have seen, certainly made its contribution to the mood that led us into Vietnam. But liberal self-hatred can go too far. To regard this in some exclusive sense as "the liberals' war" with the implication that conservatives, generals, Republicans, businessmen, right-wing ecclesiasts and so on were against it is absurd. It cannot be called "the liberals' war" unless "liberal" is capaciously defined to include such characters as John Foster Dulles, Richard Nixon, Strom Thurmond, the Joint Chiefs of Staff, Cardinal Spellman, Ambassador Nolting, William F. Buckley, Jr., and others not usually accorded top seeding in liberal rank lists.

It was above all the absolutist conviction, cherished by American conservatism, of the fixed and final division between the forces of good and the forces of evil that prepared the way for Vietnam by persuading America that all communist threats were equal and identical and therefore all required direct American military reaction. Once again, a doctrine rational in its essence underwent expansion and began to be applied without discrimination. Indeed, in time it began to be applied without thought.

5. *The Rise of the Warrior Class*

Thus postwar American foreign policy grew from a series of legacies — Stimsonian collective security, Rooseveltian social evangelism, Dullesian anticommunism, each bequest tempted into universalism and messianism by the power vacuums left in the wake of the Second World War. It was this combination of factors that beguiled America into a course which much of the world today regards as imperialistic and which even Americans must concede as imperial — the course that has reached its disastrous climax in Vietnam.

Yet, if there is an American imperialism, it is imperialism of a peculiar sort. The classical theories of imperialism derive from the European experience, and it is hard to fit American policy into the conventional categories. The attempts of pious Marxists, for example, to account for the American presence in Vietnam in Leninist terms — as the result of the need for investment outlets — is self-evidently absurd. The American government has already poured more money into Vietnam than American business could hope to get back in a century. Nor is it convincing to argue that we "needed" to spend $22 billion a year for Vietnam in order to preserve business profits at home. The effect of the Vietnam spending has been to overheat the economy, to stimulate inflationary pressures and to require an unpopular tax increase. Except for firms specifically dependent on production for Vietnam, everyone would be happier if the war spending came to an end. Business leaders have not been notably enthusiastic about the war — especially once the Army stopped relying mainly on poor whites and blacks and started drafting their own sons.

A more sophisticated version of the Marxist thesis is that the United States must suppress revolution everywhere because, if revolution succeeds in a country without American investment, the contagion of success may lead to revolutions in other countries *with* American investment. This Leninist version of the domino theory is faintly more plausible as an argument than the strict thesis, except for the fact that American policy in the Third World, while it has been uniformly anticommunist, has by no means been uniformly antirevolutionary. Nor do nationalist revolutions in the Third World invariably lead to communist rule; quite the contrary — the communists have come to power in only three new nations in the last quarter century: China and North Vietnam, because they put themselves at the head of nationalist movements during the Second World War, and Cuba, because Fidel Castro for reasons of his own steered his revolution, undertaken on other grounds, into the communist empire. Actually the American government has accepted nationalist revolutions in most countries that have had them; and it has given surreptitious assistance to progressive nationalist parties and even to noncommunist revolutionaries in a number of countries in Asia, Africa and Latin America. The objection to the Cuban revolution (at least within the Kennedy administration) was not to Castro's program of internal reconstruction but to his potential role as an instrument of Soviet policy — an objection which, as the events of October 1962 showed, was hardly without point.

Nor do other classical theories of imperialism work much better. Hannah Arendt's argument (in *The Origins of Totalitarianism*) that imperialism was the result of "the alliance between mob and capital" does not apply here; there was no surging popular demand for the adventure in Vietnam. Nor do the theories tracing imperialism to the instabilities and temptations created by disparities in power explain why there were half a million American troops in South Asia rather than in South America. The theories relating imperialism to the mission of social reform (as in Bernard Semmel, *Imperialism and Social Reform*) are more relevant; as are those which relate imperialism to the protection or conquest of strategic political or military positions (as in the writings of W. L. Langer).

But of the classical theories of imperialism the one which throws most light on American behavior is that proposed by Joseph A. Schumpeter in his essay "The Sociology of Imperialism." Schumpeter saw imperialism as "the objectless disposition on the part of a state to unlimited forcible expansion" — a disposition created and sustained by the habits and interests of a warrior class. There would always be, he said, rational pretexts for military action — national security, treasure and so on — but the essential urge would come from the sheer momentum of the military machine in motion.

European imperialism of the late nineteenth century, in Schumpeter's view, was the work of martial and feudal elements surviving in bourgeois society. Believing that the instinct for physical combat was fading rather quickly in the industrial world, he felt that imperialism would be a passing phase in a society which had "neither warlike instincts nor structural elements and organizational forms oriented toward war." He was particularly optimistic about the United States, which among all capitalist countries seemed to him "least burdened with precapitalist elements, survivals, reminiscences, and power factors" and would therefore be "likely to exhibit the weakest imperialist trend." But what Schumpeter omitted in his argument, though it was implicit in his theory, was the possibility that war among industrial states might produce new structural elements and organizational forms oriented toward war, a new warrior class and new forms of imperialism.

Has not something like this happened in the United States? The American imperialism of the turn of the century was a clear case of Schumpeterian atavism. Men like Theodore Roosevelt and Henry Cabot Lodge, who as historians had celebrated the Federalist vision of the American role, reached back as politicians and strategists to the Federalist past in the hope of redeeming the new commercial society by giving it a martial purpose. But, lacking a serious institutional base in that society, neo-Federalist imperialism could not, and did not, last. Half a century later, however, two world wars had brought a great military establishment into existence, and the Cold War made it permanent.

During the war, Roosevelt relied more on military advisers like General Marshall and Admiral Leahy than he did on his State Department. After the war the establishment of the Department of Defense and the National Security Council consolidated the military influence on national policy. For many years the military have absorbed by far the largest portion of the federal budget. Defense contracts have enlisted large sections of the industrial community in the military effort. With America predisposed to foreign involvement by the legacies of collective security and social evangelism and, in a sense, propelled into such involvement by the power vacuums of the postwar world, with, in addition, the unitary communist movement of the age of Stalin posing a quite genuine threat and generating crusading absolutism in response, the new warrior class became the agency for both the militarization and the enlargement of our interventionist policies.*

One must not overdo all this. The military machine suffered a succession of restraints — first, from within, by the Second World War generals of the Marshall-Eisenhower-Bradley generation; then, from without, by Presidents Truman, Eisenhower and Kennedy as well as by civilian elements of the national security bureaucracy, by such men as Acheson (when he was in office, though not much thereafter†),

---

* I would sharply distinguish this proposition from the argument offered by R. J. Barnet in his interesting book *Intervention and Revolution* (New York, 1968). Mr. Barnet traces the imperialist impulse to what he calls the National-Security Managers. As the next paragraph makes clear, I question the notion of the national security bureaucracy as any sort of unified monolith. I would also contend that military conceptions, far from determining our policies in the postwar years, predominated only in certain areas and at certain moments, and often as a matter of last resort. Nor do I accept the assumption of bureaucratic determinism that argues that militarization and escalation were bound to win out. For a discussion of these issues, including Mr. Barnet's rebuttal, see the record of the meeting at the Adlai Stevenson Institute in Chicago in June 1968 in R. M. Pfeffer, ed., *No More Vietnams? The War and the Future of American Foreign Policy* (New York, 1968), pp. 50–114.

† Mr. Acheson's letter on China of March 15, 1949, to Senator Connally contains wisdom that could have been usefully applied to Vietnam:

There is no evidence that the furnishing of additional military material would alter the pattern of current developments in China. There is, however, ample evidence that the Chinese people are weary of hostilities and that there is an overwhelming desire for peace at any price. To furnish solely military material and advice would only prolong hostilities and the suffering of the Chinese people and would arouse in them deep resentment against the United States. Yet, to furnish the military means for bringing

Harriman, Lovett and, in later times, McNamara. The National Security Council was never very effective as a source of national decisions. Nor has the military caste always been united in its views. In 1954 the Navy and the Air Force favored American intervention in Vietnam; the Army, forcefully represented by Generals Ridgway and Gavin, opposed intervention and carried the day. In 1962 General Shoup of the Marine Corps dissented from the recommendation of the other Joint Chiefs for a surprise air attack on the nuclear missile bases in Cuba. Secretary McNamara was engaged throughout his time at the Pentagon in argument with the Chiefs. By 1967 he had become the particular custodian of the negotiating interest within the government, leading to that peculiar exchange of roles by which the Secretary of Defense sat in his office trying to figure out how to start negotiations with Hanoi while the Secretary of State sat in *his* office picking out bombing targets (perhaps in part because, as Mr. Rusk revealed in an interview, he was "within three days" of taking his oath as a career military officer in 1946 when General Marshall offered him a civilian post in the State Department). In the last year of the Vietnam war the CIA and the Secretary of Defense were far more skeptical than the Joint Chiefs or the Secretary of State about the effectiveness of American bombing.

Yet, if the national security bureaucracy is often divided in its views, the warrior caste, as a powerful element in that bureaucracy, has had increasingly behind it the power of

---

about a reversal of the present deterioration and for providing some prospect of successful military resistance would require the use of an unpredictably large American armed force in actual combat, a course of action which would represent direct United States involvement in China's fratricidal warfare and would be contrary to our traditional policy toward China and the interests of this country.

sheer momentum — especially in a time when new military technologies, by making America vulnerable to attack from almost any spot on the planet, gave the invocation of "national security" an unlimited application and when duty required the military of one nation to advocate constant growth to forestall potential adversaries from gaining technological superiority. "Created by wars that required it," Schumpeter wrote of the military establishment in ancient Egypt, "the machine now created the wars it required." His account of Rome from the Punic Wars to Augustus has an uncomfortable contemporary relevance:

Here is the classic example of that kind of insincerity in both foreign and domestic affairs which permeates not only avowed motives but also probably the conscious motives of the actors themselves — of that policy which pretends to aspire to peace but unerringly generates war, the policy of continual preparation for war, the policy of meddlesome interventionism. There was no corner of the known world where some interest was not alleged to be in danger or under actual attack. If the interests were not Roman, they were those of Rome's allies; and if Rome had no allies, then allies would be invented. When it was utterly impossible to contrive such an interest — why, then, it was the national honor that had been insulted.

The fight was always invested with an aura of legality. Rome was always being attacked by evil-minded neighbors, always fighting for a breathing space. The whole world was pervaded by a host of enemies, and it was manifestly Rome's duty to guard against their indubitably aggressive designs. They were enemies who only waited to fall on the Roman people. Even less than in the cases that have already been discussed, can an attempt be made here to comprehend these wars of conquest from the point of view of concrete objectives.

In whatever sense America can be said to be an imperial state, the active carriers of that imperialism are not our bankers or our foreign investors or our traders — not any of the conventional Marxist villains. The carriers are our politicians, our diplomats and, most particularly, our military leaders. It is our military leaders who — for military, not for economic reasons — have conned both the executive and legislative branches of the government into voting enormous military appropriations and into building enormous military installations, largely irrelevant in the missile age, all over the world (and who, as the price we must pay, insist we must do nothing to offend such splendid countries as Portugal or South Africa). It is they who argue for military intervention. It is they who forever oppose agreements (like the test ban treaty of 1963) designed to slow up the arms race and who forever demand new systems of offense and defense.

The forward role of the military has been notably evident in Vietnam. First, they succeeded in defining the problem in the terms stated by General Wheeler in November 1962: "It is fashionable in some quarters to say that the problems in Southeast Asia are primarily political and economic. . . . I do not agree. The essence of the problem in Vietnam is military." Subsequently, at every point along the way, the generals promised that just one more step of military escalation would at last bring the victory so long sought and so steadily denied. The Pentagon, in addition, has seen Vietnam as an invaluable training ground and testing ground for new weapons and new techniques.

Here surely lies a major cause of our imperial drift: the incessant pressure of the professional military in an age of international crisis. The warrior group, because of its own internal needs and preoccupations, constantly demands more money, more weapons systems, more military involvement, more military intervention. Its members invoke the emotions of virility and patriotism to strengthen their case. Their importunities affect the way choices are defined and the atmosphere in which decisions are made; the pressure is often effective in amorphous situations and with irresolute leaders. But this is *not* a question of bureaucratic determinism. The warrior group does not inevitably control United States policy, nor are the warriors evil men or war criminals. They are professional men trying to do a professional job and making exactly the arguments the nature of their profession requires. It is foolish to be surprised by the advice they give or to blame them for it. It is far more to the point to blame those who take their advice.*

* One of the oddities of the Vietnam period was the reverence accorded General Westmoreland by the American press as well as by the President of the United States. Westmoreland's assessments of the Vietnam problem are worth recalling: "I am optimistic and we are making good progress" (June 20, 1964); "I believe the whole operation is moving in our favor" (July 8, 1964); "This is the time to be more aggressive and take the offensive" (April 14, 1965); "It is doubtful if we will ever have anything in the way of opposing land forces as in the Korean War" (July 9, 1965); "Backed at home by resolve, confidence, patience, determination and continued support, we will prevail in Vietnam over the Communist aggressor" (April 28, 1967); "We have achieved all our objectives, while the enemy has failed dismally" (July 13, 1967); "Senator Henry Jackson said that Westmoreland . . . 'feels quite confident. He sees the enemy losing steadily and continuously'" (November 17, 1967); "I am absolutely certain that, whereas in 1945 the enemy was winning, today he is certainly losing. . . . In general he can fight his large forces only at the edges of his sanctuaries. . . . His guerrilla force is declining at a steady rate. . . . I see progress as I travel all over Vietnam. . . . The enemy's hopes are bankrupt" (November 22, 1967); "Through careful exploitation of the enemy's vulnerabilities and application of our superior firepower and mobility, we should expect our gains of 1967 to be increased manyfold in 1968" (January 1, 1968); "Although the enemy has achieved some temporary psychological advantage, he suffered a military defeat. . . . I do not believe Hanoi can hold up under a long war" (February 26, 1968); "Militarily we have never been in a better relative position in South Vietnam. . . . The spirit of the offensive is now prevalent throughout Vietnam" (April 8, 1968); "The enemy seems to be approaching a point of desperation. His forces are deteriorating in strength and quality. . . . Time is on our side" (May 30,

What matters is not that the military bureaucracy makes certain recommendations but that Presidents and Secretaries of State take these recommendations seriously. President Kennedy accepted the recommendations of the Joint Chiefs of Staff on one major decision in his administration — the Bay of Pigs. He rejected pressures for direct military intervention in Cuba twice — after the failure of the Bay of Pigs and again during the missile crisis. He was entirely skeptical of military plans for intervention in Laos. He declined to follow JCS counsel on Berlin in 1961 or on the test ban treaty of 1963. President Johnson, on the contrary, seems to have flinched from overruling the Joint Chiefs, except on occasion by not giving them quite all the troops or bombing targets they wanted. The essential problem, in short, is not organizational; it is substantive. It does not lie in the existence of the military establishment but in the judgment and will of the civilian leadership.

6. The Nemesis of Universalism

The tragedy of Vietnam is the tragedy of the catastrophic overextension and misapplication of valid principles. The original insights of collective security and liberal evangelism were generous and wise. But compulsive Stimsonianism and

1968); "The enemy is getting nowhere militarily. . . . He is frustrated to the point where he is desperate" (June 9, 1968).

What an astonishing record of misconception and misjudgment! If someone had compiled this record in business, where money is involved, he would have long since been fired. But if he is a general and only spends lives, he is decorated and promoted.

compulsive New Dealism, stimulated by the illusions of Superpowership, rigidified by an absolutist anticommunism and pressed ever forward by the professional demands of the new warrior class, brought American universalism in time into a messianic phase. "History and our own achievements," President Johnson said on February 12, 1965, "have thrust upon us the principal responsibility for protection of freedom on earth. . . . No other people in no other time has had so great an opportunity to work and risk for the freedom of all mankind."

This messianic phase led us to lose our sense of the relation between means and ends. I do not see that our original involvement in Vietnam was *per se* immoral. What was immoral was the employment of means of destruction out of all proportion to rational purposes. The wreckage we wrought in Vietnam had no rational relationship to a serious assessment of our national interest or to the demonstrated involvement of our national security.* The messianic phase transcended and transformed the constituent elements of our past foreign policy. Yet the existence of these traditional elements gave the Johnson administration a sense that it was executing a legacy and endowed it therefore with an overweening conviction of the rectitude of its mission, the purity of its motives and the wickedness of its critics. It was this that must have led Secretary Rusk to say on February 9, 1968: "There gets to be a point when the question is,

---

* The total bomb tonnage dropped on Vietnam, North and South, through October, 1968, was 2,948,057 tons. The total tonnage dropped during the Second World War in both the European and Pacific theaters was 2,057,244 tons. This means that American planes dropped almost 50 percent more tons of explosives on this hapless country than were dropped on Japan, Germany and other enemy territories during the last world war. (I owe these figures to the pertinacity of I. F. Stone, who elicited them from the Pentagon press office and published them in his highly erratic but sometimes useful *Weekly*.)

whose side are you on? Now, I'm Secretary of State of the United States, and I'm on our side!" *

Given the perhaps excessive self-righteousness which could lead a Secretary of State to suggest that his critics must be on the side of Ho Chi Minh, given too the reluctance of proud and stubborn men to admit that they could possibly have made mistakes, only the abject failure of the policy could force its supporters to draw back. The failure of the Vietnam policy had long been evident to most detached observers. The evidence against the effectiveness of military escalation was just as strong, for example, on March 31, 1967, as it was on March 31, 1968; and, if President Johnson had given his speech a year earlier, many Americans and many Vietnamese, now dead, would today be alive. But in the end the failure of the policy became so plain that even the President had to admit it — everyone had to admit it except, inevitably, General Westmoreland and Joseph Alsop.

What was announced on March 31 was more than simply the collapse of the American policy in Vietnam. What was announced was the collapse of the messianic conception of the American role in the world — indeed, the end of the entire Age of the Superpowers. To understand the reasons for

---

* Compare Mark Twain in "To the Person Sitting in Darkness": "Having laid all the historical facts before the person sitting in darkness, we should bring him to again, and explain them to him. We should say to him: 'They look doubtful, but in reality they are not. There have been lies; yes, but they were told in a good cause. We have been treacherous; but that was only in order that real good might come out of apparent evil. True, we have crushed a deceived and confiding people; . . . we have invited our clean young men to shoulder a discredited musket and do bandits' work under a flag which bandits have been accustomed to fear, not to follow; we have debauched America's honor and blackened her face before the world; but morals, high principles, and justice cannot do an unright thing, an unfair thing, an ungenerous thing, an unclean thing. It knows what it is about. Give yourself no uneasiness; it is all right.' "

this collapse we must return for a moment to the Superpowers at high noon.

There were always decisive differences between the Superpowers on internal values and polities. But their views of the world outside had remarkable similarities. Each Superpower saw mankind as divided between forces of light and forces of darkness. Each assumed that the opposing bloc was under the organized and unified control of the other. Each insisted that every nation line up on one side or the other and condemned neutralism as anomalous if not as immoral. Each expected its own side to accept its own ideas of political propriety and economic organization. Washington supposed that what was then known as the free world should reshape itself on the American model, Moscow that the communist world should reshape itself on the Russian model.

These were the dreams of glory of the Superpowers. But, alas, the world itself did not sit still; it began to change. And the most basic change of all was the rise of a new force in revolt against the reign of the Superpowers — or rather the resurgence of an older force now endowed in the years after the war with new potency and purpose. That force was nationalism; and the rise of nationalism meant growing opposition to the United States in the Western bloc, growing opposition to the Soviet Union in the communist bloc and growing opposition to both America and Russia in the Third World.

Nationalism means first of all the determination to assert national identity, national dignity and national freedom of action. It can also mean, as the memory of prewar Germany, Italy and Japan reminds us, the determination to assert these things at the expense of other nations; and in this sense nationalism has been and will be a source of tremendous danger to the world. But the nationalism that arose after the Second World War was, in the main, not the aggressive and hysterical nationalism that had led nations before the war to try to dominate other nations. It was, rather, the nationalism generated by the desire to create or restore a sense of nationhood.

In the years since 1945 nationalism has redrawn lines of force around the planet. Take Europe, for example, which Churchill described twenty years ago as "a rubble heap, a charnel house, a breeding ground for pestilence and hate." Economically shattered, politically demoralized, militarily defenseless, Western Europe in the forties was absolutely dependent on America for social reconstruction and military protection. Then the Marshall Plan set in motion the process of economic recovery. Economic recovery led to the revival of political self-confidence, and political self-confidence to a determination to assert European autonomy. No doubt the turn given this mood in recent years by General de Gaulle is exaggerated and extravagant. But it would be a great error, I believe, to suppose that Gaullism does not spring from a profoundly real impulse in contemporary Europe: a deep pride in European traditions and capacities, a growing will to reaffirm European independence against the twin colossi. And even those who reject the narrow nationalism of de Gaulle do so in the name of the larger nationalism of Europe.

The contagion of nationalism runs everywhere. Today nationalism is seeking home rule in Scotland and Wales; it is dividing the country of Belgium; it is threatening Canada with the secession of French Quebec; in our own country it finds expression in the mystique of black power. And it has wrought even more spectacular changes within the empire Stalin once ruled so calmly and implacably. The Yugoslav heresy of 1948 represented the first serious rebellion of national communism against Russian primacy. In another decade China burst forth as an independent communist state, increasingly determined to challenge Russia for the domination of Asia and for the leadership of the international communist movement. With the clash between China and Russia, the unified communist empire began to break up. Moscow long ago had to accept the Yugoslav heresy, and on Yugoslav terms. It has conceded a measure of national initiative to the once cowed and compliant satellites of Eastern Europe. Albania and Rumania are going their own way. In a desperate effort to preserve the dominant Russian position, the Soviet Union had to resort to military intervention in order to discipline communist Czechoslovakia. Even Poland, even East Germany, may some day insist on national freedom. "Everyone chooses the truths he likes. In this way faith disintegrates." This was Pope Paul VI, but it might as well have been Brezhnev.

The unity of communist discipline, the unity of communist dogma — all are vanishing as international phenomena, crumbling away under the pressure of nationalism. In the contemporary age of polycentrism there is no longer any such thing as "world communism." A communist takeover no longer means the automatic extension of Russian, or even of Chinese power. Every communist government, every communist party, has been set free to begin to respond to its own national concerns and to pursue its own national policies. One communist state, Cuba, has even performed the ingenious feat of being simultaneously at odds with both Moscow and Peking.

As nationalism has transformed the democratic and communist worlds, so too it has transformed the Third World. After the war, many people — communists and anticommunists alike — supposed that communism was the wave of the future and accepted the thesis of its inevitable triumph. In particular, it was anticipated that Marxism would sweep through the developing world like a prairie fire. With Asia, Africa and Latin America shaken by deep-running revolutionary demands for economic development and social justice, new states everywhere, it was believed, would turn to communism, if only as the most efficient technique for modernization. Some in the West became mesmerized by the notion that, when a nationalist revolution began in an underdeveloped country, communism was bound to win out.

This has not happened. There has been an abundance of nationalist revolutions in these years. But the striking fact is plainly the failure of the communists to ride to power on nationalist upheavals. We have noted that since the war, communism has triumphed in only three nations in the Third World — China, North Vietnam and Cuba. For the rest, it has been a washout as a revolutionary creed.

The reason for the failure of communism in the developing world is the same as the reason for the expulsion of colonialism from that world: what the new nations want more than anything else is the assurance of their own national freedom of decision. And this very fact too, while it has endowed the new nations with spirit and audacity, has prevented them from forming, as some once feared they might do, a unified bloc against the West. Today they are unified only in their determination to stay out of the Cold War — and in the hope of shaking down the developed countries, Russia as well as America, for all the economic aid they can get. Beyond that, they too are deeply divided by nationalist resentments and rivalries.

Nationalism has thus changed the relations between America and the Western world and Russia and the communist world, and it has defeated expectations of Russian and American influence as well as of a unified neutralist bloc in the Third World. It has emerged as the most powerful political emotion of our time. And the result has been to alter the conditions which a quarter century ago produced the Age of the Superpowers. This era came about, we have noted, as the response of two dynamic states to the vacuums of power left in the wake of the Second World War. In the years since, the reinvigoration of nationalism — in Europe, within the communist empire, in the Third World — has begun to fill these vacuums. These have been, in short, the years of the clash between nationalism and Superpowership — and the result has been to place limits on the power of America and Russia. The Age of the Superpowers is coming to an end.

7. *The Last Hurrah of the Superpowers*

Or at least this is evident to everyone — except to the Superpowers themselves. A main source of trouble in the world today is, as often before, the failure of Superpowers to recognize a new historical situation. This is natural enough. England and France, though knocked out of the running after the Second World War, continued to try and act like great powers as late as their attempt in 1956 to control the Middle East and humiliate Arab nationalism. Superpowers are always slow to realize the decline in their capacity to command events. So America and Russia, operating on the momentum of ideas generated in the immediate postwar years, have persisted, despite a new age and a changed world, in those habits of thought and action that worked more or less between 1945 and 1955. The illusion of Superpowership thus lay behind the long American attempt to determine the destiny of Vietnam. It lay behind the Soviet attempt to enter the Caribbean in 1962, as it lies behind current Soviet attempts to dominate the Middle East and dictate the future of Czechoslovakia.

In 1967 Chairman Kosygin visited the United States and had a meeting with President Johnson in New Jersey. He came at a moment when Russia and America were in sharp disagreement over the two most urgent items on the meeting's agenda — Vietnam and the Arab-Israeli war. Yet, in spite of this disagreement, the meeting itself was surprisingly cordial. This caused puzzlement at the time. In retrospect there is no great mystery why this should have been so. The two leaders were evidently brought together by considerations deeper than conflicts in Southeast Asia or the Middle East. They were brought together by a common sense of international frustration and a common fear that their mutual interests in world management were under challenge. They shared most of all a deep perplexity and anguished exasperation over the inability of their two countries to run the world any longer. The partnership of Holly Bush was above all a partnership in irritation and chagrin.

The world had for some time been approaching the point when the common American-Russian interest in global management was becoming more important than their disagreement on ideological issues or than the clash of their national interests. The irony, of course, is that these two countries were not at all concerned with collaboration during the Era of the Superpowers — at a time when such collaboration might have gone far toward ordering the planet. But, as the recovery of national initiative in the rest of the world began to threaten the very idea of Superpowership, the tendency grew to consider it more important to share world domination with the other than to open up the game. So, like two cartels that have been competing bitterly against each other for the world's supply of a vital commodity — in this case, power — they now tend to prefer to divide the market between themselves as against the risk and uncertainty that would follow from the admission of new competitors.

The clearest expression of this drawing together can be seen in the attempt to limit the control and availability of nuclear weapons. I do not suggest that the test ban treaty of 1963 and the treaty to stop nuclear proliferation are not excellent things in themselves. They are surely the greatest formal strides toward peace the world has taken in this generation. But it is important also to consider how these proposals look to the non-nuclear nations. Their obvious effect — and, some cynics have suggested, their secret intention — is to exclude the rest from the nuclear club and thus to preserve American-Russian nuclear dominance. This is why, of course, these treaties have been so bitterly denounced by the two great rebel states — France in the Western bloc and China in the communist bloc.

Alas, the drift of the Superpowers toward collaboration,

generally encouraging as this new mood may be, has come too late, at least too late to save their joint hopes of world domination. "What forces in the world could resist us?" Kosygin said to *Life* in February 1968. "Nobody." Kosygin is wrong. The pathos of the present situation is that, just as America cannot unilaterally impose its will on Southeast Asia and Russia cannot unilaterally impose its will on the Middle East, so America and Russia together, even if they agreed on every detail of policy and worked together to put a common policy over, can no longer settle affairs in Southeast Asia and the Middle East. The events in the rest of the world have developed a life of their own — a future as well as a past of their own — and they are passing beyond the reach even of joint American-Russian dictation.

Indeed, the very process of Russian-American rapprochement hastens the end of Superpowership by reducing the fear that independent national action is likely to provoke the great powers into nuclear war; it thereby increases every nation's sense of its own freedom of maneuver. Nothing exhibits more arrestingly the decline of Superpowership than the spectacle in recent years of Superpowers pushed around by their satellites — the Soviet Union by East Germany, Cuba and North Vietnam; the United States by South Korea, South Vietnam and Taipei. The influence of the Superpowers in the next phase of world affairs will become increasingly marginal. Tocqueville's forecast — America and Russia, each "marked out by the will of Heaven to sway the destinies of half the globe" — has had, in the end, an exceedingly short run.

It would clearly be better for the world if the Superpowers began to acknowledge the limitations history has now imposed on their role. But, as we have seen, this is never an easy thing for a state to do. Ordinarily it takes defeat in war to persuade a Superpower that it has been living beyond its means. Sometimes one defeat is not enough. It took two defeats, for example, to convince Germany it was not a Superpower; there are those who fear that the Germans may not have learned this lesson yet. Great Britain, on the victorious side in the Second World War, persisted in the illusion until the defeat at Suez terminated her imperial dream. The American failure in Vietnam has produced a striking reassessment of the world position of the United States. Vietnam has been an expensive and horrible education; but no one can question the fact that most Americans are now determined to have no more Vietnams. Bitter experience has thus compelled the Germans, the Japanese, the Italians, the British and finally, I believe, the Americans to recognize they cannot live as Superpowers in the modern world. Only the Soviet Union, sustained by a dogmatic faith in the infallibility of its ideology, still seems dogged in the pursuit of Superpowership, and this in spite of spectacular setbacks in Cuba and the Middle East. The world must hope that Czechoslovakia may in time have the same effect on Russia that Suez had on England and Vietnam on the United States.

8. *After the Superpowers*

The last-ditch champions of the American Vietnam policy like to argue that the only alternative to universalism is isolationism. This, of course, is a self-serving definition of the issues; and the debate should not be established in these terms. A headlong dash from the world, a retreat to our own shores, even a retreat to our own hemisphere — all these are impossible options. An isolationist course would be as false to our interests as it would be false to our ideals. The United States cannot resign from the task of helping to build a rational world order.

But what form is this world order likely to take? As Franklin Roosevelt construed the universalist world a quarter of a century ago, it would be a world in which order would be enforced by the great powers. The decline of the Superpowers dooms this world. But it would appear equally to doom the sphere-of-interest world sought by Stalin. Thoughtful people still argue that spheres of influence offer the only alternative to universalism. But is it probable that, in the age after the Superpowers, the sphere-of-interest policy will be as easy to work as it was in the past? Confronted by nationalism in Czechoslovakia, Russia had to use military force to maintain its sphere of influence in Eastern Europe. Confronted by nationalism in the Dominican Republic, the United States had to use (or thought it had to use) military force to maintain its sphere of influence in the Caribbean. Both Superpowers got away with their military intervention in the short run. But both know that, where they are unwilling to use military force, they can no longer count on the automatic compliance of the countries of Eastern Europe or Latin America. It is highly doubtful whether China will be any more successful in putting together a submissive sphere of influence in East Asia.

The sphere-of-influence idea, in short, seems another casualty of the end of the Age of the Superpowers; it no longer presents a real alternative to universalism. My guess is that the most realistic evolution in the future would be along the lines of the proposal made by Churchill in 1943 — a development of regional groupings within the United Nations, thereby merging universalist and sphere-of-influence conceptions, strengthening the "middle powers" and discharging the great powers from the supposed obligation to rush about putting down every presumed threat to world peace. Lester Pearson of Canada has already suggested the division of the UN into regional assemblies.

This would be a policy neither of universalism nor of isolationism but of discrimination. It would imply the existence of what President Kennedy called the "world of diversity" — "a robust and vital world community, founded on nations secure in their own independence, and united by allegiance to world peace." And it would imply the recognition of the limits of American power. As Kennedy put it in 1961, "We must face the fact that the United States is neither omnipotent nor omniscient — that we are only 6 percent of the world's population — that we cannot impose our will upon the other 94 percent — that we cannot right every wrong or reverse each adversity — and that therefore there cannot be an American solution to every world problem."

Alas, Kennedy's profound insight was forgotten when his successor reinstated Dullesism and plunged ahead with the policy of overkill. But today, in the melancholy aftermath of Vietnam, we must at last understand more urgently than ever that "there cannot be an American solution to every world problem" and that we must therefore demand a sense of proportion and priority in the conduct of our foreign affairs.

A more discriminating policy on the part of the United States would also correspond to the rhythms of American interest in foreign affairs. Professor Samuel P. Huntington has recently called attention to a striking essay written in 1951 by Frank L. Klingberg describing the alternation of "extrovert" and "introvert" moods in American foreign policy. Examining American history since 1776, Klingberg found four introvert phases, averaging about 21 years in length, and three extrovert phases, averaging about 27 years. The fourth phase of extroversion began, in his view, around 1940 and, by his theory, would last to about 1967; "it seems logical to expect America to retreat, to some extent at least, from so much world involvement, and perhaps to do so sometime in the 1960's." *

One need not surrender to theories of cyclical determinism to acknowledge the possibility of a condition of national weariness and exhaustion after a time of intense activity and strain. Nor is such a condition confined to the United States. Our shifts to the extrovert phase, Klingberg notes, have "always occurred at a time of active European or world

* Klingberg further suggested that "the major problem of this coming [introvert] period will carry heavy moral implications. . . . The aspirations of the people of Asia and Africa could well furnish the chief issue, along with special repercussions from America's own racial problem." See Frank L. Klingberg, "The Historical Alternation of Moods in American Foreign Policy," *World Politics*, January 1952. My father offered a cyclical interpretation of American domestic politics in "Tides of American Politics," *Yale Review*, December 1939, later revised and reprinted in Arthur M. Schlesinger, *Paths to the Present* (New York, 1949).

diplomacy." Many nations today, for one reason or another, are entering inward-looking phases of their own. They are more concerned with questioning their own societies and meeting their own problems than with maneuvering for international position.

In light of the Vietnam tragedy and of the current world mood, what would be the basic principles for a new American policy? What are the lessons of Vietnam?

First, that everything in the world is not of equal importance to us. Asia and Africa are of vital importance for Asians and Africans, and they are of some importance for us. But they are not so important for us as they are to Asians and Africans, nor are they as important for us as are Europe, Latin America and Soviet Russia. In the last three years we have given most of our attention and resources to a marginal problem on the mainland of Asia while our position has steadily deteriorated in parts of the world far more indispensable to our national security.

Second, that we cannot do everything in the world. The universalism of the older generation was spacious in design and noble in intent. Its flaw was that it overcommitted our country — it overcommitted our policy, our resources and our rhetoric. It was tinged with messianic pretension. It estranged our friends without intimidating our enemies. The time has surely come to stop going abroad in search of monsters to destroy. Vietnam should teach us that in the last half of the twentieth century armed white men cannot determine the destiny of a nation on the mainland of Asia. It should teach us, more generally, that the Age of the Superpowers is over, and that any American policies which involve the denial of local nationalism are doomed to failure. It should teach us that "nation-building" is something which

can only be done by the people of the nation themselves —
that, as Robert Kennedy said in April 1968, "All the might
and power of America cannot provide or create a substitute
for another government, or for the will of another people."

*Third, that we cannot be the permanent guarantor of
stability in a world of turbulence.* Violence is epidemic in
the developing world; and we cannot regard each outbreak
as a summons for the American fire brigade. "Every country," a wise Englishman said, "has a right to its own Wars of
the Roses." Not every revolution, not every change in political and economic systems, not every assertion of belligerent
nationalism is necessarily a mortal threat to the security of
the United States. Above all, as Robert Kennedy has said,
"We cannot continue as we too often have done in the past
to automatically identify the United States with the preservation of a particular internal order . . . or confuse our own
national interests with the rule of a particular faction." He
added, "The worst thing we could do would be to take as our
mission the suppression of disorder and internal upheaval
everywhere it appears."

*Fourth, that all problems in the world are not military
problems, and that military force is not necessarily the most
effective form of national power.* So long as we continue to
define our world problems in military terms, so long we will
strengthen our own warrior class and plunge the nation into
further military intervention. This is a self-defeating course.
We have never had more military power in the world than we
have today — and we have seldom in recent times had less
influence. As General de Gaulle observed to President Kennedy in Paris in 1961, the French had learned that exerting
influence in Southeast Asia and taking military action there
were almost incompatible. We should ponder this state-

ment. And, as we free ourselves from the military hang-ups of our foreign policy, we can begin to combat the militarization of our domestic thought and institutions.

Fifth, that the basis for our international influence in the coming period will lie less in the power of our arms than in the power of our example. As the Superpowers themselves begin to realize that their time is over, then they will recognize that future world leadership will demand persuasion as well as power. Political ties, economic assistance, cultural relations: these we must strengthen as we can. But military intervention is another matter.

We should undertake military intervention only (a) when the national security of the United States is directly and vitally involved, (b) when the people whom we think we are supporting display a capacity for resistance themselves and (c) when, in addition, there are reasonable prospects for success — all conditions rejected and trampled on by those who made American policy for Vietnam. We must take advantage of the fact that modern military technology — intercontinental missiles, nuclear submarines, rapid means of airlift — reduces the need for the physical presence of American troops and bases in foreign lands. The time has come for a policy of "selective disengagement."

Of course, it seems easier in the short run to throw military weight around like an international bully than it is to appeal to the reason and conscience of mankind and to validate that appeal by the values we display in our national community. Yet we have exerted our greatest influence in the world precisely when, as in the days of Woodrow Wilson, of Franklin Roosevelt, of John Kennedy, American leadership, in great part because of its identification with progressive policies at home, has been able to command the confidence of ordinary people everywhere. Mr. Nixon's campaign goal of "clear-cut military superiority" will never be a substitute for American idealism as exemplified in action.

We can restore our influence only as we contract our military presence around the world and begin to display reason, restraint and magnanimity in our dealings with other nations. Above all, we can restore our influence only as we live up to our highest ideals in our national community. "Those are not wrong," Carl Schurz wrote seventy years ago, "who maintain that the nation which would assume the office of a general dispenser of justice and righteousness in the world . . . should be held to prove itself as a model of justice and righteousness in its own home concerns." The industrial order is undergoing vast and fundamental changes as the mechanical society created by the first industrial revolution is evolving into the new electronic society. "Because your country is further on the path of industrial development than ours," Jean-Jacques Servan-Schreiber told a meeting of American intellectuals, "many of the crises you are living through today are the ones we shall increasingly have to face in the future." If America is in turmoil, he continued, this was not the proof of decay but the price of progress. America seems in crisis because Americans have reached the point in social transformation where they are raising and debating fundamental questions long buried in tradition and dogma: the relationships between rich and poor, between black and white, between parent and child, between structure and spontaneity. "From the answers that you will find to this new set of questions will come a new 'social contract,' a new definition of the relationship between man and society with this second industrial revolution."

The experience of Vietnam has shown that we cannot run

two crusades at once — that we cannot wage even a small war against an underdeveloped country and at the same time move creatively to meet the problems of our own land. The policy of total involvement in the world is incompatible with the policy of social reconstruction at home. It would appear that in the years ahead America will exercise international influence less by trying to run the planet than by trying to solve the new problems of the high-technology state — the accelerating pace of technical change, the humanization of the city, the dilemmas of racial justice, the reform of education, the plight of the individual in a world of great organizations. In the period ahead the world will heed America less because of our armed might than because of our capacity to heal the disruptions and fulfill the potentialities of the electronic society. If this is so, then national and international interests converge in providing new and exhilarating, if remarkably difficult, goals for the boundless energies of American life.

V

JOE COLLEGE,
R.I.P.

THE CRISIS OF AMERICAN CONFIDENCE comes in part from the readiness of the most active among the poor, the blacks, the intellectuals, the young and (in a different way) the low-income whites to reject American society — a rejection that in time begins to rattle even those most accustomed to that society or profiting most from it. Still, among the defecting groups, the poor and the blacks have always been outsiders, and intellectuals are notoriously wayward and inscrutable. It is the revolt of the young, taking place in the heart of the American middle-class family, which has plucked most painfully at the nerve of American self-confidence.

1. *The New University*

Throughout American history parents have made their children the bearers of the family's aspirations in the struggle of life; and now, more than ever before in any country in history, success in that struggle is believed to require "going to college." Never have so many young Americans pursued their baccalaureates. College is beginning to come within the grasp of everyone, or at least of everyone in the middle class. In 1900 one out of every twenty-five Americans from 18 to 21 was in college; in 1939, one out of seven; in 1968, almost one out of two. In the decade between 1957 and 1967, college enrollment more than doubled. The United States today has nearly 6 million college students — 46 percent of all young people from 18 to 21. In California four out of every five high school graduates now go on to college. By the early seventies there will be more than 7 million students in institutions of higher learning. The founding fathers saw America as a rural society; already college students outnumber farmers by more than a million.

The rush of young men and women into higher education coincides with, and is partly caused by, the entry of the university itself into a new era in its relation to society. During most of American history, the university was hardly a functional necessity in American life. College training was considered useful for ministers and professors, later for doctors and lawyers and scientists; but it was not supposed terribly important for those who did the serious work of American society — those who ran the corporations and plantations and ranches and government. Now the coming of the high-technology society has changed all that. The increasing knowledge and specialization demanded by the electronic age, the increasing technical sophistication of the environment of work, the increasing complexity of economic and cultural problems — all this makes higher education functionally essential as never before.

The new assignment of the university is to supply business and government with the specialists and the knowledge the great organizations need for operation and growth. Yet, even while the university has become the indispensable source of professional and technical expertise, it still clings to its traditional assignment as the place for independent and critical intellectual inquiry. The crisis of the contemporary university springs in great part from this double role. Education is a treacherous servant; it can never be wholly co-opted by any society, whether corporate or communist. Thinking is a dangerous habit which, once acquired, cannot easily be kicked, or stopped from leading its devotees down forbidden roads. If the contemporary university sustains and staffs the world of organization, it also incites and nourishes the mutiny against organization. If its faculties include those whose highest ambition is to serve the organizations, it also includes those who unsparingly expose and condemn them. If some of its graduates become happy technicians, others become ardent critics of technical society. As a result, the American university today, simultaneously a center of collaboration and a center of resistance, is in a state of incipient schizophrenia.

With the university at once more popular, more powerful and more divided than ever before, the quality of the educational experience has begun to change. The more college students we have, the more baffling they seem to become. For years adults saw college life in a panorama of familiar and reassuring images, derived from their own sentimental memories (or from the movies) — big men on campus, fraternities and sororities, junior proms, goldfish-swallowing, panty raids, winning one for the Gipper, tearing down goalposts after the Big Game, homecoming, twenty-fifth reunions. College represented the "best years of life," a time of innocent frivolity and high jinks regarded by the old with easy indulgence. But the stereotypes don't work any more. Students today have a new set of rituals: demonstrations, strikes, sit-ins, interrupting classes, locking up deans, howling down eminent visitors, seizing college buildings, fighting cops. To the older generation the new undergraduate seems a strange, even a menacing, phenomenon, committed to frenetic agitations, consumed with mysterious resentments.

Many adults look on college students today as spoiled and ungrateful kids who don't know how lucky they are to be born in the greatest country on earth. Even men long identified with liberal views find the new undergraduate, in his extreme manifestations, almost unbearable. The hard-working student, Vice President Humphrey tells us, "is being replaced on our living room televisions by the shouter of obscenities and hate." President Nathan M. Pusey of Harvard speaks of "Walter Mittys of the left . . . [who] play at being revolutionaries and fancy themselves rising to positions of command atop the debris as the structures of society come crashing down." George F. Kennan talks of "the extremely disturbed and excited state of mind of a good portion of our student youth, floundering around as it is in its own terrifying wilderness of drugs, pornography and political hysteria." All these things, on occasion, have been true. Yet the very magnitude of student discontent makes it hard to blame the trouble on individual malcontents and neurotics. A society that produces such an angry reaction among so many of its young people perhaps has some questions to ask itself. Disraeli concluded *Sybil* with an exhortation about Young England in 1845 that applies to Young America a century and a quarter later: "We live in an age when to be young and to be indifferent can no longer be synonymous. We must pre-

prepare for the coming hour. The claims of the future are represented by suffering millions; and the Youth of a Nation are the trustees of Posterity."

2. The New Generation

Yet, despite the conspicuous discontent, most students still go to college to prepare themselves to earn a living in our present society. Most have the same political and economic views as their parents. Most, until 1968, supported military escalation in Vietnam. Most believe safely in law and order, the Republican and Democratic parties, the capitalist system and God. Some may even tear down goalposts and stage panty raids, if only to preserve parental illusions about college life. The typical college freshman in 1968, according to a survey of 100,000 freshmen by the American Council on Education (as summarized by the *Washington Post*), was "white, Protestant, grew up in a small town or suburb, wants to go into business or engineering, has a confused concept of civil liberties and has his eye firmly fixed on the buck." Nor is there anything new about the existence of an insurgent minority. Children have rebelled against their parents before; and in America, at least from the days of the Transcendentalists, the young have freely condemned the hypocrisy and conformism of their elders. After all, Emerson himself used to inveigh against the "establishment" and recommend "doing your thing."

Still something sets this generation of college students —
quiescent majority and rebellious minority alike — apart
from their parents. And, if a parent is really concerned to
find out what is worrying his children, he must make the
imaginative leap, always difficult for an older generation,
into the shoes of the young. He will find first of all that this
college generation has grown up in an era when the rate of
social change is faster than it has ever before been in human
experience. The constant acceleration in the velocity of history means that lives alter with startling and irresistible rapidity — that inherited ideas and institutions live in constant jeopardy of technological obsolescence. For an older
generation, change was still something of an historical abstraction, dramatized in occasional spectacular innovations,
like the automobile or the airplane; it was not a daily threat
to identity. For our children, it is *the* vivid, continuous over-
powering everyday fact, suffusing each moment with tension
and therefore, for the sensitive, intensifying the individual
search for identity and meaning.

The presumed indispensability of a college education for
success in life compounds the tension; one has only to watch
high school seniors worrying about the fate of their college
applications. And college itself, in a society that is beginning to value academic grades more than social status, may
determine the student's whole future and is therefore grimly
competitive as never before. It can all easily become too
much. Brian McGuire, who had the highest marks in the
College of Letters and Science at Berkeley in 1968, wrote after
graduation, "My four years of university education, instead
of helping me to become a man, have nearly turned me into
an unfeeling, unthinking zombie, totally removed from the
world outside my own specialized field. . . . I was letting

the system dominate me and demolish me as an individual. . . . In America we have become a society of anticipation and anxiety. We are losing meaning, values and purposes."

Nor does one have to be a devout McLuhanite to heed Marshall McLuhan's emphasis on the fact that this is the first generation to have grown up in the electronic epoch. Television affects the young in diverse ways: by its strong and early communication of styles and possibilities of life; by its horrid relish in crime and cruelty; by providing a public stage for student demonstrations and leaders with, as a result, the quickened spreading of the contagion of unrest from one campus to another. It affects the young still more fundamentally by its creation of new modes of perception. "The instantaneous world of electric informational media," McLuhan has argued, basically alters the way people perceive their experience. Where print culture gave experience a frame, viewing it in logical sequence and from a distance, electronic communication is simultaneous and collective; it "involves all of us all at once." This is why the children of the television age differ more from their parents than the parents differed from their own fathers and mothers. Both older generations, after all, were nurtured in the same typographical culture; television plunges the contemporary young from early childhood into the very thick of things.

Another factor distinguishes this generation — its affluence. The postwar rise in college enrollment in America, it should be noted, comes not from any dramatic increase in the number of youngsters from poor families but from sweeping in the remaining children of the middle class. For most students, in the words of the young radical Tom Hayden, status and affluence are "facts of life, not goals to be striven for." "This is the first generation of students," says

the president of the *Harvard Crimson,* "which is not going to
school for purely economic reasons." In the past, economic
pressures encouraged students to buckle down and conform;
today, as another young radical has put it, "Our minds have
been let loose to try to fill up the meaning that used to be
filled by economic necessity." Never have students felt so
free to heed their consciences and follow their ideals.

The velocity of history, the electronic revolution, the affluent society — these have given today's college students
a distinctive outlook on the world. And a fourth fact must
not be forgotten: that this generation has grown up in an age
of chronic violence. Their parents had been through depressions, crime waves, riots and wars; but for them episodes of
violence were still exceptional. For the young, violence has
become routine. They are the children of Hiroshima, the first
generation to come of age in the first (and only) country to
drop an atomic bomb. Their childhood memories are of the
Korean War; indeed, the United States has been at war as
long as many of them can remember. The war in Vietnam
seems to them particularly odious and brutalizing; most have
come to feel that the insensate destruction we have wrought
in a rural country on the mainland of Asia has far outrun
any defensible claim of the American national interest.
Within their own land, moreover, they live under the shadow
of violence provoked by racial injustice. Even petty crime
has acquired a new importance. Some have never known a
time when it was safe to walk along the streets of their home
city at night.

Above all, they have seen three men shot down who in-
carnated for them the best in our traditions and our hopes;
and the impact can hardly be overstated. The murder of
John F. Kennedy in 1963 made many young people sud-

denly wonder what the point was of striving to improve American society if this was to be the reward. "What has happened to our country?" my weeping daughter said. "If this is the kind of country we have, I don't want to live here anymore." Professor Kenneth Keniston of Yale, a most sensitive observer of the contemporary undergraduate, has written, "The change in student attitudes toward political life and social reform since the assassination of President Kennedy seems importantly connected to the rise of drug use." Is this farfetched? Dr. Robert Coles of Harvard, another extremely perceptive observer, agrees: "I'm not sure that the rise in the use of drugs is not related to the fall of opportunities for idealism in this country that came around 1964 and 1965."

The murders of Martin Luther King and Robert F. Kennedy five years after Dallas strengthened a terrible premonition about America. Also, by removing two leaders to whom the young could relate, these assassinations deepened their predicament; as a Columbia student put it, they "severed America's most vital links between youth and age." Our national reaction to this parade of horrors — brief orgies of remorse followed by business as usual and the National Rifle Association triumphant — has only validated disillusion and distrust.

3. The International Guerrilla War

Together these developments have given American youth an unprecedented immediacy of involvement in what many of them have come to regard as a monstrous society. For, even when American society refrains from evil deeds, it fills the young with an awful sense of individual powerlessness. The great organizations surround them, tower over them, inundate them with advertising and propaganda, undermine their feelings of personal identity by threatening to turn them all into interchangeable digits on IBM cards, not to be bent, folded, spindled or mutilated. They see the system as using, manipulating and consuming them, for its and not for their purposes.

Such feelings have set off the guerrilla warfare of contemporary students against the existing structures of society not only in the United States but throughout the developed world. (There is student unrest, of course, in underdeveloped countries too; but this is more predictable and has different sources and significance.) Uprisings in Berkeley and Morningside Heights are paralleled by uprisings at the Sorbonne and Nanterre, in the universities of England and Italy, in Spain and Yugoslavia and Poland, in Brazil and Turkey and Japan.

Every country has local grievances which detonate local revolts. American undergraduates first fixed on racial injustice as the emblem of a corrupt society. This remained the major issue until about 1968. Until then, most college students had supported the war in Vietnam — so long at least as less privileged young men were fighting it. It used to exasperate Robert Kennedy when he asked college audiences in 1966 and 1967 what they thought we should do in Vietnam — hands waving for escalation; and then asked what they thought of student deferment — the same hands waving for a safe haven for themselves. Finally, as the draft began to cut deeper, the colleges began to think hard about the war; a minority of students, indeed, had been doing just that since the teach-ins of the spring of 1965. The more they thought about it, the less sense the prospect of going to Vietnam made. In 1967–1968, according to the Educational Testing Service, Vietnam led the list of issues causing student protests. Thirty-eight percent of the institutions surveyed reported demonstrations against the war; next came demonstrations against dormitory regulations (34 percent), for civil rights (29 percent), for a larger voice in university policy (27 percent) and against the draft (25 percent).

No one should underestimate the intensity of the resistance to the war. "I am sorry about defacing the walls," went a student graffito at Hamilton Hall in Columbia, "but babies are being burned and men are dying and this University is at fault quite directly." Not all students who hated the war burned draft cards or fled to Canada. Many — and this may have been as courageous a position as that of defiance — felt, after conscientious consideration, that they had to respect laws with which they disagreed so long as the means to change these laws remained unimpaired. Yet even they regarded friends who chose to resist with sympathy. One who was himself prepared to go to Vietnam said to me, "Every student wants to avoid the draft. Every student, realizing that the method to this end is very individual, respects any method that works — or attempts that do not."

The antidraft revolt somewhat diminished after President Johnson's speech of March 31, 1968, the Paris negotiations and the McCarthy and Kennedy campaigns. But it will resume, and with new ferocity, should there be a reintensification of the war. In April 1968 a four-page advertisement appeared in the *New York Times* headed: "We, Presidents of Student Government and Editors of campus newspapers at more than 500 American colleges, believe that we should not be forced to fight in the Vietnam war because the Vietnam war is unjust and immoral." In June a hundred former presidents of college student bodies and campus editors declared: "We publicly and collectively express our intention to refuse induction and to aid and support those who decide to refuse. We will not serve in the military as long as the war in Vietnam continues."

In the meantime, the war has left a melancholy residue not just in philosophical disillusion about a supposedly democratic system but in wrecked personal lives. Many young Americans today are in jail in the United States or living miserably as draft-evaders or deserters in Canada and Sweden. More are wandering like nomads around the planet. Never in our national existence has America had so many young men without a country.

Yet the war and the draft remain not so much primary causes of the unrest as visible symbols for what the young perceive as a profounder absurdity and depravity in their society. Americans who expect that the end of war will mean the end of undergraduate discontent have too shallow a view of the matter. Another inadequate view, even though espoused by such moral philosophers as Richard M. Nixon and the Reverend Dr. Norman Vincent Peale, blames student turbulence on permissive child-rearing ideas: thus the doctrines of Dr. Benjamin Spock (which Dr. Peale summarizes as "feed 'em whatever they want, don't let them cry, instant gratification of needs") are alleged to have produced "a student generation that thinks it can get what it yells for." A little reflection exposes the superficiality of these theories. The students of Paris were not rioting because their government was about to send them to Vietnam; nor are the students of Poland, Turkey, Spain and Japan in revolt because their parents were devotees of *Baby and Child Care*.

Every country has its local issues. In Paris students live in conditions that have not improved materially since the Middle Ages and endure a rigid examination system that has hardly altered in half a century. In Poland and Czechoslovakia they detest a sterile, dogmatic and pretentious ideology. As Stephen Spender has remarked, the militant students of Paris and West Berlin think they want to be proletarianized, the militant students of Prague and Warsaw to be bourgeoisified. All this suggests that the diversity of local motive may conceal a deeper shared disquietude. Modern society seems to menace the integrity of the young — democratic states in one way, communist states in another — and the result is a determination by the young to resist incorporation into the system, a determination to win identity and potency by assaults upon the tyranny of structure and by demands for a voice in their own future. Among political leaders, General de Gaulle, of all people, seems to have the clearest understanding of the problem, even if he has not notably acted on his insight. The "anguish of the young," the old General said after his own troubles with French students in the spring of 1968, was "infinitely" natural "in the mechanical society, the modern consumer society, because it does not offer them what they need, that is, an ideal, an impetus, a hope, and I think that ideal, that impetus, and that hope, they can and must find in participation."

4. *The Ethos of the Young*

Not every American student exemplifies this anguish or demands this participation. The rebellious mood appears, for example, more in large colleges than in small, more in good colleges than in bad, more in urban colleges than in rural, more in private and state than in denominational institutions, more in the humanities and social sciences than in the physical and technological sciences, more among bright than among mediocre students. Yet, as anyone who lectures on the college circuit can testify, the anguish has penetrated surprisingly widely — among chemists, engineers, Young Republicans, football players and even into those last strongholds of the received truth, the Catholic and fundamentalist colleges.

How to define this anguish? It begins with a profound dislike, aggressive among the activists and muted, but nonetheless real, among many more, for the society which produced them. The world, as it roars down on them, seems a series of impersonal structures lying in wait to suppress their individualities and computerize their futures. They call it, if they vaguely accept it, "the rat race," or, if they resist it, "the System" or "the Establishment." They see it as a conspiracy against idealism in society and identity in themselves. An outburst on a recent Public Broadcasting Laboratory program conveys the flavor. The System, one student said, "hits at me through every single thing it does. It hits at me because it tells me what kind of a person I can be, that I have to wear shoes all the time which I don't have on right now. . . . It hits on me in every single way. It tells me what I have to do with my life. It tells me what kind of thoughts I can think. It tells me everything." Another student added, with rhetorical bravado: "Regardless of what your alternatives are, until you destroy this system, you aren't going to be able to create anything."

More typically, this mood finds private and quiet expression. With unassuming but resolute passion students yearn to seize control of their own future. My generation had the illusion that man made himself through his opportunities (Franklin D. Roosevelt); but our children believe that man makes himself through his choices (Jean Paul Sartre). They now want, with a moving urgency, to give their own choices transcendental meaning. The Beats of the fifties helped set the mood, but the kids of the late sixties have moved beyond the Bohemian self-indulgence of Allen Ginsberg and Jack Kerouac. "We do not feel like a cool swinging generation — " a Radcliffe senior said in a 1968 commencement prayer, "we are eaten up by an intensity that we cannot name. Somehow this year more than others, we have had to draw lines, to try to find an absolute right with which we could identify ourselves. First in the face of the daily killings and draft calls . . . then with the assassinations of Martin Luther King and Senator Kennedy."

The contemporary student generation can see nothing better than to act on impulses of truth: *"Ici, on spontane,"* as a French student wrote on the walls of his college during the Paris insurgency. They are going to tell it, as they say, like it is, to reject the established complacencies and hypocrisies of their inherited existence, to come out, in a favorite if barbarous phrase, for "unstructured free growth." One student said to me:

Basically the concept of this "do your thing" bit (as ludicrous as it sounds) may be the key to the matter. What it means is similar to Mill's *On Liberty* because it allows anybody to do what he wants to do as long as it does not intrude on anyone else's liberty. Therefore, nobody tries to impose anything on anybody, nor do they not accept a Negro, a hippy, a clubby, etc. I really believe that today we see beyond superficial appearances and thus, in the end, will have a society of very divergent styles, but that will be successfully integrated into a really viable whole. . . . We test out old thoughts and customs and either dispose of them or retain them according to their merits.

Along with this comes an insistence on openness and authenticity in personal relationships. A 1968 graduate — a girl — puts it clearly:

I think in personal conduct people admire the ability to be vulnerable. That takes a certain amount of strength, but it is the only thing which makes honesty and openness possible — it means you say the truth and somehow leave open a part of your way of thinking — of course you cannot be vulnerable with everyone or you would destroy yourself — but it is the willingness to be open, not just California cheerful open, which is almost a mask, since it is on all the time, and therefore cannot be truthful — it is a little deeper than that. . . . It means being strong enough to reveal your weaknesses. This willingness to be vulnerable — and those you are vulnerable with are your friends — coupled with ability to be resilient — to be strong but supple — those are good qualities, because inherent in them are honesty and humor, and the good capacity to love.

This is the ethos of the young — a commitment not to abstract pieties but to concrete and immediate acts of integrity. It leads to a desire to prove oneself by action and participation — whether in the Peace Corps and VISTA or by meeting local tests of college and community existence. The young prefer performance to platitude. The self-serving rhetoric of our society bores and exasperates them, and those who live by this rhetoric — e.g., their parents — lose their respect.

5. The Generation Gap

It is understandably difficult for parents, who have worked hard for their children and their communities, to see themselves as smug and fraudulent. But it is also understandable that the children of the sixties should have grown sensitive to the gap between what their parents claim their values to be and what (as they see it) their values really are — the gap made vivid in a land of freedom and equality which has so long, so unthinkingly and so shamefully condemned a tenth of the population to tenth-class citizenship. "It is quite right that the young should talk about us as hypocrites," Judge Charles E. Wyzanski, Jr., recently said at Lake Forest College. "We are."

And, more often than they know, parents themselves unconsciously signal to their children a cynicism about the System or a disgust for it. Every father who bewails the competitive tensions of his career, who says he "lives for the weekend," who conveys to his children the sense his life is unfulfilled — they are all, as Professor Keniston has put it, "unwittingly engaged in social criticism." Sometimes parents even find compensation for their own frustrations in the rebellion of their children; there is what one observer has described as the proud "my son, the revolutionary" reaction, as with the mother of Mark Rudd, the Columbia student firebrand who emerged briefly in the spring of 1968 as the Che Guevara of Morningside Heights.

Some children now regret, or affect to regret, that their parents did not take a harder line. Steven Kelman, a Harvard junior, quotes a Harvard sophomore: "They never did force any arbitrary system of values on me — what I find is that with so much freedom, I'm left with no value system, and in certain ways I wish I had a value system forced on me, so that I could have had something to believe in." Such complaints, however, are not convincing and have the air of an alibi. Suppose those parents had tried to impose an arbitrary value system! As another Harvard junior more wisely observes, "I think students feel indifferent about their parents because they don't really have control over their kids any more. If they do, then revolt." And revolt against parents is no longer a major issue. There is too little to revolt against. Seventy-five years ago parents had unquestioning confidence in a set of rather stern values. They *knew* what was right and what was wrong. Contemporary parents have been too much swept along themselves by the velocity of history to be sure of anything. They may be square, but they are generally too doubtful and diffident to force their squareness on their children.

Parents today are not so much intrusive as irrelevant. Mike

Nichols caught one student's-eye view of his elders beautifully in *The Graduate*, with his portrait, so cherished by college students today, of a shy young man freaked out by the surrounding world of towering, braying, pathetic adults. A girl who finished college last June sums it up:

> People like their parents as long as their parents do not interfere a whole lot, putting pressure on choice of careers, grades, personal life. . . . I think freshmen tend to discuss and dislike their parents more than seniors. By then, supposedly you have some distance on them, and you can afford to be amused or affectionate about them. For instance, if your parents are for Reagan or were for Goldwater, you know the space between you and them on it, and the impossibility of crossing it, so you let them go their imbecilic way and stand back amused. Other people say with obvious delight that they really like their parents. But nobody wants to go back home. For any length of time, it is usually a bad trip.

One student even looks forward to an ultimate "communion of interests" between today's students and their parents, only "with the younger half having gone through more (which may be necessary in this more complicated, difficult, tense, scary world) to get to the same place."

6. Student Power

No, the boys and girls of the nineteen-sixties, unlike the heroes and heroines of Dreiser, Lewis and Wolfe, are not generally mad at their families. Often they regard their father and mother with a certain compassion as the casualties of the system that they themselves are determined to resist. In many cases — and this is even true of the militant students — they are trying to *live* the values their parents affirmed; they are not so much rebelling against their parents' attitudes as applying them. They reject their families much less than they do the dominating social institutions — the "structures" — of which they consider their parents as fellow victims. And the nearest structure for them to reject, at least in its present form, is the college itself — the instrument they see as ordained by society to tame and bridle the young and turn them into faithful servants of the great organizations.

When students challenge their colleges, they often cite plausible academic grounds — classes too large, professors too inaccessible, curricula too rigid, and so on. Generally such points are well taken. But one wonders whether educational reform is the real reason for student self-assertion, or just a handy one. The colleges most in need of reform are ordinarily not those where the agitation takes place. The biggest troubles happen at the best institutions and often involve the most successful students. One sometimes suspects that the common cry against Clark Kerr's "multiversity" is a pretext. Hal Draper, the radical historian of the Berkeley Free Speech

Movement, agrees that "dissatisfaction with the quality of education given by the university played no major role in motivating the fight."

This does not mean, though, that "student power" is a fake issue. But the object is only incidentally educational reform. No one really supposes that smaller classes, chummier professors and more "relevant" courses would solve the problem. The essential purpose of student power is to remind the authorities that students exist as human beings; a democratization of university government, it is felt, might weaken the university's ties to a corrupt society and give the young a better chance of seizing control of their lives and fulfilling themselves as free individuals. For, oddly enough, American higher education, that extraordinary force for the modernization of society, has failed to modernize itself — a fact which not only antagonizes students but gives them a sense of moral justification. Harold Howe II, the Commissioner of Education in the Johnson administration, has pointed out that "professors who live in the realm of higher education and largely control it are boldly reshaping the world outside the campus gates while neglecting to make corresponding changes to the world within." Students cannot understand "why university professors who are responsible for the reach into space, for splitting the atom, and for the interpretation of man's journey on earth seem unable to find the way to make the university pertinent to their lives."

An "academic revolution" has taken place in recent years; but in some senses it has only made the problem worse. As analyzed by David Riesman and Christopher Jencks in their recent book by that name, it involves the increasing domination of undergraduate education by the methods and values of graduate education. While spreading professionalization has improved the quality of American universities, it has also produced professors more concerned with colleagues and research than with students. It has consequently increased discontent among undergraduates — especially among those who do not have their professional or vocational future all worked out by their freshman year — and a longing, in the words of Riesman and Jencks, for "a sense that an adult take them seriously, and indeed that they have some kind of power over adults which at least partially offsets the power adults obviously have over them." An eastern undergraduate puts it this way: "Students want more excitement from their courses and, especially, more courses which have something to do with their life. They want to align the universities with their new concepts of freedom and their new interests. The pettiness, traditional values, useless regimen that we feel we are removing from our lives is more difficult to remove from bureaucratized, self-interested universities. Combined with this problem is that students don't feel overworked nor do they really want to work hard — but they want to work with less tension and more exciting stuff."

Academic government, in most cases, is still foolishly autocratic. Many institutions operate on the memory of rules devised when they were boys' academies in the early nineteenth century. This situation has been accepted with astonishing docility by faculty as well as by students. To this day, for example, the Harvard faculty, long the most distinguished in the country, is excluded from the governing boards of the university; it has no clear voice in the choice of a president (or of recipients of honorary degrees) or in the allocation of resources within the university; indeed, until recently faculty members could not leave town during term time for more than four days (even during the reading period when

216 JOE COLLEGE, R.I.P.

no classes meet) without requesting permission, like school-
boys, from the university authorities. A Harvard professor,
modifying a famous phrase, once described his institution as
"a despotism *not* tempered by the fear of assassination." Yet,
as Professor Galbraith has pointed out, government and business, confronted by difficult problems, rarely seek out the eminent lawyers and bankers who constitute the Harvard Corporation: "when tasks of vast technical or social complexity must
be done, and done well, it is to the university faculty that society turns. Only for running the modern university is it
imagined that they are too stupid or otherwise incompetent."

In most institutions the faculty now has control over appointments and curriculum. Students, however, have lingered
outside the magic circle, denied any voice in university decisions. As a Columbia undergraduate recently put it, "American colleges and universities (with a few exceptions, such as
Antioch) are about as democratic as Saudi Arabia." The students at Columbia, he adds, were "simply fighting for what
Americans fought for two centuries ago — the right to govern themselves."

What does this right imply? At Berkeley in 1964 students
boldly advocated the principle of *cogobierno* — joint government by students and faculties. This principle has effectively ruined the universities of Latin America, and no
sensible person would wish to apply it to the United
States. However, many forms of student participation are
conceivable short of *cogobierno* — student attendance, for
example, at faculty and trustee meetings, student control of
discipline, housing and other nonacademic matters, student
consultation on curriculum and examinations, student membership on academic committees, campus ombudsmen and
so on. These student demands may be novel, still it is a little

hard to argue that they are unreasonable. The freshmen surveyed in 1968 by the American Council on Education were predominantly conservative; yet nearly 90 percent said that students should help design the curriculum. But most college administrations for years have rejected such ideas with about as much consideration as Mussolini, say, would have given a petition from a crowd of Sicilian peasants. The situation of college students today is like that of organized labor before the Wagner Act.

One can hardly overstate the record of student submissiveness under this traditional and bland academic tyranny. As recently as 1960 Professor Riesman, noting undergraduate complaints about college and society, could write, "When I ask such students what they have done about these things, they are surprised at the very thought they could do anything. They think I am joking when I suggest that, if things came to the worst, they could picket!" But the circumspect student generation of the fifties was already passing away. Soon John F. Kennedy and the civil rights freedom riders, then the Vietnam war, stirred the campuses into new life. Still college presidents and deans, like Tom Girdler and Ernest Weir in face of the CIO in the thirties, ignored the signs of protest. The initiative consequently went to student extremists, who welcomed the chance to prove that force was the only way to make complacent administrators and preoccupied professors listen to legitimate grievances. "Our aim," as an Oxford student leader put it in 1968, "is to completely democratize the University. We shall look for particular cases on which we can confront authoritarianism in colleges, faculties and the University." Or, in the words of Mark Rudd of Columbia, "Our style of politics is to clarify the enemy, to put him up against the wall."

7. The Student Left

The present spearhead of undergraduate extremism is that strange organization, or nonorganization, called Students for a Democratic Society. SDS began half a dozen years ago as a rather thoughtful movement of student radicals. Its Port Huron statement of June 1962, a humane and interesting if interminable document, introduced "participatory democracy" — that is, active individual participation "in those social decisions determining the quality and direction of his life" — as the student's solution to contemporary perplexities. In its early years SDS performed valuable work in combating discrimination and poverty; and this work generated a remarkable feeling of fellowship among its members. But the Port Huron statement no longer expresses official SDS policy: SDS itself has increasingly become an excellent example of what Lenin, complaining about left-wing communism in 1919, called "an infantile disorder."

This is not to suggest that SDS is communist, even if it contains Maoist and Castroite (or Guevaraite) factions. The official American Communist party detests it — a feeling cordially returned by many SDSers, who regard the Communist party as itself part of the System. "We have within ranks," observed Carl Davidson, an SDS vice president, "communists of both varieties, socialists of all sorts, three or four different kinds of anarchists, anarcho-syndicalists, social democrats, humanist liberals, a growing number of YAF [Young Americans for Freedom] libertarian laissez-faire capitalists, and, of course, the articulate vanguard of the psychedelic liberation

front." The basic thrust of SDS is, if anything, anarcho-syn-
dicalist, but the historical illiteracy of the membership assures
it a most confused and erratic form of anarcho-syndicalism.
Davidson says that the "shock troops," which may constitute
85 percent of the organization, are not ideological. "They are
usually the younger members, freshmen and sophomores, rapidly moving into the hippy, Bobby Dylan syndrome. Having
been completely turned off by the American system of com-
pulsory miseducation, they are staunchly anti-intellectual and
rarely read anything unless it comes from the underground
press. . . . In one sense they have no politics. But . . . they
turn out regularly for the demonstrations. They are morally
outraged about the war, cops, racism, poverty, their parents,
the middle class and authority figures in general. . . . They
long for community and feel their own isolation acutely."

The anarchist impulse extends to SDS organization: the
passion for decentralization is so great that organization
hardly exists (the joke is "the Communists can't take over
SDS — they can't find it"). The impulse also extends to its
program: the belief in the creative power of action is so great
that there is no program. The SDS gallery of heroes suggests
its diversity: Che Guevara, of course, various heroes-for-a-
day like Mario Savio in Berkeley, Rudi Dutschke in West
Berlin, Danny Cohn-Bendit in Paris, Regis Debray in Bolivia;
Herbert Marcuse, the California savant who denounces tolerance and justifies the forcible repression of wicked ideas;
Paul Goodman, the affable anarchist who has taken recently
to chastising some of his followers; the late Frantz Fanon, the
brilliant champion of violence against colonialism; Noam
Chomsky of M.I.T., an innovator in linguistics and an hys-
teric in politics.

Anarchism, with its unrelenting assault on all forms of

authority, is a natural response to a world of structures. As a French student scribbled on the wall of his university at Nanterre, "*L'anarchie, c'est je*." But the danger of anarchism has always been that, lacking rational goals, it moves toward nihilism. The strategy of confrontation turns into a strategy of provocation, intended to drive authority into acts of suppression supposed to reveal the "hidden violence" and therefore the true nature of society. Confrontation politics requires both an internal sense of infallibility and an external insistence on discipline. Soon the SDS people began to show themselves, as one student put it to me, "exclusionary, self-righteous and single-minded. I feel that they (along with certain McCarthy people) are the one group that does not think that everybody should do their thing, but rather do the SDS thing." The impatience with reason and order became in time a theatrical relish in emotion and destruction. "You've got to let yourself get angry — and maybe violent as well," wrote Michael Rossman of the Berkeley Free Speech Movement (four years later), "— before you can find out who you are." The contempt for tolerance became in time a virtual rejection of participatory democracy. Professor William Appleman Williams of Wisconsin, whose own historical writing stimulated this generation of student radicals, ended by calling them "the most selfish people I know. They just terrify me. . . . They say, 'I'm right and you're wrong and you can't talk because you're wrong.'" At Columbia SDS was prepared, as a liberal professor put it, to "exact a conformity that makes Joe McCarthy look like a civil libertarian."

In 1967 SDS began to discuss in its workshops how confrontation politics — seizing buildings, taking hostages and so on — could be used to bring down a great university. Such SDS scheming should not be taken too literally. The Cox

Commission, which investigated the disturbances at Columbia in the spring of 1968, was undoubtedly right in rejecting the theory that the trouble at Morningside Heights was all the result of an organized SDS conspiracy. But it was also probably right in suggesting that the "endless hours of SDS discussions of revolutionary tactics . . . accustomed many reform-minded students to the idea that resort to disruption is an acceptable method of pursuing one's goals if only the goals can be called conscientious." This follows the Marcuse doctrine that "there is a 'natural right' of resistance for oppressed and overpowered minorities to use extralegal means if the legal ones have proved inadequate." When a maladroit university administration mishandled the questions of a projected new gymnasium and the university's relations to the Institute for Defense Analysis — questions which for the students symbolized the issues of racial justice and Vietnam — SDS took full advantage of the opening. Then brutal police intervention transformed an SDS putsch into a general student insurrection.

At Columbia the SDS leaders displayed even less interest than the university administration in negotiating the ostensible issues. Some months later Mark Rudd, the SDS leader, told the *Boston Globe:* "We manufactured the issues. The Institute for Defense Analysis is nothing at Columbia. Just three professors. And the gym issue is bull. It doesn't mean anything to anybody. I had never been to the gym site before the demonstrations began. I didn't even know how to get there." The SDS interest was power. "If we win," Rudd wrote in a "Dear Grayson" letter to President Kirk, "we will take control of your world, your corporation, your University and attempt to mold a world in which we and other people can live as human beings. Your power is directly threatened, since we will have to destroy that power before we can take over. . . . I'll use the words of LeRoi Jones, whom I'm sure you don't like a whole lot: 'Up against the wall, mother-fucker, this is a stick-up.'"

After the Columbia putsch, Tom Hayden set forth the revolutionary future. The goal, he said, mimicking Che Guevara's pledge to "create two, three, many Vietnams in Latin America," was to "create two, three, many Columbias . . . to expand the strike so that the U.S. must change or send its troops to occupy American campuses. . . . Many of the tactics learned can also be applied in smaller hit-and-run operations between strikes: raids on the offices of professors doing weapons research could win substantial support among students while making the university more blatantly repressive." The student militants, said Hayden, "are, in Fidel Castro's words, 'guerrillas in the field of culture.'"

As the SDS leaders get increasing kicks out of their revolutionary dramatics, they have grown mindless, arrogant and, at times, vicious in their treatment of others. In recent months the young men who incite riot and talk revolution have encouraged acts of exceptional squalor — not only the denial of free speech but the rifling of personal files, the tearing up of an unpopular professor's research notes and a general zest in destruction for the sake of destruction. Their influence is to turn students into what John Osborne, one of Britain's "angry young men" of the fifties, has called "instant rabble." And, in the end, SDS may become a victim of its own tactics. At the national convention in 1968, one SDS leader complained about the militant or "Jesse James" faction, "We've got to be able to stop a clique of people from putting down any kind of dissent — or rational argument

— in order to manipulate and gain control. It could be an extremely dangerous precedent." It could indeed.

What is the future of SDS? No one, including its own national office, can be very sure how many members SDS really has. In the spring of 1968 *Time* and *Newsweek* generously awarded it 35,000, and in the autumn SDS itself claimed 40,000. But J. Edgar Hoover, who is not addicted to minimizing the enemy, told Congress on February 23, 1968, that in 1967 SDS had 6372 members, of whom 875 had paid dues since January 1. Whatever the number, it is an infinitesimal fraction of the six million students enrolled in American colleges.

8. *The Demonstrations*

Yet this fact should not induce complacency in the country clubs. Many students who would not dream of joining SDS share its sense of estrangement from American society and have been "radicalized" by SDS activity. "Although the activist students usually make up only a minor percentage of the total enrollment," Commissioner Harold Howe said in May 1968, "they very often appear to mirror the real even if unspoken desires of the majority for greater participation in the administration of the institutions they attend." Commissioner Howe limited his point unduly. The activists very often appear to mirror the real if unspoken desires, or at least concerns and anxieties, of the majority on a wide range of issues, social and political as well as academic.

In 1958 the Gallup poll reported that one student in five had taken part in protest demonstrations — a statistic suggesting not only that a million students may be counted as activists but that the proportion has probably doubled since the estimates of student rebels in the spring of 1966 as one in ten (Samuel Lubell) and one in twelve (the Educational Testing Service). In January 1969 *Fortune*, after extensive polling, estimated that of the college population about 60 percent were pursuing conventional career objectives, while the remaining 40 percent, defined "mainly by their *lack of concern* about making money," were critical of official values. The *Fortune* conclusion was that about 750,000 students now "identify" with the position of the New Left. All studies, moreover, indicate that the activists are good students, that they abound in the best universities and that they are, in the main, the sons and daughters of the relatively affluent. "Their backgrounds show," the Louis Harris poll reports, "that they are far more likely to come from homes with incomes of $15,000 a year and over, from the cities and suburbs, have fathers who are creative men, and have parents with a college or post-graduate degree."

A recent episode at Antioch explains why the majority often goes along with the activists. Although on other campuses Antioch is considered a paragon of democracy — its students, for example, can attend the meetings of its board of trustees — this fine old experimental college in Yellow Springs, Ohio, evidently still has problems of its own. A year ago the board of trustees met before an audience of seventy-five or so students. One member began to read the report of the committee on the college investments. As he droned along, a student suddenly jumped up and shouted, "This is all a lot of fucking bullshit." A second student then arose and said, with elaborate irony, "You shouldn't talk that way. These wonderful trustees are giving of their time and substance to help us out." Next, in quick succession, half a dozen other students got up and called out caustic one-line sentences at the startled trustees. At this point the lights went out. When they came on thirty seconds later, the trustees were confronted by a tableau: one masked student standing with his foot on the chest of another masked student prostrate on the floor. The boy on the floor said, "Massa, is it all right if I use LSD?" The standing student replied, parodying a phrase cherished by academic administrators, "It is all right if you follow institutional processes." A series of similar Q and A's followed. The lights went out again; there were sounds of scurrying; and, when the lights came on, all but a dozen students had gone.

A moment of silence followed. Then the trustee who had been reading the report from the committee on investments resumed exactly where he had left off. This was too much for a colleague, who broke in and said reasonably, "Mr. Chairman, I don't think that we ought to act as if nothing had happened." The chairman asked what he proposed, and the trustee suggested that they invite the students still in the room to tell them what this had been all about. The students responded that, while they had not approved of the demonstration, they were now delighted that it had forced the trustees to listen to them. "You may not like what you saw," one said. "But now you are discussing things that you would never be discussing on your own initiative."

This story illuminates a disastrous paradox: that the extremist approach often works. "I feel like I just wasted three and a half years trying to change this university," a Columbia senior said after the troubles in the spring of 1968. "I played the game of rational discourse and persuasion. Now there's a mood of reconstruction. All the logjams are broken — violence pays. The tactics of obstruction weren't right, weren't justified, but look what happened." The activists understand what has till recently escaped the attention of the deans: that a small number of undergraduates, if they don't give a damn, can shut down great and ancient universities. As a result, when the activists turn on, the administrators at last jump to do things which, if they had any sense, they would have done on their own long since — as Columbia is revising its administrative charter for the first time (the *New York Times* tells us) since 1810. Commissioner Howe says: "Perhaps students are resorting to unorthodox means because orthodox means are unavailable to them. In any case, they are forcing open new and necessary avenues of communication." Both Berkeley and Columbia will be wiser and better universities as a result of the student revolts. One can hardly blame the president of the *Harvard Crimson* for his conclusion: "All the talk in the world about the unacceptability of illegal protest, all the use of police force and all the repressive legislation will not change the fact that attention is drawn to the evils in our universities in this way. As long as students have no legitimate democratic voice, attention is drawn only in this way."

The secret of protecting the intellectual life of the university in an age of undergraduate turbulence lies in avoiding situations that might drive the great majority of moderate students into an alliance with the tiny minority of extremists. Rigid insistence on "law and order," especially when enforced by city police or the state National Guard, is not usually the best way to keep the moderates and the crazies apart. When university administrations pursue irrational policies, they tend to unite the students behind irrational leadership. Only by pursuing rational policies can administrations hope to isolate the extremists.

The key, it seems to me, lies in the assessment of the student demands. If the demands make sense, a college administration would be ill advised to reject them or defer their consideration even when student manners are bad unless the provocation is indeed immense; stalling on procedural grounds only discourages the moderates and facilitates their radicalization. If the demands don't make sense, the administration ought to be able to explain why in terms that hold the moderate support. Thus the agitation for black studies programs is eminently sensible; American universities should have had such programs long since. But the stipulation that only black scholars should teach in such programs makes very little sense. According to this principle, only southerners should teach southern history, only Germans German history, only communists the history of communism and so on. University administrations will succeed when they stand reasonably against patently unreasonable proposals and actions.

9. *Personal Meaning*

The students' demand for a "legitimate democratic voice" in the decisions that control their future is part of a larger search for control and for meaning in life. The old sources of authority — parents and professors — have lost their hold.

Nor does organized religion retain much power either to impose values or to advance the quest for meaning. Nominal affiliation has not faded away as much in American colleges as, say, at Cambridge University in England, where a recent poll showed 37 percent agnostic or atheist, 35 percent Christian and 27 percent indeterminate. (The Churches Correspondent of the London *Daily Telegraph* commented, without evident irony, "The figures confirm the belief that interest in the Christian faith continues at a high level in the older universities.") But religious belief in the traditional sense is no longer widespread in American colleges. A Catholic girl recently said that "there definitely is no interest in any doctrine about the supernatural. The interest is in human values." The Radcliffe commencement prayer this June began: "We pray that You will hear us as we think about our graduation, even though we have trouble using the traditional language for talking to You and though many of us no longer feel a part of a religious community." "Nobody thinks about religion," reports an eastern sophomore, "but probably respect people who have religion because it is so rare."

Finding so little sustenance in traditional authorities, students today have to evolve their own values. The most thoughtful want to live according to their own standards of authenticity. It is hard, however, to fix these standards with great confidence, because undergraduate mores fluctuate constantly. Students, like everyone else, are rushed along by the velocity of history. The electronic age produces, consumes and discards with extravagant speed. Television in particular accelerates certain forms of growth, or at least of knowing sophistication. As the Dean of Students at Northwestern put it, if Booth Tarkington were writing *Seventeen* today, he would have to call it *Eleven*. So, in contemporary colleges, students fresh from high school may become the pacemakers, with things to teach to seniors. One finds not only the now notorious conflict between the generations. One finds conflicts emerging within the younger generation — a development recognized at the conclusion of the film *Wild in the Streets* when, after the fifteen-year-olds have taken over the country, an eleven-year-old is heard to mutter darkly, "Never trust anyone over twelve."

The search for meaning in life often takes forms that an older generation can only regard as grotesque or perilous. Thus drugs become a means by which, if people cannot find harmony in the world, they can instill harmony in their own consciousness. "The persons attracted to drugs," writes a member of the class of 1964, "were looking for a new dimension in life, which, they believed, would expand their powers of creativity and enable them to pursue more fulfilling lives. They wished to leave an ugly and destructive society for a more beautiful, significant environment among people of non-competitive, non-political, non-material tastes." To some it will no doubt seem blasphemous to regard drugs as a substitute for religion. Yet one can hardly doubt that William James, if alive today, would have included ecstatic states induced by drugs in his *Varieties of Religious Experience.* For many young people drugs offer the closest thing to a spiritual experience they have; their "trips," like more conventional forms of mysticism, are excursions in pursuit of transcendental meanings in the cosmos. This is why the young so much admire the conclusion of Stanley Kubrick's *2001: A Space Odyssey* — a conclusion that only bewilders the older generation.

The invasion of the life of the young by drugs is relatively recent; and it provides a good illustration of the intra-generational conflict. "When I was a freshman in 1960," a venerable figure of twenty-five, just out of law school, tells me, "drugs were really a fringe phenomenon. Today pot is *the* pervasive form of nightly enjoyment for students. How can parents understand this if a person like myself, hardly four years older than my sister, isn't able to understand it?" His sister, who had just graduated from college, reports, "You see, the people who have been coming in as freshmen since even my first year, '64, and with a big boom, in '66, have been turned on. Once again, as last year, the biggest pushers are in the freshman class." And a younger brother, now a college junior, says:

> The newest generation of college students I already feel somewhat cut off from and scared of. Whereas we may be uncommitted, they have absolutely no conception of being committed and therefore don't worry about it. The problem is that they got into drugs while they were in high school, or even earlier. They may have lacked certain of the reservations that we had. They may have lacked the sense of responsibility which is so necessary in tackling serious problems. Perhaps therefore they went too fast too soon. Anyway, I wonder what is left for them when they get into college — what will be their kicks?

As for the drugs themselves, marijuana is a staple. It causes little discussion in its purchase, use or non-use. On the sophisticated campuses "everybody" has smoked it at one time or another; or at least this is a common student impression. A more precise estimate — from Dr. S. F. Yolles, director of the National Institute of Mental Health — is that about two million college and high school students have had some experience with marijuana. Fifty percent of those polled said they had had no effects. Presumably most of the rest find in the chemical expansion of consciousness an occasional means of relaxation or refreshment, as liquor is for their parents. It is hard to persuade students (and many doctors too) that pot is any more lethal than tobacco or alcohol; and parents achieving a high on their fourth martini are advised not to launch a tipsy tirade against marijuana. Dr. Yolles says of the student drug taker, "The academic standing of the occasional user was better than average, while the heavily involved drug user had lower than average scholastic grades."

LSD, on the other hand, is quite another matter, and its vogue has notably waned in the last year or so. Students, reading about its possible genetic effects and hearing about the "bad trips" of their friends, simply reject it as too risky. Undergraduates, it should be added, are very rarely hippies; when drugs begin to define a whole way of life, students drop out, and studies go by the board. It is hard to carry a course load and pursue the passive, often timeless, existence of the hippie community. A few students who experiment in hard drugs may now be turning from "acid" to "speed," or Methedrine. But an interesting departure, reported from Cambridge, Massachusetts, is the resurgence of simple old-fashioned drinking. "Younger kids who really started right off with grass often missed the whole alcoholic thing, and now they stop you on the street and say wow they got drunk and what a trip it was." No doubt this development will reassure troubled parents.

Love is another medium in which the young conduct their search for meaning. Against Vietnam they cried: "Make love, not war." "The student movement," one girl observed, "is not a cause. . . . It is a collision between this one person and that one person. It is an *I am going to sit beside you.* . . . Love alone is radical." The culmination of love is personal relations (or, as students corrupted by their professors of sociology prefer to say, "interpersonal" relations).

Here attitudes have relaxed, though it is not clear how much the change in sexual attitudes has produced a change in sexual behavior — to some degree, certainly, but not so much as some parents fear. A 1968 poll at Oberlin showed that 40 percent of the unmarried women students had (or claimed) sexual relations. Dr. Paul Gebhard, who succeeded the late Dr. Alfred Kinsey as director of the Institute for Sex Research at the University of Indiana, observes that sexual relations among college students are "more fun nowadays," especially for women, and create less guilt. An Institute for Sex Research survey estimates that about 25 percent more college students have had intercourse today than would have had twenty years ago but describes the increase as gradual and attributes it in great part merely to an earlier start in patterns of courtship. One girl undergraduate says, "I am convinced there is a greater naturalness and acceptance and much less uptightness about sex in the present college era than in the one earlier."

Unquestionably the pill has considerably simplified the problem. "No longer is it [again a girl is speaking], oh I can't sleep with anyone because sex is sinful or risky or whatever; it is, rather, do I want to sleep with this person and, if I do, how will it affect me or the relationship. . . . The emphasis is on satisfying whole, friendly, honest relationships of which sex is only a part. Where sex is accepted as an extension of things, then nobody really talks about it that much, except as a pleasant thing."

The new naturalness has encouraged the practice known to deans as "cohabitation" and to students as "shacking up" or "the arrangement" — that is, male and female students living together in off-campus apartments. Rolling with the punch, colleges are now experimenting with coeducational student housing. Nearly half the institutions represented in the Association of College and University Housing Officers now have one form or another of mixed housing. What may be even more shocking to old grads is the vision of the future conveyed by the report that at Stanford the Lambda Nu fraternity proposes next year to go coed.

The new freedom of sex and drugs may be less depraved than it seems. "We might take drugs and cohabitate and do other things which may have been looked down upon ten years ago," a junior says, "but I think they are all done within a similar-type Puritan ethic. Action within this ethic has been enlarged while the ideology remains the same. . . . The responsibility factor remains the same."

10. Heroes and Hopes

Though students today no longer find models, if they ever did, in parents, professors or pastors, though many seek fulfillment in their personal code of authenticity or in drugs or love, they have not abandoned heroes. Nearly all regard John F. Kennedy with admiration and reverence. Many in 1968 followed and then mourned his brother; many others followed Eugene McCarthy (and cut their hair and beards in order to be "clean for Gene"); many liked John Lindsay. Among writers, the situation is more puzzling. J. D. Salinger

(*Catcher in the Rye*) and William Golding (*Lord of the Flies*) were the literary idols of youth in the fifties; but they seem to have passed their time. "We read Salinger and Golding when we were kids," a college senior tells me, "and that is where they stand; they are camp almost." The press reports an enthusiasm on the campuses for J. R. R. Tolkien and *The Lord of the Rings*; but I must confess sympathy for a perceptive girl who says: "When I stand in lunchlines, I see people holding Tolkien in their hands, but they aren't the people I know. I guess that people like it because it hands them a whole society and set of symbols and passwords which they can use to describe themselves, set off the cliques. It gives people a whole world of the imagination without having to use their imagination." The German writer Hermann Hesse with his novels about romantic quests for self-knowledge is having a current whirl; an electronic rock group on the West Coast calls itself "Steppenwolf"; but one can confidently predict that in a few years Hesse will be back with Salinger and Golding in the high schools.

The testimony is general that the old, whether in public affairs or in literature, don't count for very much in the colleges. "The models for today's students," a sophomore writes, "probably come more from their contemporaries than any other group — the latest draft card burners, people with the guts to live the way they want despite society's prohibitions, etc. — or from older people who sympathize with them and give intellectual prestige to their feelings."

Above all, students find in music and visual images the vehicles that bring home reality. "THE GREAT HEROES OF THIS DAY AND AGE," a girl affirms in full capitals, "ARE BOB DYLAN AND THE BEATLES." Dylan "gave us a social conscience and then he gave us folk-rock and open honest talk about drugs and sex and life and memory and past." One student thinks Dylan "may have a profounder influence than the Beatles because he is American and sings about America — and his evocative powers are profound — to affect those poor people and us — *John Wesley Harding* is a wandering, obscure and sad album, but it is also gentle and tender and necessary. . . . Sometimes you just can't listen to Dylan any more, it is too much of an emotional experience."

As for the Beatles, "Well, they taught us how to be happy. We evolved with the Beatles." The evolution was from a simple happiness to a more complex form of sensibility — from the first Beatle songs, with their insistent beat, to the intricate electronic songs of today and their witty, ambiguous lyrics. "When you really listen to *Sergeant Pepper*, it can be an exhausting, amazing, frightening experience. Especially 'A Day in the Life' which is a hair-raising song because it is about our futures too and death."

What these heroes stand for, in one way or another, is the determination to affirm the integrity of the private self against the enveloping structures and hypocrisies of organized society. They embody styles of life which the young find desirable and admirable. "Let there be born in us," the Radcliffe commencement prayer in 1968 concluded, "a strange joy, that will help us to live and to die and to remake the soul of our time."

Yet college students have no easy optimism about the future. "When people talk about the future," one remarks, "they either talk of utopias, desert islands populated by their chosen friends, or revolution." "People don't talk about the future," says another. "That's too depressing because it means growing old and having responsibilities and the even-

tual capitulation to the System, because it won't change."
"People don't think of the future in panoramic terms," still
another says. "They simplify and hope for the end of arti-
ficialities. They want to see people who they can trust in
power. Their model will come when they seize power and
purify power with their own energy and spirit."

For the moment they are determined, in the words of the
student orator at the 1968 Notre Dame commencement, not
to be satisfied to "play the success game." More college
graduates every year hope for careers of public and community service. The acquisitive life of business holds less and
less appeal. "Mostly," says one of them, "students know
what they *don't* want to be: they don't want to be tied
down to a hopeless, boring regimen; they don't want to give
in to the establishment, after spending most of their youth
avoiding it; they don't want to profit through special interest groups and to the detriment of people in need. Mostly
they want to make the society they live in better, richer for
all, more fun. The problem is that they lack the plans to
accomplish the ends."

One can hardly doubt that a good many — perhaps most
— of these defiant young people will be absorbed by the System and end living worthy lives as advertising men or insur-
ance salesmen. Hal Draper, the old radical musing on the
800 sit-inners arrested at Berkeley at the height of the Free
Speech Movement, wrote, "Ten years from now, most of
them will be rising in the world and in income, living in the
suburbs from Terra Linda to Atherton, raising two or three
babies, voting Democratic, and wondering what on earth
they were doing in Sproul Hall — trying to remember, and
failing."

One must hope for the sake of the country that some of

this fascinating generation *do* remember — not the angry and senseless things they may have done, but the generous hopes that prompted them to act for a better life. But who can say? — certainly not their elders. Yet the attempt at understanding may even be a useful exercise for the older generation. I discovered this in talking to students for the purposes of this piece. And I treasure a note from one who patiently cooperated. "Even as I distrust anybody of the older generation who tries to write about the younger," the letter said, "I think it will be interesting to see how you figure it out."

VI

THE PROSPECTS
FOR POLITICS

THE CRISIS OF AMERICAN CONFIDENCE, extends far beyond the reach of politics. Political leadership, however wise or noble, cannot hope to resolve aesthetic or moral or metaphysical perplexities; it certainly cannot hope to abolish the impulses of hate and destruction within the human heart. Yet, if politics cannot do everything to improve the state of man, it can do something. In particular, it can help create conditions that restrain and temper the forces of inhumanity and chaos. It does so by the very act of forming a social order; it does so whenever in that order — as, for example, in the relationship between capital and labor — it begins to substitute rational for arbitrary processes. George Bancroft well defined the political function when he wrote in 1834, "The feud between the capitalist and laborer, the house of Have and the house of Want, is as old as social union, and can never be entirely quieted; but he who will act with moderation, prefer fact to theory, and remember that every thing in this world is relative and not absolute, will see that the violence of the contest may be stilled."

American politics in our age faces two assignments. The first is the age-old business of the republic: safe and peaceful relations with the world; justice, order and economic opportunity at home. But to these abiding tasks politics in the nineteen-seventies must add a second and more specific goal: the restoration within the United States of a vital sense of national community. For our nation is in a state of incipient fragmentation. A series of tensions severely strain the social fabric: tensions between young and old, between poor and rich, between black and white, between educated and uneducated, between intellectuals and know-nothings. "Of all dangers to a nation," wrote Walt Whitman, ". . . there can be no greater one than having certain portions of the people set off from the rest by a line drawn — they not privileged as others, but degraded, humiliated, made of no account." The urgent problem of our politics is to give the presently alienated groups a feeling of membership in the national process — to include all Americans in a genuine commonwealth of reason, justice and opportunity.

1. *The Anatomy of Alienation*

The alienated groups consist of two sorts: the estranged and the excluded. The estranged are those who in the past have formed part of the national community — the intellectuals, the young, the lower-middle-class whites, for example — and are disaffected on recent and particular grounds: the intellectuals and the young because of the Vietnam war; the lower-middle-class whites because of the Negro revolution. For them one can speak of the "restoration" of social ties. The excluded are those — the traditionally poor, the blacks, the Indians, the Puerto Ricans, the Mexican-Americans — who have never been full members of this nation. For them the issue is not the restoration but the achievement of national status.

Both the sense of estrangement and the sense of exclusion have been reinforced by the changes accumulating and intensifying within American society. The velocity of history has never been greater; and the momentum of technological change is whirling us past the mechanical into the electronic society.* The world we are about to enter will be dominated by the capacity to deal instantaneously and precisely with a vast number of factors. This capacity requires and fosters the development of great organizations; and it is already beginning to revolutionize communications, research, education, production, transport and nearly every other aspect of our lives. This second industrial revolution, by computerizing the social structure and speeding the pace of change, may have political and psychological consequences almost as profound as the first.

No social emotion in consequence is more vital in America today than a sense of personal helplessness, uselessness and impotence. It is always pleasurable to suppose that this feeling of powerlessness is confined to oneself. But, as Jules Feiffer delights in pointing out, nearly everyone in American society feels powerless — not only the young, the poor, the blacks, the intellectuals, but conservatives, businessmen,

---

* Daniel Bell, to whom we are all indebted for his thoughtful and imaginative extrapolations into the electronic future, writes of the "post-industrial" society. I find this term puzzling. Surely the new society will continue to be an industrial society. "Post-mechanical" society would make more sense; but why not simply the "electronic" society?

publishers, millionaires, Secretaries of State, Presidents. This impression of individual powerlessness has steadily increased as science and invention have proceeded to depersonalize, organize, mechanize and now automate the processes of life. Everyone more or less has the sense of existing in the shadow of vast uncontrollable structures, impervious to human desire or need.

The impending electronic revolution, the new world of great organizations, alarm the intellectuals, who feel that it will render them obsolete as thinkers and absorb them only as technicians. It baffles and menaces as well as excites the young. As for the lower-middle-class whites, the most conservative group in American society, the vision of unchartered and inexorable change fills them with fear. The premonition of disruption haunts the background of American life, while the prospect of inundation by what Daniel Bell has called "the greatest bombardment of aural and visual materials that man has ever experienced in his history" looms horribly ahead of us.

For the new technology is highly ambiguous in its impact. If the organizations it breeds threaten to stamp individuals into a common mold, at the same time the experience it makes possible endows the individual with new appetites, new choices, new ideals. At the same time, for example, that the electronic society confirms the estranged groups in their estrangement, it holds out to the excluded groups tantalizing images of change and possibility. In the relatively slow-moving mechanical society, the outcasts tended to remain passive and invisible. But the stimuli of the electronic society are incessant; a moral revolution accompanies the technological revolution; and one step toward a better life leads rapidly to the next.

The excluded groups today are mostly better off than they were a generation ago. They receive more attention, have more influence and exert more pressure on society than ever before. Yet they grow more drastic and importunate as their status improves. This should surprise no one. As Tocqueville observed of the discontent that led to the French Revolution, "Patiently endured so long as it seemed beyond redress, a grievance comes to appear intolerable once the possibility of removing it crosses men's minds. For the mere fact that certain abuses have been remedied draws attention to others and they now appear more galling; people may suffer less, but their sensibility is exacerbated." So, while the failure to continue improving the objective situation will only make matters worse, we cannot rest in the comfortable supposition that continued improvement will solve our problems. The operative idea here is what the sociologists call "relative deprivation" — that is, a sense of frustration measured not against the past but against the future, not in terms of how little people once had but of how much they now expect.

The electronic revolution can thus be counted on, for a time at least, to heighten the strains within the national community. In the short run, our internal schisms may grow worse rather than better. We have faced comparable crises twice before: in the eighteen-fifties and in the nineteen-thirties. In the eighteen-fifties the problem was intractable and the leadership feeble. The social tensions could not be contained within the democratic process; the result was national dissolution. In the nineteen-thirties, the problem, though deep and difficult, could yield to intelligent leadership, and the leadership was superb. Today we face a third time the problem of whether our inner tensions will burst the bonds of the democratic process and seek solution through secession (the black nationalists, the hippies) or violence. The answer to that problem lies in politics.

For, contrary to the dreams of those from Saint-Simon to Veblen who have supposed that technological change will convert political into technical problems, modern society will almost certainly continue to make its major decisions through political means. This will be as true of totalitarian as of democratic states. Totalitarianism may drive politics underground; but, as the experience of Nazi Germany and of communist Russia and China shows, this does not destroy politics; it only makes political struggle more desperate and murderous. And in democratic states — i.e., states where the rule of the majority is limited by the assurance to minorities of the freedom to convert themselves into new majorities — politics will continue paramount. The high-technology society will certainly increase the number of decisions taken on technical grounds; but, as more and more decisions are removed from the impersonal and quasi-automatic mechanisms of the market, the competition among social groups to influence and control the making of decisions will become more visible and therefore more acute.

American statecraft in the seventies will thus confront the problem of bringing estranged and excluded groups into the national community at a time of unprecedented technological change in a society dominated by great organizations and under constant threat of individual dislocation and social disruption. We shall therefore "have to test anew whether a nation organized and governed such as ours can endure." Why is the outcome by no means certain? One cause of the crisis of American confidence today is surely the nagging doubt whether our political leadership — whether, indeed, our political structure — will be adequate to the woes that beset us.

2. Enter the New Politics

Throughout American history the political problem has had a series of redefinitions at the hands of Presidents who responded decisively to the challenges of their generation. The last fundamental redefinition came from Franklin Roosevelt. He was the creative political genius of his age; and, in meeting the economic and social crisis of the Great Depression, he established the framework of thought and action which has more or less governed national politics ever since. He set the issues, delineated the constituencies and refined the techniques.

The Great Depression facilitated Roosevelt's task of political reconstruction; but at the same time it left its distinctive imprint on the substance of that reconstruction. For the New Deal was born in an age of scarcity. It emerged as a protest against the conservative doctrine of human impotence in face of economic crisis. Its concern was with the problems of a society that could not feed, clothe, house or employ all its people. It contended — and rightly, I believe — that the national government was the best instrument available to the people for reviving and reforming the stricken economy. And it rallied a coalition of trade unions, city machines, ethnic minorities, family farmers and intellectuals — a disparate and often diverging group, based on the poor and the uneducated and unified by FDR's political skill. It was this coalition that produced the vast rearrangement of political and economic power in the thirties. It was this coalition that, perhaps less from conviction about the policy than from confidence in the leader, supported the internationalist course in foreign affairs in the forties. And it was this coalition that made the Democratic party the majority party in the nation.

The New Deal coalition, its ideas, policies and methods, thus sprang from depression. But the United States has changed in the years since the thirties — in great part, because of the New Deal. Most strikingly, it has become an affluent society. Because our affluence is spread very unevenly, and because many New Deal ideas and policies were relevant not just to depression but to social decency, the New Deal approach had continuing contributions to make to the age of affluence. But the very success of New Deal policies began to undermine the New Deal coalition.

A sense of common desperation had created the original alliance; but, by using the affirmative state to protect jobs, homes, bank accounts and farm prices, by assuring compensation for the unemployed and pensions for the old, the New Deal reduced that sense of desperation. The component elements began to lose their early feeling of solidarity and to pursue their divergent interests. In 1952 the Republicans came back to Washington. It is true that this was less because of the popularity of the Republican party than because of the popularity of the Republican candidate. Yet something was changing in American politics. As one Democratic politician put it after the 1952 election, "The trouble is that we ran out of poor people." This was not, of course, true; for plenty of poor people remained in our society. But, unlike the ambitious immigrants of the eighteen-nineties or the politically aggressive unemployed of the nineteen-thirties, the poor of the fifties were all too often a demoralized and inarticulate minority who in many cases had inherited their poverty and passively accepted it as a permanent condition. As for the despairing job-seekers of the thirties, many were prosperous suburbanites by the fifties and the sixties. The "forgotten men" of FDR, as James Reston has pointed out, have become the "forgotten Americans" of Richard Nixon. Affluence thus tended to subvert the old New Deal coalition.

At the same time, the rise of the affluent society has given new questions prominence in our politics. The issues of the New Deal were fundamentally those of what might be called quantitative liberalism. The New Deal program tackled the elemental needs of the American people — a job, a suit of clothing, three meals a day, a roof over one's head and a measure of security for old age. Because the New Deal secured the material basis of life for so many, the issue of post-New Deal liberalism became less to raise the standard of living than to raise "the quality of life," a phrase first introduced into politics by Adlai Stevenson in 1956. Qualitative liberalism identified new areas for action — such areas as civil rights, civil liberties, education, the humanization of our cities, the relationship between life and environment, the state of the arts. Foreign policy, which until the end of the thirties was a subordinate and marginal consideration, became a central question. Moreover, as Simon Patten predicted half a century ago, the shift from a deficit to a surplus economy brought with it a transvaluation of values. Consumption began to become as important as production, leisure as important as work, self-fulfillment as important as economic discipline. The search for personal honesties in life might often seem (and often be) sheer hedonism and irresponsibility from the perspective of the Puritan ethic; but no one could doubt that a new mood — permissive rather than compulsive — was entering the American polity.

While affluence was thus thrusting forward new problems and values, the electronic revolution was beginning to have a startling impact on American politics. Changes in the means of communication — above all, the rise of television and of public opinion polls — hastened the decay of the traditional political structure. For a century a series of institutions — the political machine, the trade union, the farm organization, the ethnic federation — had mediated between the politician and the voter, passing back and forth between them and representing each to the other. But television started to change all this. Increasingly the voter began to base his judgment not on what his party boss or labor or farm or ethnic leader told him but on what Walter Cronkite and David Brinkley showed him.

One result has already been to sap the strength of the traditional mediating institutions and to begin the liquidation of the traditional brokers of American politics. Another has been to increase the sense of individual helplessness, since the broker can no longer serve as the voter's channel to government. The citizen can't argue with the image on the tiny screen, and all he has is the vague hope that he might some week be selected to register his views by George Gallup or Louis Harris. Soon candidates will be left to stand face to face with a diffused, frustrated and irritable public opinion. The Old Politics is now a self-perpetuating myth — a myth kept alive by the political professionals, who have a vested interest in its preservation, and by newspapermen, who spend most of their time interviewing political professionals.

The combination of the affluent society and the electronic revolution is bringing into existence what has come to be known as the New Politics. For politics in the thirties divided essentially according to the level of income. The poor demanded, and the rich opposed, that complex of measures which brought about so beneficial a redistribution of opportunity, income and power in American society. But new issues create a new order of battle. Quantitative liberalism appealed to those of low income; qualitative liberalism appeals to those of high education. The level of education has become increasingly the dividing line of the politics of the sixties as economic issues begin to yield to moral and cultural issues.

Consider such foreign policy questions as the Vietnam war, foreign aid, negotiated disarmament, East-West trade, admission of mainland China to the United Nations; consider such domestic questions as racial justice, open housing, civil liberties, students, law and order, federal aid to cities, federal aid to education, even air and water pollution, even cigarettes and billboards. On these issues, it is the less educated, low-income whites who tend to be the most emotional and primitive champions of conservatism — who want to crack down on the "niggers," imprison the long-haired college kids and bomb hell out of the North Vietnamese. The affluent and better educated, on the other hand, tend to care more about rationality, reform and progress. Louis Harris summed up the testimony of public opinion polls when he said recently, "The privileged have become the progenitors of change, while the underprivileged whites have become the steadfast defenders of the status quo."

The electronic revolution has meanwhile sharpened this change by creating a new constituency. For the fastest growing group in American society is the one defined by the Bureau of Labor Statistics as "professional, technical and kindred workers." In 1900 that group constituted 4 percent of the labor force and as late as 1940 less than 8 percent. Now it is about 12 percent, and it is continuing to increase at more than twice the average rate for other fields of employment. If one adds to this group the expanding proportion of those defined as "managers" and "officials" in the category "managers, officials and proprietors, excluding farm," one has a figure already approaching 20 percent of the labor force.

This is the group that J. K. Galbraith has called the "technostructure" — "all who bring specialized knowledge, talent or experience to group decision-making." They are predominantly college-educated (Louis Harris estimates that 28 percent of the electorate in 1968 went to college; by 1976 the figure should be more than 40 percent). They live predominantly in the suburbs (today more Americans live in suburbs than in the cities). If this professional-technical-managerial class is by no means unified in its views or values, its high level of education and aspiration creates both an active interest in issues and a formidable determination to take part in public affairs — and this at just the time that, as a consequence of the electronic revolution, the New Politics of instantaneous mass involvement is replacing the Old Politics of the mediating institutions. As more and more people go to college, we have never in our history (at least since the seventeen-nineties) had so large a proportion of well-informed, independent and (to use the jargon) "issue-oriented" voters, or so many eager to influence the course of events. This aggressive new constituency regards the old political establishment with mistrust and tends to respond to any candidate who sets himself against it. It has no great faith in parties and adores split tickets. It has endowed the New Politics with its distinctive goal — the goal of the broadest possible *participation* in the processes of national and social decision. It is this idea of participation which expresses the revolt against the great impersonal structures and which will probably provide the key to the reconciliation of the estranged and excluded groups with the national community.

It is important, I think, to distinguish the New Politics from the New Left (and from the New Right). The same conditions — the electronic revolution, the affluent society, the rise of the great organizations, the emergence of the technostructure, the decline of economic issues, the rise of moral and cultural issues — have produced the New Left and the New Right as well as the New Politics. Neither the New Left nor the New Right is a united or homogeneous movement. Each embraces a wide variety of people and doctrine. Within each there are strong disagreements over tactics and goals. Yet the New Left and, less clearly, the New Right share a common view: that is, that the American democratic process is corrupt and phony, that it cannot identify or solve the urgent problems and that American society as at present organized is inherently incapable of providing justice to the alienated groups — for the New Left, the poor, the blacks, the young, the intellectuals; for the New Right, the lower-middle-class whites.

In particular, the New Left and the New Right are agreed in their condemnation of the central institutions of American power, whether real (the national government), semi-mythical (the Establishment) or mythical (the power elite). However much they detest each other, the two extremisms have common methods and common targets. "The real enemy of the radical left in America," writes the New Left *Washington Free Press*, "is and always has been liberalism." Karl Hess, who as Senator Goldwater's speechwriter in 1964 reputedly wrote that "extremism in the defense of liberty is no vice," recently said, "I take my stand with the anti-authoritarians, and so does the New Left. . . . This is one of the reasons I find many of the statements and actions of SDS very satisfying."

It is a happy symbiosis. George Wallace needs Tom Hayden and Eldridge Cleaver; Tom Hayden and Eldridge Cleaver need George Wallace. As Hayden put it in Chicago in August 1968, "America is reaching a point of bankruptcy and decay so complete that only military tools can protect the political institutions. . . . As reform has failed, the reliance on police power has become more visible. . . . Our victory lies in progressively demystifying a false democracy, showing the organized violence underneath reformism and manipulation." This is exactly what Wallace requires for *his* followers; and Wallace's promise to save law and order by stationing paratroopers twelve feet apart on every block is exactly what Hayden and Cleaver require for *their* followers. Thus New Left and New Right verify each other's claims and witness each other's pretensions. For all their vast differences in values and objectives they end as tacit partners in a common assault on civility and democracy.

The idea of the New Politics is very different. The New

Politics acknowledges the existence and urgency of the questions that fill the extremists with apocalyptic despair. But it believes that these questions can be met and resolved by democratic means. The point of the New Politics is to force these questions on the national agenda — to make the party system recognize them, take account of them and move to meet them. Some individuals may waver, say, between the New Politics and the New Left, which is why the two are occasionally confused. But no one should ignore the fundamental and radical difference between, on the one hand, the determination to master and use the existing political system and, on the other, the determination to reject and overthrow that system. A test question would be whether the Vietnam war is seen as the result of particular decisions taken by particular men in a situation where other men might have taken other decisions; or whether it is seen as the predetermined expression of an evil system that would have imposed an imperialistic policy on whatever body of men sat in the councils of state.

Those who believe in the New Politics as against the new extremisms have one salient advantage — that is, that in the past the American democratic tradition has shown sufficient resilience and initiative to meet urgent problems. The power of this democratic tradition is still very considerable. It is felt, I believe, by all the disaffected groups; all would prefer to preserve the process of peaceful change. This is demonstrated by the alacrity with which these groups, given half a chance, respond to leadership which seeks to fulfill their objectives within that process. Walt Whitman well expressed the common sense of American democracy: "It is the fashion among dilettants and fops to decry the whole formulation of the active politics of America, as beyond redemption, and to be carefully kept away from. See that you do not fall into this error. America, it may be, is doing very well upon the whole, notwithstanding these antics of the parties, and their leaders, these half-brain'd nominees, and many ignorant ballots, and many elected failures and blatherers. It is the dillettants, and all who shirk their duty, who are not doing well. As for you, I advise you to enter more strongly into politics. I advise every young man to do so. Always inform yourself, always do the best you can; always vote."

The New Left and the New Right exist and, to some degree, prosper because the Old Politics has failed to provide the leadership and programs that would meet the real issues in American society. The question is whether the New Politics can bring about for the seventies the reconstruction of our politics that Franklin Roosevelt brought about for the thirties. Doubts about the answer to this question contribute to the crisis of national self-confidence.

3. *Jefferson vs. Hamilton*

The idea of participation obviously implies decentralization in the making of decisions and as great a shift as possible from national toward local control. This prospect has great appeal to all those frustrated by the Old Politics. It appeals to the New Right as the means of reestablishing states rights, putting blacks in their place and stopping government regulation of business. It appeals to the New Left as the means of turning the ghettos over to the blacks, the schools to the parents, the antipoverty programs to the poor and the universities to the students. And it appeals to the followers of the New Politics as the means of bringing government back to human size, restoring the vitality of democracy and releasing the diverse energies of creativity in the land.

Participation and decentralization have many aspects. In France, for example, workers in the euphoria of June 1968 sought a voice in management. Oddly enough, not even the New Left in the United States has shown much interest in participation and decentralization in industry. Here government, and especially the national government, has been the principal target.

The New Deal a generation ago brought about a striking centralization of power and decision in Washington. This was essential given the urgent need for reform and recovery in the Great Depression. It was inevitably strengthened by the Second World War. But the centralizing impulses of the New Deal should not be exaggerated. Roosevelt himself, while he wanted national authority to meet national problems, well understood the values of diversity and local experiment. He took care to incorporate debate in the center of government by surrounding himself with strong men urging a variety of approaches and views. He introduced forms of popular referendum into his agricultural programs and his labor policies. The industrial side of the First New Deal represented an attempt to bring about industrial self-government; the industrial side of the Second New Deal represented an effort to restore free competition. In neither phase did the New Deal propose centralized industrial planning. David Lilienthal's conception in the Tennessee Valley Authority of "grassroots democracy" — the "decentralized administration of centralized authority" — expressed a fundamental part of the New Deal philosophy.

Nonetheless, the New Deal years undoubtedly encouraged Americans to turn to Washington for solutions. They also left a legacy in the forms of federal controls — controls which, when institutionalized and bureaucratized, began to lose contact with local needs and feelings. In time, this led to a tendency to make decisions that had local impact without consulting local wishes. Conservatives had long inveighed against New Deal centralization; after a generation, many liberals, when they inspected the ossified remains of the New Deal in, for example, the welfare and farm programs, started to take up the cry. In the thirties, the right used to quote Jefferson: "Were we directed from Washington when to sow, and when to reap, we should soon want bread." In the sixties the same quotation began to fall from the lips of the left.

The recoil against centralization is the contemporary expression of an old argument in American democracy — essentially the argument Hamilton and Jefferson started in the first decade of the republic. Hamilton, of course, insisted on the indispensability of affirmative central authority to advance the national welfare at home and the national interest abroad; Jefferson on the indispensability of the distribution of power, local control and individual liberty. Actually this was less an argument of principle than of emphasis. Both men, in their ways, were right. Most of our great Presidents — Jefferson himself, Jackson, Lincoln, Wilson, Franklin Roosevelt, Kennedy — were at once Jeffersonians and Hamiltonians. Together the two views represent the systole and diastole of American democracy, and each has served historically as the corrective of the other.

In this century Herbert Croly, reacting against the governmental impotence of the McKinley years, defended the Hamiltonian view. "Hamilton's policy was one of energetic and intelligent assertion of the national good. . . . Jefferson's policy was at bottom the old fatal policy of drift." Then, against Theodore Roosevelt, probably the only unqualified Hamiltonian to sit in the White House, Wilson revived the Jeffersonian thesis that (as stated by Croly) "the vitality of a democracy resided in its extremities, and it would be diminished rather than increased by specialized or centralized guidance." As Croly had reinforced Roosevelt's views, so Louis D. Brandeis reinforced Wilson's; and the rival theses warred against each other once more in the nineteen-thirties, where the First New Deal in a sense expressed the spirit of Hamilton/Roosevelt/Croly and the Second the spirit of Jefferson/Wilson/Brandeis. The most assiduous proponent of the Jeffersonian view in the New Deal was Felix Frankfurter. There is an historical felicity in the fact that the most thoughtful and eloquent advocate of this view today is a former law clerk of Justice Frankfurter's, Richard N. Goodwin.

The contemporary revival of the ideas of participation and decentralization began in the years after the Second World War. It showed itself first of all, I think, in the unexpected improvement in city government. In 1888 Bryce had pronounced municipal government to be "the one conspicuous failure of the United States," and there had seemed little reason to quarrel with this judgment in subsequent years. In the nineteen-thirties, when I went to college, few students attended courses on municipal government, and no one would have dreamed on graduation of preferring city hall to Washington. Yet, beginning in the forties, a number of very able men became mayors of leading cities. Today, in the main, city government shows more imagination and vitality than state government, and bright students would rather work for John Lindsay or Kevin White than for Richard Nixon.

Then the Eisenhower administration came to office committed to the notion of decentralization. The vision of transferring countless federal functions to the states was close to Eisenhower's heart; and, when his Commission on Intergovernmental Relations failed to come up with a comprehensive program for such transfers, he appealed personally in 1957 to the Governors' Conference for action. After working for a year, the resulting committee of governors and federal officials could find only two minor programs, costing $80 million, to recommend for transfer from federal to state hands. For the rest, the Eisenhower administration did succeed in turning over the offshore oil lands to the states and valuable power sites to private corporations. This formalistic approach to decentralization proved ineffective; and it certainly failed to satisfy the desire of anyone, except bankers, oilmen and private utilities, for participation.

As usual, a liberal Administration proved more adept at innovation, even for what had been assumed to be a conservative objective. The particular champion of decentralization in the Kennedy years was Robert F. Kennedy, then Attorney General. Using the President's Committee on Juvenile Delinquency as his instrument, Kennedy stimulated cities to come up with coordinated plans to help boys and girls in the slums; and, to make sure that these would not just be schemes benevolently imposed by social workers and welfare agencies, he insisted on bringing the poor into planning and execution. This experience fostered the concepts

of "community action" and the "maximum feasible participation" which later entered President Johnson's war against
poverty. Moreover, in the Johnson years, the so-called Heller
plan, envisaging a distribution of federal tax funds to the
states, offered a fruitful new approach to the problem of decentralization. The Johnson Model Cities program requires
slum residents to vote on plans to rebuild their neighborhood
and provides for their participation in carrying out such plans.

This piecemeal devolution of national functions has been
accompanied by a new statement of the Jefferson-Brandeis
philosophy. Central direction cannot do so much as we think,
Richard Goodwin writes, because the problems "are far too
large for the limited abilities of a few administrators." We
must therefore allow "communities, private groups, cities,
and states to make public decisions that are now vested in
the central government. . . . *The general guide should be
to transfer power to the smallest unit consistent with the scale
of the problem.*"

This has undoubted appeal as a principle. But it assumes
that the governmental unit "closest" to the people is more
likely to act for the general welfare than the more remote
unit. This assumption, alas, is hardly borne out by experience,
which of course is why the national government has steadily
acquired power through American history. The local unit,
unless carefully redefined, tends to be controlled by the local
rich, not by the local poor. It is often the last stronghold of
reaction. What would happen, for example, to the Bill of
Rights, to racial justice or to the conservation of natural resources if communities, private groups, cities and states were
to make the decisions now vested in the central government?
Segregation was one of the prices Lilienthal paid for the
decentralization of TVA. Do we have an indefinite supply

of men strong enough in their localities to withstand the pressure of powerful local interests? And do we have an indefinite supply of men devoted enough in their localities to resist the temptation of money flowing through their hands? The difficulties of the Human Resources Administration in New York City are hardly encouraging.

Mr. Goodwin correctly warns that decentralization will not mean any decline in national spending, nor can it be permitted to mean "the absence of rigorous national standards for the use of national revenues." But does not this take us back to the New Deal doctrine of "decentralized administration of centralized authority"? It is important, I think, not to go overboard on Jeffersonianism in a day when the neighborhood is no longer a self-sufficient unit. Centralization is not only necessary to set standards. It is also less vulnerable to selfish local pressures; it offers greater flexibility in the transfer of resources; and it assures the most economical use of trained and specialized public personnel. The growth of central power in this century, far from diminishing the significance of the individual citizen, has given a majority of individuals — workers, Negroes, members of other ethnic minorities, even intellectuals — much more significance than they would otherwise have possessed. It has been the national government that has strengthened individual rights against state and local governments as well as against concentrations of private power — whether in the legal (collective bargaining, equal rights) or the economic domain. The individual freedoms destroyed in this century by the increase in national authority have been, in the main, the freedom to loot and waste our national resources, the freedom to deny a tenth of the nation their rights as citizens, the freedom to work small children in the mills and immigrants in the sweat-

shops, the freedom to pay starvation wages and require barbarous working hours, the freedom to deceive in advertising
and in the sale of securities — all freedoms that, one supposes, a decent country can easily do without. Nor can
it be said that the increase in national authority has weak-
ened local government. As noted earlier, local government
today is greatly more honest, aggressive and imaginative than
it was in the nineteenth century, when national authority was
considerably weaker.

This does not mean that the pressure for decentralization
is not healthy. Mr. Goodwin is surely right in saying that the
national government has tried to do too much. And it certainly does not mean that such pressure represents an anachronistic reversion to Jeffersonian simplicities. For the electronic revolution itself, by transforming the modes of calculation and communication, makes the coordinated devolution
of authority far more feasible than it has ever been before.
The computer, with its provision for instantaneous feedback
and self-correction, will, when applied to social decisions,
both increase the capacity of a system for self-regulation and
widen the potential representation of the individual in the
process; it will solve many technical problems in both decentralization and participation. American politicians have not
yet tried to figure out the impact of cybernetics on democracy; but they should ponder the observation of Anthony
Wedgwood Benn, Minister of Technology in the British La-
bour government: "The evolution of modern management
science will ultimately allow every single individual to be taken
into full account in the evolution of social planning, taxation
and social security policy."

Yet, in other respects, the logic of science and industry is toward centralization; and the theory of decentralization must be much more carefully thought out than it has been up to now if the individual is to have a genuine voice. Participation that turns out to be only decorative and symbolic would increase the sense of frustration. Decentralization that would simply turn power over to state and local governments and to private business (including, it should be added, the recent fad of private business management of public programs) — decentralization on the Eisenhower-Goldwater model — would be retrogressive, and very often wasteful and corrupting. If democratic participation is the objective, decentralization on the Lilienthal model is infinitely more promising and should be imaginatively explored.

Most promising of all, from the viewpoint of direct participation, is the Robert Kennedy model, which involves not a resort to the state and municipal political units that had so long toadied to the local moguls but the creation of "new community institutions that local residents control and through which they can express their wishes." Such new institutions, Kennedy hoped, could build "self-sufficiency and self-determination within the communities of poverty," help the poor shape their own destiny and bring "not just individual residents but the entire community into the mainstream of American life." For Kennedy, the community-development corporation was one chosen instrument. Of course, such corporations could not succeed without federal support, including direct investment as well as tax credits for firms moving into poverty areas. But the vital aspect was the enlistment of the concern of the ghetto, along with the capital of the surrounding community, in the effort at regeneration. He showed what he meant in 1966 when he organized two corporations — one composed of residents of Bedford-Stuyvesant, the second largest black ghetto in the country, the other of august New York financiers — to work together for the humanization of life in a sad and wasted New York enclave. The community-development corporation as such is appropriate only to a particular range of problems; but steps toward community control of schools, police and so on would seem to offer paths for discriminating exploration.

Decentralization can easily become, as with the New Right and the New Left, a demagogic crusade against the national government. But the New Politics, I take it, would join decentralization with a wise use of the national authority. This could well lead to a burst of administrative and institutional invention that could do much to combat the conviction of powerlessness in the high-technology society and to bring all our citizens into vital relation with the national community. And, if we deny all legitimate demand for reasonable participation, we are going to force the passion for participation into illegitimate and destructive outlets.

4. Before 1968

The New Politics, I have suggested, is the expression of an emerging national mood created by the electronic and organizational revolutions, the affluent society, the emergence of the technostructure, the decline of economic issues, the rise of moral and cultural issues. Its distinctive impulse is the passion for greater participation in the decisions which determine one's life. For most of those swayed by the New Politics, the critical issue was the Vietnam war — a war that by 1968 had reached proportions which no one outside the National Security Council could remember ever having voted for or been consulted about. The war seemed to compress in itself the secretiveness and dissimulation that made a New Politics imperative. (For those on the right who shared the contempt for the Old Politics and the new passion for self-determination, the critical issue was the Negro revolution which they, for their part, could not remember having voted for or been consulted about.)

Because it represented a national mood, the New Politics began to speak through both major parties (as well as, in distorted and deranged ways, through the New Right and the New Left). It had its greater impact, though, in the Democratic party. This was natural enough. It is an axiom of American history that the great political debates tend to take place first within the majority party. Only if the majority party shows itself incapable of dealing with urgent national issues does the minority party have a serious chance to create a new majority. So the debate over slavery tore the Whig party to pieces in the eighteen-fifties and enabled the Republicans to establish a new political consensus; so too the expulsion from the Republican party in 1912 of its progressive wing prevented the Republicans from meeting the problems of social justice in an industrial society and gave Franklin Roosevelt his opportunity to devise new programs and make the Democrats a new majority party.

This does not mean, of course, that minority parties do not experience their own inner debates between the stand-patters and the modernizers. As men like W. H. Seward had tried to make the old Whig party face up to the problems identified by Jackson, so in the last thirty years liberal Republicans have tried to make their party face up to the issues identified by FDR. And they have been just enough more successful than Seward to keep their party in intermittent connection with the vital issues of the age.

Both parties, then, have had to wrestle with the implications of the recent revolution in political issues and techniques. Yet in each party the pull of the past has been very great. Like all human institutions, political parties tend to cling to accustomed ways of perceiving and doing things. Moreover, older men, which means men whose ideas were formed in another time and often in a rural environment, tend through the sheer attrition of seniority to occupy positions of authority in a political party. This is notably true, of course, of Congress, which is why (to adopt James Mac-Gregor Burns's useful distinction) the congressional wings of each major party tend to be more standpat than the presidential wings.

The inherent conservatism of political organizations thereby increased the gap between the Old Politics and the new times. In the case of the Democratic party, the coalition put together by Roosevelt in the thirties was in trouble by the sixties. The city machines had mostly fallen into disrepair. (Chicago was almost the last remaining example of the old-fashioned boss; perhaps the Daley organization should be preserved in the Museum of Natural History — or, since it is a machine, in the Museum of Science and Technology.) Trade union membership had declined both relatively and absolutely; by 1968, only about one fifth of the labor force was organized and, in any case, labor leaders could no longer reliably deliver a labor vote. The south was straggling — in many instances, rushing — out of the party. The ethnic minorities had been turned against each other by the Negro revolution. The intellectuals were disaffected. The combination of the new, noneconomic issues with the new means of mass communication was subjecting the New Deal coalition to severe strain. It would have required creative political genius equal to that of Franklin Roosevelt's to reconstruct and revitalize that coalition.

I have no doubt that President Kennedy had precisely that genius and was well on his way to finding new terms for old alliances when tragedy terminated his gallant life. It is an irony of history that his successor, Lyndon Johnson, a devoted son of the New Deal, should have administered the *coup de grâce* to the New Deal coalition. In domestic affairs President Johnson's vision of the Great Society offered genuine promise of reconstituting the old alliances. But he nullified this wise and admirable effort by his policies in foreign affairs and by his attitudes toward the national Democratic party.

The traditional foreign policy of the Democratic party — the policy of Wilson, Roosevelt, Stevenson and Kennedy — has been a policy that united realism and idealism. These leaders acquired their great influence around the planet because they understood that a fundamental component of national power is the capacity to move the conscience and reason of the world. The traditional foreign policy of the Republican party, on the other hand, has been to deprecate the relevance of world opinion and to base American policy rather exclusively on the theory that military power is the only thing the other side understands. In Vietnam, the Dominican Republic and elsewhere, President Johnson, by casting the United States in the role of an international bully, rejected the traditional foreign policy of the Democratic party in favor of the traditional foreign policy of the Republicans.

In so doing, he badly confused his own party, leaving it torn between loyalty to the Democratic President and loyalty to historic Democratic principles. After holding out his splendid conception of the Great Society with its promise of justice to the poor and the blacks, he now proceeded to sacrifice the Great Society to a squalid and irrelevant war. Vietnam was the essential cause of the Democratic defeat in 1968; and the men who persuaded President Johnson that he should embark on the course of military escalation were the men directly responsible for that defeat. In particular, the Vietnam blunder drove the intellectual community into opposition to the Democratic administration. For better or worse, intellectuals in our society wield a political influence out of all proportion to the votes they cast. No Democratic President of this century has been elected without their active and enthusiastic support. The intellectuals in the thirties had been the lynchpin of Franklin Roosevelt's coalition. In estranging them, Lyndon Johnson hastened the demoralization and intensified the crisis of the Democratic party.

Nor could the President save the party by other means. A supreme congressional politician, President Johnson was an incompetent and ineffective national politician. This should not have been too surprising. After all, he had had experience in only two national campaigns: one, when he was the vice presidential candidate; the other, when he was running for President against a man Noam Chomsky could have beaten. In his political instincts, Johnson was more a South American *caudillo* than a North American leader. He had little knowledge of the Democratic party outside the south, little understanding of the forces that animated and inspired it, indeed little interest in its national organization. In the Johnson years, for example, the White House systematically snubbed, spurned and starved the Democratic National Committee. Nor could personal magnetism compensate for party disorganization. The President as a man impressed increasing numbers of Americans as high-handed, devious and disingenuous, the embodiment of a political system that willfully deceived the people and denied them a voice in vital decisions. The President's personal compulsions completed the crisis of the party.

The New Politics was now on the march. The vital question in 1967 was whether the goal of political participation could be pursued within the established political process. The Democratic party of Lyndon Johnson seemed impenetrable; the Republican party of Barry Goldwater and Everett Dirksen unimaginable. The young saw the institutions of American society as organized to shut them out; and the more radical among them began to conclude that exclusion was inevitable in a system controlled, as they believed, by a military-industrial complex. Thus Mark Rudd of the Columbia SDS viewed the war in Vietnam "as an inherent part of the political-economic system that dominates our country." As the estrangement grew more acute and embittered, the more romantic or irrational students began, with sublime unrealism, to speculate about destroying the system through violent revolution.

5. The 1968 Election

This was the situation at the start of 1968. Then in March the New Hampshire primary took place. The nation owes a good deal, I think, to Senator Eugene McCarthy for his demonstration that protest had means of expression within the democratic process. McCarthy's first cause was rationality in Vietnam; but he soon moved beyond this to touch the larger issue of the reassertion of popular control. He coolly attacked the institutions which seemed to deny men mastery over their own lives — the Pentagon, the military-industrial complex, the selective service system, the Federal Bureau of Investigation, even the political machines of his own party. He communicated to people, especially on the campuses and in the suburbs, the idea that it was (I quote Richard Goodwin) "within their power to bring about change." And he displayed himself as entirely his own man in the teeth of the consumer society, unwilling to say a word or make a gesture false to himself for the sake of the mass media.

After New Hampshire, the revolt of the New Politics was strengthened by the decision of Robert Kennedy to enter the contest. Kennedy had been against the war a good deal earlier and more sharply than McCarthy; and he added another essential part of the New Politics to which McCarthy, before 1968, had been indifferent — that is, the need for self-determination by the poor and the blacks. The New Politics scored its first triumph when, two weeks after Kennedy's declaration, President Johnson withdrew from the presidential contest and ended the escalation in Vietnam.

The murder of Robert Kennedy removed the ablest and most powerful leader of the New Politics. But the protest continued to seek outlets within the process — behind McCarthy and later George McGovern in the Democratic party; and, in the absence of its natural leader, John Lindsay, behind Nelson Rockefeller in the Republican party. In the end, though, neither party rose to the challenge. Both conventions selected men of the past — men whose minds had been formed a generation ago and who tended to see the nineteen-seventies in the image of the nineteen-forties. Both candidates represented the Old Politics, and their designations accentuated the sense of mass frustration, a condition dramatized in the disorders of the last days of the Democratic convention.

Among the intellectuals the reaction, for a season, was disgust and withdrawal. Among the nonintellectuals the reaction, for a season, was a drift to the only remaining means of registering protest against the Old Politics — that is, by supporting George Wallace. Commentators expressed astonishment that men and women who had been for Kennedy or McCarthy in March were for Wallace in September; but no one should have been all that surprised. The Wallace effort for a moment moved beyond its racist base and became a repository for general resentment and rancor throughout the land.

In the meantime, the major party campaign was markedly vacuous. Mr. Nixon, by evident design, waged a campaign of mechanical banality and evasion. This was intended, of course, to minimize the risk of saying anything that might offend anybody; and in the end his anticampaign worked, though only barely. Mr. Humphrey, carrying the burden of an unpopular President, an unpopular administration and an unpopular war, seemed for a while frantic and ineffectual.

The closeness of the contest may be attributed in the short run, I believe, to a conflict between two fundamental principles of American politics. One principle has long since been formulated: it is TURN THE RASCALS OUT. If a party has done badly in office, the sound reaction of the American voter is to give the opposition a chance. The Johnson administration had permitted the American involvement in Vietnam to deepen and harden beyond any rational justification. It hardly seemed that the men who plunged us deeper and deeper into the Vietnamese futility should be rewarded by reelection. Many voters felt — and understandably so — that the Democrats simply did not deserve four more years of power.

This was one instinct at work in the electorate. But it was countered by another instinct. This second principle has not been so clearly formulated as the first; but it can be expressed, I think, somewhat as follows: HUMAN BEINGS ARE BETTER THAN MECHANICAL MEN. The fact that this principle has not been formulated should not lead anyone to underestimate its potency. In alliance with the first principle, it led to Franklin Roosevelt's decisive victory over Herbert Hoover in 1932 — the victory that established the Democratic party as the majority party for more than a generation. And, when the two principles came into conflict in 1948, the second overcame the first; the electorate in the end, despite dissatisfactions with his administration, chose the vivid and fallible humanity of Harry S. Truman over the unctuous calculation of his opponent. The two principles were again in conflict in this election. As the campaign wore drearily on, more and more voters were obviously beginning to be depressed by the idea of a mechanical man in the White

House. As each week went by, moreover, Hubert Humphrey was more himself. He began to emerge at last from under his burden, to speak with his own voice and seem at last his own man. As he did this, he started to win back the trade unionists from Wallace and the intellectuals from apathy. Had there been another week — perhaps another seventy-two hours — he would probably have won the election.

In the short run, this conflict of political instinct helped shape the 1968 result. And, though the election hardly grappled with the issues raised by the New Politics, it did not altogether fail as an educational experience. While the candidates did little positive to clarify issues, the voters themselves began to crystallize their judgments in the course of the year, and the candidates had at least the sense to acquiesce. There is no more astute observer of political tendencies than Samuel Lubell; and I am impressed by the conclusion Mr. Lubell reached on the eve of the election. "On the two most emotional issues — Vietnam and our racial crisis," Mr. Lubell wrote, " — my interviewing does indicate that the campaign has gained general public acceptance for policies which in time could unify the country."

On Vietnam, the electorate impressed on the parties the growing demand that we bring a hopeless war to an end and withdraw our military forces from the mainland of Asia. In the past Mr. Humphrey had been a steadfast supporter of President Johnson's policy of military escalation, and Mr. Nixon's only disagreement had been that President Johnson did not escalate fast enough. Yet both candidates — Mr. Nixon by silence and Mr. Humphrey by declaration — seemed to agree with the growing conviction that we must de-escalate the war and move as soon as possible toward a negotiated settlement.

As for racial justice, the Wallace movement may have had the useful effect of making many voters think about the consequences of their prejudices. Wallace tempted them for a while; but then in the end they drew back, and Wallace's appeal contracted rather swiftly to the lower Confederacy. Probably Mr. Lubell is also right in suggesting that "the strength of Wallace's backing . . . shocked many liberals and Negroes into realizing that excesses on the Negro side have to be curbed." In any case, I would agree with his conclusion that "the preponderant part of the electorate, in most of the South as well as in the North, is prepared to support a 'middle course' policy that would curb racial violence while still continuing Negro progress."

This clarification of national opinion is an immense gain. But it expressed the process of democracy rather than the leadership of the candidates; and this implies a dangerous disconnection between politicians and reality — a disconnection which, if continued, will encourage further secession from the democratic system. The lasting answer to this disconnection can only lie in moving beyond the Old Politics and making our major parties responsive to the issues and the methods of the nineteen-seventies.

In the perspective of history, the 1968 election may well go down as the last hurrah of the Old Politics of this period — as, say, the 1928 election in retrospect was the last hurrah of the Old Politics of the twenties. And, as the 1928 election foreshadowed the political developments of the next decade — for example, in the rising Democratic strength in the cities — so the 1968 election may, if we read it aright, tell us something about the shape of American politics to come.

Two questions will be decisive. The first is: Will the major parties now start to do what they failed to do in 1968 —

will they understand and accept the political imperatives of the new age? If they fail to do this, then we can expect a serious growth among both the New Right and the New Left, nominally at each other's throats but each feeding on the existence of the other and both united in their desire to abolish the institutions of accommodation in our society. But, if the major parties succeed in the task of modernizing their ideas and methods, then we can hope to continue to fight out our battles within the political system, as, except for the Civil War, we have done throughout our history.

The second question is less important but still not altogether devoid of interest. It is: Which party will create the framework for the politics of the coming time, as Franklin Roosevelt's Democratic party created the framework for the politics of his time? Each party, it should be noted, has its assets in the contest for the future.

6. *The Republican Response*

The great Republican asset is the possession of the Presidency. For the Presidency is the most influential office in the land; there is no better vantage point from which to bring a new political consensus into existence. The problem is whether the new Republican President has the imagination or the desire to do this. The Republican party has at this moment a great opportunity to return to its early and best traditions — the traditions of Abraham Lincoln and Theodore Roosevelt. This liberal generation has tended to write off the Republican party as constitutionally devoid of intelligence and initiative; and, indeed, the record of the last half century would go far to sustain this judgment. Yet one must not forget that, when an alliance of Conscience Whigs and Jacksonian Democrats formed the Republican party more than a century ago and when Lincoln became the first Republican President, it was a broadly based party devoted to the cause of human freedom. Nor should one forget that sixty years ago, when men like Theodore Roosevelt and Robert M. La Follette were Republican leaders, the Republican party was in the forefront of the struggle for progressive reform.

Moreover, the shift from quantitative to qualitative issues — from the economic conflict of the thirties to the cultural conflict of our own day — is sociologically favorable to Republican prospects. The Republican party, after all, is the party of the more affluent and therefore of the better- (or at least the longer-) educated. It has a natural base in the suburbs and the technostructure. It has a collection of young and attractive leaders. Will it now be able to seize the leadership of the New Politics?

"The Republican party," Nelson Rockefeller said in the primaries, "must become again a national party, the voice of the poor and the oppressed." To do this, it would have to embrace the ethnic minorities; it would have to welcome the Negro; it would have to fight for civil rights and civil liberties. It would have to believe in the national government, like Hamilton, as well as in localism, like Jefferson; it would have to contend for federal aid to education, like Lincoln, and for federal protection of natural resources, like Theodore Roosevelt. With Roosevelt, it would have to say: "The more we condemn unadulterated Marxian Socialism, the stouter should be our insistence on thoroughgoing social reforms." Above all, it would have to renounce the theory that the only freedom worth worrying about is the freedom of businessmen to make money, and that the only people worth listening to are those who have made a great deal of money. Again TR provides an instructive text:

> We stand equally against government by a plutocracy and government by a mob. There is something to be said for government by a great aristocracy which has furnished leaders to the nation in peace and war for generations; even a democrat like myself must admit this. But there is absolutely nothing to be said for government by a plutocracy, for government by men very powerful in certain lines and gifted with "the money touch," but with ideals which in their essence are merely those of so many glorified pawnbrokers.

Can President Nixon do such things? Can he avail himself of his quite extraordinary opportunity to reconstruct his party and form a new majority coalition? Perhaps he can. No one can predict the impact of ultimate responsibility: the chemistry of the Presidency can turn routine politicians into purposeful leaders, as in the cases of Polk and Truman, as it can turn eminent public figures into gloomy losers, as in the cases of Buchanan and Hoover. In addition, forecasters may be not only fallible but prejudiced. I had certainly better declare my own interest: my enthusiasm for Mr. Nixon has always been well under control, and I strongly opposed his election.

Yet it is only realistic to recognize that President Nixon stands a chance of pulling it off. In the end, it depends in great part on his own perception of his problem. He has always been an unpredictable and elusive figure. Part of this elusiveness lies, I think, in a remarkable fact about him: that is, his rootlessness. Nearly every other American President has had sturdy roots geographically and socially — Johnson in Texas feudalism, Kennedy in eastern patrician life, Eisenhower in the military world, Truman in the middle border and so on. In contrast, Mr. Nixon, born in California, trained to the law in North Carolina, lately resident in New York, elected to the Vice Presidency from one state and to the Presidency from another, a boy from the lower middle class who has made good, seems sectionless and classless. His nearest equivalents are the British political leaders Harold Wilson and Edward Heath. Nixon, Wilson and Heath are all products of the mobility of the new technical society: and they carry a special appeal to those other rootless, sectionless, classless, mobile "new" men who inhabit the suburbs and the technostructure.

The technostructure has, of course, its hip wing which in the main followed Senator McCarthy in 1968. But its square majority in the suburban foxholes saw themselves contentedly, if not quite ecstatically, in Mr. Nixon. The highly programmed character of the Nixon campaign faithfully expressed the technical virtuosity of the new men, as the campaign's intellectual emptiness reflected their conviction that technique matters more than substance. Mostly salaried employees, moving from one place to another at the organization's behest, they are beset by taxes, mortgages, installment debt, social permissiveness, rebellious children and racial integration. In the campaign Mr. Nixon called them "the forgotten people . . . those who are not breaking the law, those who do pay taxes, those who do go to work, those who do support their churches and their schools." These "forgotten Americans," he said, "finally have become angry . . . because they love America and don't like what has been happening to America for the last four years."

These angry people give Mr. Nixon both his peculiar constituency and his signal opportunity. He came from among them, and his closest associates are men, like himself, who sprang from the lower middle class and made it in a big way. The "forgotten Americans" have a basic role in the quest for national reconciliation. As Eisenhower, if only by not doing anything about it, persuaded the business community to accept the New Deal, and as Johnson did his mighty best to persuade the south to accept racial justice, will Nixon bend his energies to persuading the disgruntled white lower middle class to accept the imperatives of modern life? If he is able to do this, he would do a good deal to diminish internal tensions, even if he were not able to do much else to bring the estranged and excluded groups into the national community.

It will not be easy. For one thing, action to propitiate the other alienated groups may intensify the disaffection of the white lower middle class. Though social mobility is fine, it sometimes exists at the cost of a sense of inner identity. Rootless people are often quick to feel angry and threatened. Mr. Nixon has not been entirely exempt from such feelings himself. When the American Communist party named its youth clubs after W. E. B. DuBois, the black historian, Mr. Nixon was sure the name was chosen because it sounded like the Boys' Club of America; this, he solemnly said, was "an almost classic example of Communist deception and duplicity." Whether or not this is so, it is certainly an almost classic example of Nixon's style of thought. And he said this not in his campaign against Helen Gahagan Douglas but as late as 1966.

In particular, Mr. Nixon seems obsessed with the problem of his own response to crisis. This is an odd concern. When crisis came, the Roosevelts and the Kennedys simply met it with patrician nonchalance; these were the expected tests of life, not worth the fuss of extended introspection. Nor did crisis, as such, ever worry such solidly rooted figures as Truman or Eisenhower. But Mr. Nixon has always worried; he even wrote a book called *Six Crises*, as if to find out, or prove, something about himself. He kept himself under wraps in the campaign. Only time and crisis will tell whether he has mastered himself in the face of pressure, tension and fatigue. Only his own skill and perseverance as a leader will decide whether the Republican party will continue to be, as Emerson once said of the Whigs, the "shop-and-till party" —

> timid, and merely defensive of property. It vindicates no right, it aspires to no real good, it brands no crime, it proposes no generous policy, it does not build, nor write, nor cherish the arts, nor foster religion, nor establish schools, nor encourage science, nor emancipate slaves, nor befriend the poor, or the Indian, or the immigrant.

7. The Democratic Response

It is possible, then, that the Republicans may forfeit the enormous advantage the Presidency could give them in the contest for the political leadership of the seventies. What about the Democrats? They lack, of course, the strategic advantage of the Presidency. On the other hand, they control Congress; they remain the majority party in the country; they are the natural home for the estranged and excluded groups. Freedom from power offers them a rare chance to contemplate their situation, think out their problems, reformulate their issues and open their places of leadership to young and unconventional men.

It can be said, I think, that Democrats are offered three different approaches to the job of reconstruction. These can be called the Humphrey way, the McCarthy way and the Kennedy way.

The Humphrey way is self-evident: it is to insist that the Old Politics is alive and well — and in America. I do not mean that this is the way Hubert Humphrey would necessarily have chosen if he had had a free choice. He is a sensitive and intelligent man who in other circumstances might conceivably have led the opposition within the party to the Johnson administration and the war. But he became a prisoner of the Vice Presidency; and he was also the prisoner of an old-fashioned personal style that seemed clamorous and archaic on the new medium. In any case, by 1968 he had no choice but to string along with the traditional middlemen — that is, with the bureaucracies of political organizations, of labor organizations, of farm organizations, of ethnic organizations. The result was an apparent effort to preserve the façade of the Roosevelt coalition without, it would seem, worrying too much about the mind and the soul. The hard question, of course, is whether the old bureaucracies can rally their constituencies any longer. The 1968 election does not decisively settle this question, though I am myself inclined to attribute Humphrey's last-minute surge less to the effectiveness of the power brokers than to the liberation of Humphrey himself and his subsequent capacity to move into the politics of mass involvement — this and the aid he got from practitioners of the New Politics after he finally modified his position on Vietnam sufficiently to enable them to enter his campaign.

If one is right in feeling that the Old Politics has run its course, the future would lie between the McCarthy and Kennedy ways. It should have been evident from the frictions of the primaries that these ways are not identical. Now that we can look back at the primaries with a measure of detachment, let us understand that, while Eugene McCarthy and Robert Kennedy agreed on the supreme issue of Vietnam, they emphatically disagreed on two other issues of more enduring importance. They disagreed on their conceptions of the Democratic coalition, and they disagreed on their conceptions of the Presidency. These issues may sound abstract. But they very possibly go to the heart of the question of the future of the Democratic party.

I have said that the nation owes a great deal to Senator McCarthy. His courage in entering the contest against President Johnson on the issue of Vietnam broke the ice-jam in the Democratic party and set free a flood of popular feeling that marvelously changed the politics of 1968. Senator McCarthy is a thoughtful and perceptive man. He saw why the Old Politics would no longer work. He accepted the conclusion that the level of education had superseded the level of income as the dividing line in our public affairs. Noting the steady decay of the alliance of the educated few and the uneducated many which Franklin Roosevelt had put together in the thirties, noting too the steady expansion of the technostructure, McCarthy would seem to have decided that the future required a new alliance which would now be founded on the educated many.

Some have said that the difference between the Old Politics and the New lies in the fact that Old Politicians, like Humphrey, see America as made up of interest groups while New Politicians, like McCarthy, see America as made up of individuals. One wonders whether this is really so. Surely James Madison was everlastingly right in the Tenth *Federalist* when he said that interest groups "grow up of necessity in civilized nations, and divide them into different classes, actuated by different sentiments and views." The real difference seemed to lie rather in the fact that Humphrey appealed to anachronistic interest groups while McCarthy had the wit to appeal to the emerging interest groups. When a politician tells an audience of students that he would fire General Hershey or an audience of professors that he would fire J. Edgar Hoover, he is appealing to interest groups as specifically and deliberately as any politician who, say, told a farm audience in 1960 that he would fire Ezra Taft Benson. The new interest groups — the suburban middle class, the college students, the church groups, the peace groups — may be less familiar than the wool industry or the steelworkers, less familiar even than the Negroes, the Puerto Ricans, the Mexican Americans, the Indians and the poor in general. That hardly makes them any less interest groups.

It was McCarthy's achievement to understand that voters were beginning to defect from the old interest groups. It was his effort to put together a coalition of the new interest groups. The inner logic of his remarkable campaign was to unite the college-educated, whatever their race, religion or previous condition of servitude: teachers, students, church leaders, enlightened businessmen, civic-minded suburbanites, the rising professional, managerial and technical classes. This, of course, is why his campaign was so popular in the suburbs. This is why he was the Democratic aspirant with the greatest appeal to Republicans. This too accounts for the "we happy few" flavor of the McCarthy campaign. It explains why his embattled followers on the streets of Chicago were mostly sons and daughters of the white middle class — why they received so little sympathy or support from the blacks, the workingmen and the poor.

He was attempting something novel in progressive politics — a revolution *against* the proletariat. McCarthy himself pointed up the contrast between his conception and Robert Kennedy's conception of the Democratic coalition when he told a university audience in Corvallis during the Oregon primary that public opinion polls showed Kennedy running best "among the less intelligent and less educated people in America. And I don't mean to fault them for voting for him, but I think that you ought to bear that in mind as you go to the polls here on Tuesday."

The Kennedy way, in my judgment, stands in sharp contrast to both the Humphrey and McCarthy ways. Kennedy saw the Democratic party as a coalition neither of political brokers nor of college graduates but as a link between the two Americas — between educated and uneducated America, between rich and poor America, between white and black America. Unlike Humphrey, he did not suppose that the traditional political institutions could control their constituencies in the new age of television and public opinion polls. Unlike McCarthy, he did not regard the "less educated" as necessarily the "less intelligent," and he was not prepared to surrender the working masses — even the cops and the cabdrivers — to George Wallace.

Like Humphrey and McCarthy, Kennedy began his analysis with the crisis of the Roosevelt coalition; but I think he read the Roosevelt experience with more precision and penetration. He dissented from the Humphrey way because he understood that Roosevelt did not create his coalition through the institutions to which Humphrey had committed himself; these institutions were the effect, not the cause of FDR's success. He dissented from the McCarthy way because he did not believe that the old Roosevelt coalition had splintered beyond recall, though he knew that coalition had to be extended by enlisting the technostructure and the suburbs. Where Humphrey proposed to reconstruct the Roosevelt coalition from above, through the political brokers, Kennedy proposed to reconstruct it from below, through his intense personal identification with the victims and casualties of American society, through urging programs on behalf of the alienated groups and through increasing their own direct participation in the political and administrative process.

One secret of political leadership is a creative relationship between the personality of a man and the problems of the time; even in a democracy, or perhaps especially in a democracy, the great leader to some degree "personalizes" the movement he leads. I forget whose phrase "experiencing nature" is — T. S. Eliot's, I think — but that is what Robert Kennedy had, and it accounted for his fascinating development and peculiar power as a political leader. The particular quality of his experiencing nature was his ability to perceive the world from the viewpoint of its casualties and its victims. When Robert Kennedy went into Harlem or Watts, when he visited a sharecropper's cabin or an Indian reservation, these were *his* children with bloated bellies, *his* parents wasting away in dreary old age, *his* miserable hovel, *his* wretched scraps for dinner. He saw it all, with personal intensity, from the inside; he was part of it. It was because those he came among felt this that they gave him so unreservedly their confidence and their love.

This astonishing power of identification with the outcasts of American society was the driving emotion of his political maturity. Not even his critics could deny his insistence that justice be done to those whom affluent America had considered untouchables — not only black Americans but Mexican-Americans and Puerto Ricans, California grape-pickers, migrant laborers in the Mississippi Delta, poor whites in Appalachia, despairing Indians in the southeast and northwest. In the Senate he made himself the particular champion of those who in the past had been constituents of no one. These people were predominantly outside the political as well as the economic community. Many had no fixed places of abode, or were too poor, too illiterate, too apathetic, too sad to participate in the governmental process. They did not register. They did not vote. Any political figure who spends time worrying about what our country has done to them does so out of conviction and contrition, not out of expectation of political return. That is why so few politicians bother.

Yet the future of the nation requires that we begin to draw the excluded groups into our national life. And full commitment to justice for the excluded groups is not only necessary to preserve their confidence in the democratic process. It is also necessary to win the ability to protect that process when it is under attack. For we obviously cannot permit violence, from whatever source, and retain a rational society. The national government must have the moral strength as well as the legal authority to defend the peaceful processes of change. It will be hard for any President to do this without tearing the country apart unless he has shown profound personal involvement in the cause of racial justice.

Robert Kennedy showed in the spring of 1968 that this approach might work. His success, for example, in both Negro and backlash districts, far from demonstrating (as his critics used to say) duplicity in his tactics, demonstrated that he had the personal power to rally disparate groups behind rational policies — as Franklin Roosevelt had rallied disparate groups behind rational policies in the thirties. Paul Cowan of the *Village Voice*, reporting in July on George Wallace in Massachusetts wrote, "I realized for the first time how important Robert Kennedy's candidacy had been. He was the last liberal politician who could communicate with white working-class America." Because he could also communicate with brown and black America, he was — however divisive he might be considered in the boardrooms and the country clubs — the most unifying figure in our politics.

So the Democrats face a choice after 1968 — whether to follow the Old Politics of the Humphrey way, the elitist politics of the McCarthy way or the national politics that one hopes will continue to move forward in the spirit of Robert Kennedy. As a Democrat, I am inclined to believe that my party is more likely to succeed not as a collection of obsolescent power blocs nor as a semiprecious rally of the *illuminati* but as a truly national party, embracing the poor as well as the rich, the black as well as the white, the young as well as the old, the uneducated as well as the educated, in a common fight for a just and liberal America. Both the Kennedy primaries and the Humphrey resurgence in the last days of the general election suggest that the reports of the death of the Roosevelt coalition may well have been exaggerated. But the revival of the Democratic party clearly requires the redefinition of the coalition of the thirties in terms of the problems of the seventies. Does it also require a commitment to positive national leadership?

8. The Future of the Presidency

This leads to the second issue that divided McCarthy and Kennedy: the nature of the Presidency.

For several reasons, not only because of his revulsion against the activist Presidency of Lyndon Johnson but also because of his confidence in his coalition of the college-educated and his desire to release energies he felt had been blocked by undue centralization of power, McCarthy emphasized in his 1968 campaign that "the New Politics requires a different conception of the Presidency." The conception he rejected he identified especially with John F. Kennedy. "What I regret," McCarthy told the London *Sunday Times* in August 1968, "is the way he personalized the Presidency. I know that Johnson has done this, but I think he has done it defensively as things have got more and more out of control. Jack did it almost deliberately. He brought all the new men in and conveyed the impression that all power radiated from the Presidency."

McCarthy declared his opposition to "the sort of presidential power which extends itself in a personal way into every institution of government." He even asked: "Has the integrity of Congress, of the Cabinet and *of the military* [my italics] been impinged upon by undue extension of the executive power?" The powers of the Presidency, he argued, should be decentralized. As against the idea of a strong Presidency on the Jackson-FDR model, he offered instead a revival of the Whig theory of a passive Presidency, though he proposed to adapt this theory to progressive purposes. "This is a good country," he once said, "if the President will just let it be." The next President, he said, "should understand that this country does not so much need leadership. . . . He must be prepared to be a kind of channel." The President's duty is to "liberate individuals so that they may determine their own lives." In a variety of ways McCarthy made clear his fear of strong presidential leadership and his faith in greater independence among the units of government and greater initiative on the part of the people.

Kennedy, on the other hand, retained the more traditional liberal belief in a strong Presidency. If his purpose was to reconstruct the Roosevelt coalition, he knew that Roosevelt had forged his coalition and held it together through precisely the sort of presidential leadership McCarthy condemned. Roosevelt had persuaded the working class of the thirties to go along with him on issues outside their daily concern, like foreign policy, civil liberties and equal rights, not because the "less educated" then had more enlightened views on such issues than their counterparts have today, but because they had a confidence in Roosevelt founded in his leadership on the issues that *were* part of their daily concern and because, for these and other reasons, they trusted and loved him. I think that Kennedy supposed that today's white low-income groups were similarly composed of decent, if confused, people and that they could be similarly reclaimed for political rationality.

Kennedy saw personal leadership as an indispensable means of welding disparate groups together in a common cause. He also saw a strong Presidency as essential for substantive as well as political reasons. No doubt President Johnson had abused his power in foreign affairs, but a general cutback in presidential power would only increase the nation's impotence in the face of deep and angry national division. Kennedy believed that we were heading as a country into perilous times, that the ties which had precariously bound Americans together were under almost intolerable strain and that reducing presidential authority could be a disastrous error when only a strong President could enable us to meet our most difficult and urgent internal issue: racial justice. The President, in Kennedy's view, had to be the active protector of the alienated groups, the tribune of the disinherited and the dispossessed; he had to be the active champion both of racial justice and of civil peace (and he could only be the second if he had demonstrated that he was the first); and, if any President renounced these obligations, the country might well break up.

Senator McCarthy's critique of the Presidency touched on somber apprehensions and raised searching questions. It expressed a doubt that had been growing for some time among American historians and political scientists regarding their uncritical acceptance of the thesis of the strong Presidency. After all, President Johnson's conduct of the war in Vietnam had been an exemplary exercise of presidential activism along approved lines — but not for approved objectives (or at least not for objectives approved by most historians and political scientists). This forced scholars to face a troubling question: Had they promoted the cult of the strong

Presidency because, up to 1965, strong Presidents had been mostly doing things that historians and political scientists had mostly wanted done? Confronted by a strong President doing things they mostly did not want done, they were compelled to take a fresh look at the old problem of presidential power.

Vietnam, of course, was the precipitating issue. President Johnson's use of presidential powers had come to seem arbitrary and devious. Neither Congress nor the electorate felt they had been consulted about the process of escalation. (To do President Johnson justice, probably a majority of both were in favor of escalation until 1968. To do Congress and the electorate justice, they might not have been had they received an accurate picture of what was going on in Vietnam.) Moreover, the executive appeared to be swallowing up vital powers of decision as a matter of principle. When a former Attorney General, later an Under Secretary of State, told the Senate Foreign Relations Committee that the declaration of war, specifically reserved in the Constitution for Congress, had become "outmoded in the international arena" and that the SEATO treaty and the Gulf of Tonkin resolution were together the "functional equivalent" of a declaration of war, the Committee formally concluded that "the intent of the framers of the Constitution with respect to the exercise of the war power has been virtually nullified." President Johnson himself carried the supposed usurpation even further when he said at Omaha on June 30, 1966, "There are many, many, who can recommend, advise, and sometimes a few of them consent. But there is only one that has been chosen by the American people to decide." Senator Dirksen added a congressional — and Republican — blessing: "It is a rather interesting thing," he told the Senate on October 3, 1967,

"— I have run down many legal cases before the Supreme Court — that I have found as yet no delimitation on the powers of the Commander in Chief under the Constitution."

My impression is that both McCarthy and Kennedy would agree that such expressions arrogated excessive powers of war and peace to the Presidency. But they disagreed in the conclusions they drew from this situation. McCarthy concluded that the situation demanded a general limitation of the Presidency with all functions reconsidered and all powers greatly reduced. Kennedy favored a more selective approach. He feared that, in recoiling indiscriminately against abuses of presidential authority in foreign affairs, the nation ran the risk of inviting a new period of weak Presidents at a time when only a strong President could serve as the center of action and purpose to hold the country together.

The problem of the future of the Presidency resolves itself therefore into the question of whether, as the McCarthy view implies, presidential power is unitary, to be enlarged or diminished across the board, or whether, as the Kennedy view implies, the President has too much power in foreign policy but conceivably too little in domestic policy.

The argument is strong, it seems to me, that the problem of the American Presidency in domestic affairs is not too much power but too little. The President does not have in internal matters quite the same constitutional authority he has in foreign policy. The Supreme Court in the Curtiss-Wright case spoke of "the very delicate, plenary and exclusive power of the President as the sole organ of the federal government in the field of international relations," adding that this power is "in origin and essential character different from that over internal affairs." Nor can a President in domestic affairs so easily shield and enhance his authority by wrapping the flag around himself, invoking patriotism and national unity and claiming life-and-death crisis.

He is therefore much more at the mercy of Congress. From 1938 to 1968 a series of strong Democratic Presidents sought congressional approval for social programs which, had they been enacted, might have greatly alleviated some of the tensions now convulsing our national community. But in these thirty years a coalition, predominantly rural, of Republicans and southern Democrats in the House of Representatives blocked or whittled down most of the presidential proposals — except for a period of two years, 1965–1967, when, as a result of the Goldwater fiasco, enough northern Democrats were elected to create a short-lived but effective liberal majority in the House. Where the head of a parliamentary government can be reasonably sure that anything he suggests will become law in short order, the President of the United States cannot even be sure that *his* proposals will get to the floor of Congress for debate and vote. And no executive in any other democratic state has so little control over national economic policy as the American President.

In recent years a new factor has arisen to limit presidential power: that is, growth of the executive bureaucracy. The expansion of governmental functions under the New Deal produced the modern bureaucracy — a development that the conservatives of the time, with their customary prescience, regarded with consternation. The New Deal bureaucrats, in the demonology of the right, were the forerunners of radical revolution. Of course, as any sensible person should have known, the government bureaucracy has turned out to be, at least against innovating Presidents, a conservatizing rather than a liberalizing force. Its basic loyalty is to the established way of doing things; and, with age and size, it has acquired an independence that enables it to ignore or circumvent presidential initiative.

The rise of the modern bureaucracy has divided the executive branch between the presidential government and the permanent government. In this complex relationship, the presidential government has preferences and policies presumably endorsed by the electorate; but the permanent government has vested interests of its own in program, it has connections of its own with congressional committees, lobbies and the press, it has its own particular, and not seldom powerful, constituencies. Also, it is around longer. We now have, in consequence, four branches of government. An activist President may have quite as much trouble with the federal bureaucracy as with the legislative or judicial branches.

A third limitation on the Presidency in domestic affairs is the fact that nearly every President who has enlarged the power of the White House has provoked a reaction toward a more restricted idea of the Presidency, even if the reaction never quite cuts presidential power back to its earlier level. Thus Jackson and Polk were followed by a parade of weak Presidents. When Lincoln expanded presidential power, Congress took out its frustrations by impeaching his successor and establishing a generation of congressional government. Theodore Roosevelt begot Taft; Wilson begot Harding; Franklin Roosevelt and Truman begot Eisenhower. FDR, in addition, was posthumously punished by the Twenty-second Amendment for the offense of having been elected President four times.

9. The Dilemma of Presidential Power

All these considerations make the Presidency notably weaker in dealing with internal than with international problems. If this is so, the next question is whether it would be possible to think up devices that would enlarge presidential power in domestic matters and restrain presidential power in foreign matters.

A number of devices have been proposed to strengthen the domestic Presidency. There would seem no convincing reason why, for example, the President and the congressional leadership should not agree that all significant presidential proposals would reach the floor for debate and vote. This would not be a guarantee of enactment; but it would be a guarantee that proposals deemed vital to the nation by the President could no longer be filed away in committee and denied consideration by the whole. Such an arrangement incidentally would spare the Senate the perennial row over Rule XXII. Similarly there would seem no convincing reason why the President should not have the right of item veto; even the Confederate Constitution provided for this. There would seem no reason why the President should not have the authority to adjust tax rates within a specific range in order to deal with economic fluctuations; or that he should not have greater discretion in reorganizing the executive branch or in moving funds from one program to another.

Congress resists such proposals out of visceral fear that this would yield further power to the executive. Yet the basic reason why the era of congressional government came to an end was the sad fact that the Presidency seemed more accurate and enlightened in perceiving the nation's needs than did the Congress. So long as this remains the case, Congress may expect to lose ground in the war of attrition. The best hope for Congress lies not in withholding from the President powers that would benefit the nation but in modernizing itself and thereby enabling it to compete with the Presidency on judgments of policy. The place to begin, of course, would be the seniority system. Contrary to congressional impression, this system was not handed down at Mount Sinai. Many state legislatures get along very well indeed without it. Its effect in Washington is to give disproportionate influence to men born in another century and shaped by small town or rural experience — hardly people qualified to meet the problems of an urban and industrial society. Congress should also continue to improve the quality and effectiveness of committee staffs.

Structural revisions of this sort would help both the President and the Congress to deal more energetically with the accumulating troubles of our national community. Are there countervailing structural revisions on the international side which would prevent the President from running away with all initiative and decision in the conduct of foreign policy? This is the area that creates the real problem of presidential power. For, as Richard Neustadt has pointed out, acts in domestic policy are generally reversible; they are subject to revision and recall through democratic processes. But acts in foreign policy are often irreversible. President Kennedy used to say: domestic policy can only defeat us; foreign policy can kill us. Moreover, the nuclear age makes this quality of irreversibility more fateful than ever before. And foreign policy decisions very often appear in emergency contexts, real, imagined or contrived; and this fact encourages the flow of power to the White House. Is it possible through structural reform to secure for Congress and the people an authoritative and continuing voice in the basic decisions of war and peace?

The Senate Foreign Relations Committee thought hard about this question and came up in 1967 with Senate Resolution 187. This resolution declared it as "the sense of the Senate" that American armed forces could not be committed to hostilities on foreign territory for any purpose other than to repel an attack on the United States or to protect American citizens or property without "affirmative action by Congress specifically intended to give rise to such commitment." This or comparable resolutions must surely pass two tests: they must offer a plausible hope that (a) they will not tie the hands of the executive in cases of genuine national emergency, and (b) they will effectively prevent a step-by-step movement from marginal to major involvement.

These questions must be considered in specific contexts; and the answer, one fears, is that S.R. 187 would probably have prevented President Roosevelt from taking his actions of 1941 in defense of American security, but that it would not have prevented President Johnson from pursuing his course of gradual military escalation in Vietnam. The reason for this is that Roosevelt would have found it difficult to put together a congressional majority for his Atlantic policy, while, as the Gulf of Tonkin example showed, Johnson would have encountered little difficulty in getting congressional endorsement for his Vietnam policy before 1968. And this suggests, I believe, the futility of trying to solve substantive problems by structural means. The probable result of efforts to limit presidential power through institutional contrivance would be to introduce dangerous rigidities into our system of national decision, stop Presidents from doing good as well as from doing harm and cause more trouble than benefit.*

The solution to the problem of excessive presidential power in foreign affairs lies, I would conclude, in the political and educational realm. The fundamental strength of the Congress in this area springs from its capacity to shape national opinion — a proposition demonstrated in the revolt against the Vietnam policy in 1967–1968. Next to the events in Vietnam themselves, the interpretation of these events provided by the dissident senators under the leadership of Senator Fulbright and the Foreign Relations Committee and transmitted by television and otherwise to the electorate was probably the major factor in turning the balance of opinion against the escalation policy.

In particular, Congress is well placed to assail the myth with which every foreign office seeks to silence critics: that only those who see the top secret cables know enough to make intelligent judgments on questions of foreign policy. As one who has had the opportunity to read such cables at various times in my life, I can testify that 95 percent of the information required for intelligent judgment is unclassified and available to any careful reader of the *New York Times*. Indeed, the American government would have had a much wiser Vietnam policy had it relied more on the *New York Times*; the estimate of the situation supplied by American newspapermen in Vietnam was consistently more accurate than that supplied by the succession of ambassadors and generals in their coded dispatches. Secrecy in diplomatic communication is mostly

* Senator Fulbright himself acknowledged the force of this point in an article in the *Cornell Law Quarterly*, Fall 1961. He then wrote, "It is highly unlikely that we can successfully execute a long-range program for the taming, or containing, of today's aggressive and revolutionary forces by continuing to leave vast and vital decision-making powers in the hands of a decentralized, independent-minded, and largely parochial-minded body of legislators."

required to protect negotiating strategies, techniques of intelligence collection, details of weaponry and gossip about personalities. One does not require full knowledge on such points to assess a political situation. The myth of inside information has always been used to prevent democratic control of foreign policy; and, if Congress derides that myth, it may embolden others to doubt the infallibility of Presidents and Secretaries of State.

But the responsibility rests even more heavily on the President than on the Congress. A President must, above all, be a man who acts not just because he himself is sure about the wisdom of a course of action but because he is responsive to the democratic process. It is not enough for policies to be sound. In all but the most extreme cases, that soundness must be accompanied by explanation and be tested by acceptance. The President must act on the principle of self-limitation and live within the discipline of consent. He must understand the legitimacy of challenges to his own authority and wisdom. He must cherish an inner skepticism about the anointment of office and a constant awareness of what Whitman called "the never-ending audacity of elected persons." He must be especially skeptical about the unique value of information that arrives through official channels and about self-serving bureaucratic versions of anything. He must be sensitive to the diversity of concern and conviction in a nation; he must be sensitive in advance to the verdict of history; he must always pay "a decent respect to the opinions of mankind."

No structural solutions can guarantee the choice of such Presidents — or can guarantee that, once chosen as open and modest men, they will remain so amid the intoxications of the office. Yet surely the whole point of democracy is that it is not an automatic system. It involves risks, because risks are the means of growth. Rather than renounce the idea of an affirmative Presidency or surround the President with hampering restrictions, it would seem better to continue to regard presidential leadership as the central instrument of American democracy — and to exercise scrupulous care in the choice of Presidents.

Certainly it is hard to see how we can unite our tormented nation and bring the alienated groups at last into the national community without a strong Presidency. "The President," James K. Polk said, "represents in the executive department the whole people of the United States, as each member of the legislative department represents portions of them." No one else represents the whole people; and the answer to the crisis of alienation surely does not lie in the weakening of the center and the dispersion of authority to local groups. This would only turn the country over to the strongest interests in each locality — i.e., to the neighborhood bullies — and speed the disintegration of American society. If the President does not serve as the representative of the unrepresented, it is hard to see where the excluded groups will find a connection with American society. One sees no other way of restoring the moral energy of American politics and of incorporating the grave forebodings and desperate urgencies of our time into the democratic process.

The answer lies in national leadership — but not in national leadership that gulps up all authority in the conviction of its own infallibility. If we are to develop a genuine sense of national community, that will begin to come only when national leadership gives local groups full and active sense of participation and initiative within a framework of national purpose. And it will come finally only through the direct commitment of individual Americans — the commitment that will transform the public agonies of America into personal responsibilities.

We must understand the limits as well as the utilities of politics. The American schism today is bitter and angry; the crisis of self-confidence goes very deep. That schism and that crisis will not be resolved by pious exhortation, nor even by beneficial legislation and wise leadership. It will be resolved only by reaching across the barriers in our land which separate some of us from others of us — only by men and women acting in the end not as members of groups but as individuals fulfilling themselves through human relations with other individuals. The volunteers of our time — the young men and women in the Peace Corps and VISTA and civil rights and community action, the tutors in the slums and ghettos, the visitors in the hospitals and asylums, all those who sacrifice their own convenience to help the outcasts of our society achieve strength and dignity — point the way to our salvation. The mission of democracy, said Whitman, is "to train communities, through all their grades, beginning with individuals and ending there again, to rule themselves." And no one should be discouraged by the fear that his own contribution cannot make a difference. Robert F. Kennedy warned in memorable language against "the danger of futility" — against

> the belief that there is nothing one man or one woman can do against the enormous array of the world's ills — against misery and ignorance, injustice and violence. . . . Few will have the greatness to bend history itself, but each of us can work to change a small portion of events, and in the total of all those acts will be written the history of this generation.

. . . Each time a man stands up for an ideal, or acts to improve the lot of others, or strikes out against injustice, he sends forth a ripple of hope, and crossing each other from a million different centers of energy and daring those ripples build a current that can sweep down the mightiest wall of oppression.

ACKNOWLEDGMENTS
AND
INDEX

ACKNOWLEDGMENTS

A NUMBER OF THESE ESSAYS have been published previously; all have been revised for this volume. An earlier version of "Violence as an American Way of Life" appeared as a Signet Special Broadside under the title of *Violence: America in the Sixties* (New American Library, New York, 1968); a portion, originally delivered as a commencement address at the City University of New York in June 1968, was published in *Harper's* in August 1968 under the title "America 1968: The Politics of Violence." "The Intellectual and American Society" draws from "Ideas and Responsibility: The Intellectual and Society," an inaugural lecture at the City University of New York in 1966, from "Intellectuals in American Politics," an essay in *The Great Ideas Today, 1968* (Encyclopaedia Britannica, Inc., Chicago, 1968) and from a review article on Noam Chomsky's *American Power and the New Mandarins* in *Book World*, March 23, 1969. "The Origins of the Cold War" appeared in *Foreign Affairs*, October 1967. "Vietnam: Lessons of the Tragedy" is based on an epilogue written in 1968 for the Fawcett edition of *The Bitter Heritage: Vietnam and American Democracy, 1941–1968*; a portion was published in *Harper's* in March 1969 under the title "Vietnam and the

ACKNOWLEDGMENTS

End of the Age of the Superpowers." "Joe College, R.I.P." is the revision of a piece published by the Saturday Evening Post, September 21, 1968, under the title "Joe College Is Dead." I owe a special debt in connection with this piece to my children, Christina, Andrew and Stephen Schlesinger and Katharine Schlesinger Kinderman for the patience and candor with which they responded to a series of elderly questions. "The Prospects for Politics," though written specially for this volume, draws from an Alf M. Landon Lecture given at Kansas State University in November 1968 as well as from the following pieces: "The New Liberal Coalition," The Progressive, April 1967; "The Future of the Democratic Party," New York, November 4, 1968; "A Skeptical Democrat Looks at President Nixon," New York Times Magazine, November 17, 1968; and "RFK—Harbinger of Hope," Playboy, January 1969.

Gretchen Stewart typed the manuscript with the assistance of Mary Chiffriller; and I want to thank them for their invariable patience and invaluable help.

INDEX

Acheson, Dean, 169; quoted, 169–170 n
Adams, Brooks, 66, 74
Adams, Henry, 66; quoted, 68
Adams, John, 59, 60, 74
Adams, John Quincy, 66, 71; quoted, 154
Aeschylus, 54; quoted, 51
After Victory: Churchill, Roosevelt, Stalin and the Making of the Peace (Neumann), 103 n
Agronsky, Martin, quoted, 156
Alperovitz, Gar, quoted, 103–104 n
Alsop, Joseph, 176
Alsop, Stewart, quoted, 2
America, Britain and Russia: Their Cooperation and Conflict (McNeil), 103 n
American Council on Education, 198
American Power and the New Mandarins (Chomsky), 86, 92, 303
America's Economic Supremacy (Adams), 74
Arendt, Hannah, 167; quoted, 97
Aristophanes, 54
Aristotle, 54, 67, 84

Association of College and University Housing Officers, 233
Atlantic Charter, 111, 112, 113, 123, 124, 130
Atomic Bomb and the End of World War II, The (Feis), 103 n
Atomic Diplomacy: Hiroshima and Potsdam (Alperovitz), 103 n
Auden, W. H., quoted, 93
Augustine, Saint, 50
Augustus, 67, 84, 171

Badoglio, Pietro, 127
Bancroft, George, 66, 70; quoted, 238
Barnet, R. J., 169 n
Bay of Pigs, 174
Beatles, the, 234, 235; quoted, 23
Beginnings of the Cold War (Herz), 103 n
Bell, Daniel, 240 n, 241
Bellamy, Edward, 72
Ben Tre (Vietnam), 157
Benda, Julien, 83–85
Benn, Anthony Wedgwood, quoted, 260